Cookery Americana

AMERICAN REGIONAL COOKING

FAVORITE RECIPES FROM THE PAST

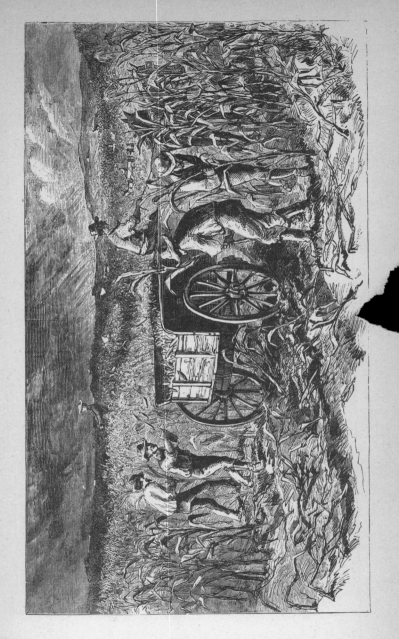

HARV

MIDWESTERN
HOME COOKERY

Introduction and Suggested Recipes

by

LOUIS SZATHMÁRY

New York · 1974

COOKERY AMERICANA is a series of 27 cookbooks in 15 volumes that chronicles a fascinating aspect of American social life over the past 150 years. These volumes provide unique insight into the American experience and follow the movement of pioneer America from the original colonies to the Great Plains and westward to the Pacific. More than cookbooks, these works were manuals for daily living: household management, etiquette, home medicinal remedies, and much more. See the last pages of this volume for a complete listing of the series.

LOUIS I. SZATHMARY, Advisory Editor for this series, is an internationally known chef, food management consultant, owner of the renowned Chicago restaurant, The Bakery, and author of the best selling *The Chef's Secret Cookbook* (Quadrangle Books, 1971). As a serious student of the history of cookery, he has collected a library of several thousand cookbooks dating back to the 15th century. All of the works in *Cookery Americana* are from his private collection.

Published by Promontory Press, New York, N.Y. 10016

Introduction Copyright © 1973 by Louis Szathmáry

Reprinted from a copy in the private collection of Louis Szathmáry

Library of Congress Catalog Card No.: 73-92638
ISBN: 0-88394-017-5

Printed in the United States of America

Contents

Introduction

According to Margaret Cook's *America's Charitable Cooks: A Bibliography of Fund-Raising Cook Books Published in the United States, 1861-1915,* the first cookbook published in the United States to aid a charitable organization came off the presses in Pennsylvania in 1861. Within the decade, the idea spread throughout the country. By 1872, the far western point was reached at San Francisco, where two charity cookbooks were being sold. The state of Washington had its Walla Walla-Whitman College project going, and "Choice Receipts" cookbooks were being sold to aid in the founding of a girls school. Of course, not only the East and Far West, but the middle states as well produced these delightful, common efforts of American homemakers.

The Presbyterian Cook Book, compiled by the Ladies of the First Presbyterian Church of Dayton, Ohio, was a typically mid-American cookbook. It was not the work of one author, but many. When leafing through any of the chapters we find that most of the contributing ladies were not necessarily natives of the town of Dayton. That their heritage was kaleidoscopic can be seen from their names. Next to the Greens, Smiths, and Browns, we spot names such as the German Gebhart, the English Craighead, the Dutch Van Ausdal, the Irish McDermont, the French DuBois. They brought from the native lands of their forebearers and from their own American past, an Okra Gumbo and a Corn Soup from the South (p. 18), Green Pea and a Pea Soup from the East (p. 20), and a unique Corn and Tomato Soup (pp. 19-20).

One lady contributed a recipe for Roast Turkey, others supplied the dressing recipes—Mrs. Brown's Plain, Excellent Stuffing, Mrs. W. A. B.'s Oyster, Mrs. Harris' Potato, as well as Apple and Chestnut stuffings (pp. 31-32). More and more of the left-over (or what to do with them) type recipes appear, such as Turkey Scallop (p. 34), with a definite economic trend to stretch, to reuse, to substitute, and to adapt.

In this book beefsteaks begin to get "stuffed," and the otherwise not too tender cuts of meat get pounded, pressed, corned, and spiced (pp. 36-37). The old large roasts of the Eastern cookbooks of twenty, thirty, and fifty years earlier are all absent, but a Traveling Lunch appears (p. 42), and Miss Hattie Brown promises the traveler in her last sentence that it "will keep fresh some time."

The Ladies of the Presbyterian Church had lots of time on their hands and were very thrifty, mixing their own mustard and making their own catsup. Four ladies contributed Tomato Catsup recipes, but others made their catsup using mushrooms, wild plums, gooseberries, and even grapes (p. 48).

Tomatoes were abundant at that time. It was rumored that in certain places in New England they were still looked upon with suspicion, as possibly dangerous to youngsters, due to some strange legend of their being an aphrodisiac—or possibly because of the legend of their amorous properties, tomatoes turned into a leading American vegetable. When comparing the first true American cookbooks with the English cookbooks of that period, one finds that perhaps only one or two vegetable recipes differ somewhat from the English. Around the time of the celebration of the 100th anniversary of American Independence, however, cookbooks in England still had very few recipes for tomatoes, and if any, not as a vegetable; whereas, tomato recipes were abundant in American cookbooks. The Presbyterian ladies from Ohio baked, broiled, scalloped, fried, and sliced their tomatoes for salads.

Among the other vegetables presented are Stewed Corn and Succotash (p. 51), Green Corn Pudding, Corn Oysters, and Corn Fritters (p. 52). The recipe for Cooking Beans "Boston Style" (p. 53) is a delightful, long poem, and the seven potato recipes (pp. 55-56) show how really popular "spuds" were becoming. Someone from New England sent in a Hubbard Squash recipe, and someone else from the South mailed in a recipe for Greens (p. 59).

The chapter on salads is an ever-growing one, and although the "hot slaw" is still around, the "cold" has already become Cole-Slaw (p. 64).

The strongest parts of the book, as in most early cookbooks, are the sections on baked and cooked sweets, desserts, and preserves. Some twenty-five recipes are presented for pie alone, and though many are well-known all-time favorites, some are rather unusual. Miss Dickson includes her Lemon Cream pie recipe, and Mrs. Degraff, Mrs. J. W. S. and Mrs. Butterfield all give Lemon Pie recipes. Mrs. Baldwin's Lemon Pie entry is called an Iowa Lemon

Waterman's Patent Lamp Tea Kettle

Waterman's Patent Coffee Filter.

Custom Made Tin Ware.

Waterman's Patent Shower Bath.

Waterman's Patent Gridiron.

Waterman's Patent Waffle Iron.

Improved Sitting Bath.

Waterman's Patent Towel Stand

Improved Clothes Horse.

Magic Cream Freezer.

NATH'L WATERMAN'S

KITCHEN FURNISHING WAREROOMS,

33 & 85 CORNHILL, BOSTON.

Established Sept'r, 1825.

The place for Families, Hotels, Steamboats and Packet Ships to obtain every article appertaining to the Kitchen department, of the best quality and at the lowest prices.

Waterman's Patent Floating Water Filter.

Improved Coffee Roaster.

Cook's Patent Polishing Iron.

Hotel Side Dishes and Coffee Urns.

Improved Bathing Pans.

Waterman's Patent Lantern.

A "VENTILATED REFRIGERATOR"—AN EARLY MODEL
WHICH WAS USED TO COOL, CHILL
AND PARTIALLY FREEZE CUSTARDS, CREAMS, ETC.

xi

Pie, and as hard as we try, we cannot figure out what makes it Iowan (pp. 67-68).

Ovens, ranges and stoves were still not very reliable, at least not in the Midwest. Otherwise, they would not have printed the following good suggestion (p. 69). "A bowl containing two quarts of hot water set in the oven of the stove prevents any article such as cakes, pies, etc. from being scorched."

Pies were made with pumpkin, squash, oranges, potatoes, sweet potatoes, and when nothing else was available, two cups of pounded crackers mixed with tartaric acid, eggs, sugar and water made a Mock Apple Pie (p. 71).

The section on *Puddings* contains some fifty recipes, among them a Valise and a Wapsie (p. 80), some mouth-watering ones such as Seven-Cent Pudding (p. 81), and some patriotic ones as the Young America Pudding (p. 82).

A large section (pp. 97-99) is devoted to recipes for one of America's all-time favorites—Ice Cream. Frozen Peaches and Frozen Strawberries (p. 99) are listed, as well as the standard favorite, Chocolate Ice Cream (p. 98), and the most popular ices—Lemon Ice and Orange Ice (p. 99).

There is one recipe for Yeast (p. 102), with such ingredients as hops, potatoes and alum; below it is one which explains the great invention of dry yeast and tells how to make and use it.

There are five different cornbread entries, and innumerable puffs, muffins, rusks, and breakfast cakes which form the greater part of the *Bread* chapter. Then come cakes, cakes and more cakes —Social Cake (p. 116), Cocoanut Pound Cake (p. 117), Cocoanut Sponge Cake (p. 117), Watermelon Cake (pp. 118-119), Bread Cake (p. 119) and so on.

The doughnut starts to lose its squareness in the three recipes on page 129, and in one we find a little hole cut out in the center with a canister top.

The housewives were canning practically everything—green corn, corn, tomato jam, orange marmalade, apple sauce, blackberries, quinces, sweet pickle cherries, walnuts, and onions. After everything is preserved and canned, the household remedies in the *Miscellaneous* chapter are lined up—one for burns, several for cuts, one to prevent lockjaw, a remedy for rheumatism, another for frosted limbs.

The entire book was a community effort—a sharing of knowledge and information. The ladies may have moved into and out of

PLANTING CORN

Dayton, but their names linger on, and they are remembered not by the color of their eyes or hair, but by their corn fritters, tomato soup or veal loaf.

In 1906 the Woman's Guild of Grace Church in Madison, Wisconsin, reissued the *Capital City Cook Book* that they originally published in 1883.

"It contained the favorite recipes of many of the good house-keepers of Madison and met with immediate and lasting success . . . Owing to the frequent demand for it the Guild has decided to publish it again."

And so, a quarter of a century later, it appeared again. People trying to remember how to make Mrs. Stevens' Black Bean Soup (p. 10), or what the differences were between Mrs. Stevens', Mrs. Schaal's and Mrs. Hawley's Tomato Soup recipes (pp. 10-11) got their answers along with some other extremely fine and unique soup recipes, such as Mrs. Ward's White Soup (p. 12) and Mrs. Ford's Almond Puree (p. 13). That Ford family of Madison, Wisconsin,

CHEESE FACTORY—TANK FOR COOLING MILK

must have been a large one with a great many friends. Mrs. Ford's Almond Puree serves twenty-four people and includes eight pounds of chicken.

A very rich Corn Soup (p. 13) and a Puree of Pea Soup (p. 14) are among the many fine soup recipes. The *Fish* and *Meat* sections, however, are very meager—mainly loafs, croquettes, casseroles, souffles, etc.—because the basic meat recipes had already been established. There are also hardy any roasts or broiled meats, but the recipe for Meat Souffle (p. 32) is delectable, and lovers of veal loaf can choose from four versions. Small gamebirds were in abundance and the recipes read as if they were written from experience.

The *Salad* section includes several chicken salads, a Grape Fruit Salad, and many dressings. Among the *Pickles* are tempting recipes for Chow Chows, Cold and Hot Slaws, and Green and Red Tomato Pickles.

This was Wisconsin, leading cheese captial of the western world, so something new and original appeared in an American cookbook—a chapter devoted exclusively to *Cheese,* including recipes for Cheese Balls (p. 51), Cream Cheese Balls (p. 51), Cheese

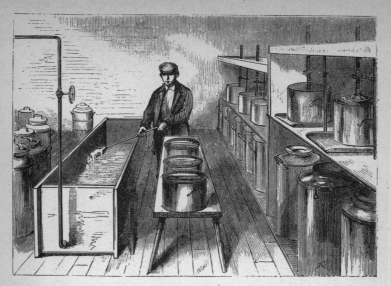

CHEESE FACTORY—TAKING CURD FROM THE VAT

Souffles (p. 51), Tarts (p. 52) and Welsh Rarebit (p. 52). The chapter on *Eggs* is impressive, indicative of the widespread raising of poultry. Included are recipes for a Curried Egg, an Egg Curry, Baked Eggs (p. 56) and international egg recipes from Mexico and France.

Among the best recipes we found in this volume were a Boston Brown Bread (p. 62), and the specialty of the famous Boston Hotel, Parker House Rolls (p. 66), Philadelphia Muffins (p. 67) and several corn bread recipes which represent various parts of the country.

In the *Pudding* section, sour cream, a strange, almost foreign substance, appears. It is interesting to note that today, fifty years later, sour cream is still not widely eaten, except on a narrow Northeast and even narrower Southwest strip. Doughnut recipes, more standardized by this time, hardly talk about shapes or frying methods. They simply list the ingredients, assuming that everyone knew what to do.

The chapter on *Cakes* is one of the largest in the book. Fruit cake and hickory-nut cake recipes are especially plentiful. Besides five different hickory-nut cakes and two walnut cakes, both of these nuts are used as ingredients in many other recipes. The berries of the Wisconsin forests—cranberries, blueberries, and huckleberries —are all worked into the cakes.

Here we find one of the staples of later charity cookbooks, regardless of denomination or geography, the Scripture Cake (p. 127), where each ingredient is connected with a verse of the Bible—"1 cup of butter, Judges, 5, verse 25, etc."—and the recipe ends with, "Follow Solomons advice for making good boys and you will make a good cake." But Mrs. Lucius Fairchild, who contributed that recipe, changes her mind—or perhaps she doesn't trust Solomon —because she adds the following: "Or proceed as in the ordinary rules for cake baking."

In this era of the freezer we find frozen fruits, ice creams, parfaits, and sherbets taking up more and more space in cookbooks. For the sweet tooth, why not try Pop Corn Balls (p. 149). There is a very good recipe for the elegant French Bar-Le-Duc (p. 148) and across from it a real American Pecan Candy to tempt the taste buds.

Besides the French, German and English recipes incorporated into American cookbooks, *The Capital City Cook Book* also includes Scandinavian and Polish recipes—a scrumptious Swedish Pudding (p. 93) and a delicious Polonaise Cake (pp. 111-112). Americans were beginning to use more and more ingredients from all parts of Europe, and the arriving immigrants were contributing to the food habits of the growing, moving nation.

We can read the recipe How to Cook Husbands (pp. 154-155) and find it amusing, nostalgic reading in this age of the Women's Liberation Movement. The book ends with delightful home-remedy formulas, such as advice for coughs, colds in the head, furniture polishes, spice bags, and useful hints such as add "a few drops of rose water to almonds to prevent their oiling when chopped or pounded," or, "Dried crumbs absorb more moisture and are better for watery dishes," or, "To make coffee for parties one pound to a gallon."

Even the advertisements are worth thumbing through: among them gas stoves, electric or combination fixtures are advertised and the coal yards offer, in addition to their heating products, slabs of lake ice for the ice box. Professor Kehl & Son offer dancing lessons in their Permanent Academy, H. Groves' Sons have a fine line of cooking brandies, and elegant Bon Ton and Royal Worcester Corsets are offered to good cooks for $5.00. Piper Bros. offers the purest olive oil, finest richest cheeses among other things; The First National Bank of Madison proudly lets the people know that their tremendous capital is $100,000; and C. Jevne & Company of Chicago informs us that their quarterly magazine, *Bon Vivant,* contains the price of every article sold in their great store.

Louis Szathmáry
CHICAGO, ILLINOIS

SUGGESTED RECIPES

The following recipes have been tested and adjusted to today's ingredients, measurements, and style of cooking by Chef Louis Szathmáry.

THE PRESBYTERIAN COOK BOOK

CORN AND TOMATO SOUP (pp. 19-20)

INGREDIENTS FOR 8:

Soup

1	pound soupbones, washed well in cold water
2	quarts of cold water
1	medium onion cut into ½ inch squares (approximately 1 cup)
2	tablespoons salt
10-12	bruised whole black peppercorns
12	ears of young, fresh corn
	Enough fresh tomatoes to make 1 quart, cut up into ½″ by ½″ pieces
1	tablespoon sugar

Dumplings

1	egg
¾	cup buttermilk
½	teaspoon salt
1¼	cups flour
½	teaspoon baking powder

METHOD: *For Soup:* Simmer soupbones with onions, salt, pepper and water over medium heat for 1½ hours. Cut the corn off the cobs and scrape any additional pulp from the cobs with a table-spoon. Add cut corn and pulp to simmering soup. Add the chopped tomatoes which have been sprinkled with the sugar. Keep simmer-ing for about 1 more hour and 10 minutes.

For Dumplings: Beat egg slightly. Add buttermilk. Mix salt and baking powder into flour. Blend into egg-buttermilk mixture. Thirty minutes before the soup will be served, dip a tablespoon into simmering soup, then remove from the dumpling dough an amount the size of an almond and float it into soup. Repeat until all the dough is used up. Serve hot, 20 minutes after last dumpling has been dropped in the soup.

HUCKLEBERRY PUDDING (p. 81)

INGREDIENTS:

    1 cup dark molasses
   ½ teaspoon cloves, ½ teaspoon cinnamon
       dissolved in ½ cup milk
    2 cups flour mixed with 1 teaspoon baking soda
    1 quart rinsed, picked over huckleberries or
       blueberries, dried on a cloth and sprinkled
       with an additional ½ cup flour

METHOD: Preheat the oven to 400°. Mix the molasses with the milk-spice mixture. Fold in the flour-soda mixture, adding it slowly through a sieve to avoid lumps. Add the flour-covered berries, and place the mixture in a well-closing, buttered pudding mold, approx-imately 5½ inches in diameter by 5 inches deep.

Immerse the pudding mold in a large pot, adding enough water to come up to 1 inch *under* the top of the mold.

Bring the water to a boil over high heat on the top of the stove, then place the pot in the oven with the pudding mold in it. Bake for 2 hours and 30 minutes, adjusting oven temperature if necessary, to keep water simmering.

Unmold, eat with cream and sugar, or with pudding sauce.

THIS DEVICE WAS HELPFUL TO HOMEMAKERS IN PICKLING AND PRESERVING FRUITS AND VEGETABLES FOR WINTER

WATERMELON CAKE (pp. 118-119)

INGREDIENTS:

- 4 cups powdered sugar, sifted
- 1 cup cold butter, cut into pieces
- 2 cups milk
- 5 cups sifted all-purpose flour
- 1½ tablespoons baking powder
  The zest (yellow part only) and juice of 2 lemons
- ¼ teaspoon red food coloring
- ½ cup raisins soaked in hot water for 1 hour then drained and patted dry, and sprinkled with 2 to 3 additional tablespoons flour

METHOD: Preheat oven to 350°. Butter and flour the inside of a 9-inch diameter, 4-inch deep cake pan.

Place the butter in a bowl and, with an electric mixer, beat it until it begins to get fluffy. Slowly add 2 cups of the sugar, constantly beating, then slowly add 1 cup of the milk. Continuing to beat, add ½ of the sifted flour, the second ½ of the milk, the remaining sugar, and finally the baking powder mixed into the second ½ of the flour. Fold in the lemon zest and juice.

Remove a little more than ½ of the batter, and to this portion add the red food coloring and the raisins. Place the smaller portion (uncolored batter) in the bottom of the pan, and with the help of a spatula, push it around the sides, but leave some on the bottom. Put the pink batter in the middle. Bake in the preheated oven for 1 hour and 45 minutes, or until a skewer comes out dry when inserted into the middle of the cake. Let the cake cool before removing from the pan.

If you wish, cover the cake with a green icing made from 1 egg white, 1½ cups powdered sugar, 3 to 4 drops green food coloring, and 1 tablespoon lemon juice.

THE CAPITAL CITY COOK BOOK

ALMOND PUREE (p. 13)

INGREDIENTS FOR 8:

1	2½-pound chicken, cut into pieces
1	pound bony veal front
1	tablespoon salt
1	parsnip, approximately 2 inches long and ½ inch in diameter, split in half
1	small turnip, about 2 inches in diameter
2	tablespoons chopped onions
2	celery stalks, chopped (approximately 1 cup)
2½	quarts water
1	tablespoon cornstarch
¼	teaspoon almond extract
32	white almonds, finely chopped, or ½ package chopped almonds, white parts only (available in stores in plastic bags)

1 cup heavy cream, whipped stiff with a small
   pinch of salt

METHOD: Place the chicken, vegetables and veal bones in a large soup pot and add the salt. Add the water and bring to a gentle boil. Boil for about 2 hours or until the chicken falls off the bones. Strain. Remove the chicken meat and skin and set aside to cool. Discard everything else. After the chicken meat and skin have cooled, cut into small pieces and blend in a blender, with some of the broth, until it turns into a pulp. Be sure to add enough stock to keep the chicken moist in the blender. Add blended meat and skin to the strained stock. Dilute the cornstarch with 1 tablespoon cold water and stir into soup. Add the almond extract, bring the soup to a boil, then reduce the heat very low, cover, and let it steep for about 30 minutes. *To serve:* place in each soup cup 1 tablespoon chopped almonds. Ladle on the soup, and add a dab of the stiffly whipped cream on top. Serve it with white croutons.

BOSTON BROWN BREAD (p. 62)

INGREDIENTS:

   1 cup molasses—light
   3 cups of buttermilk
   1 teaspoon salt
   2 teaspoons baking soda
   5 cups whole wheat flour
   2 cups raisins, soaked in hot water for 1 hour
      and then drained and dried

METHOD: With a wooden spoon, mix the molasses and the buttermilk together. Sift together the flour, salt and baking soda. Stir the dry ingredients into the molasses-buttermilk mixture, making sure no traces of the flour remain. Add the raisins. Pour the batter into 2 50-ounce cans.

Cover the cans with aluminum foil folded into fourths, and secure them with thin wire. Set the cans into boiling water which comes within 1 inch of the top of the cans. Steam for 3½ hours in a preheated 450° oven.

Let cool, then insert a thin knife to loosen sides and remove from cans. Serve cold or reheat.

WELSH RAREBIT (p. 52)

INGREDIENTS FOR 8:

- 1 pound processed American cheese
- 1 tablespoon butter
- 1 cup beer
- 1 egg yolk
- 1 teaspoon Worcestershire Sauce
- ½ teaspoon dry mustard
- 1 dash cayenne pepper
- ¼ teaspoon paprika
- ¼ teaspoon salt
- Tabasco sauce to taste
- 16 slices of buttered toast, each cut in four triangles

METHOD: Cut up cheese into ½ in. x ½ in. x ⅛ in. pieces (if sliced cheese, cut into ½ in. x ½ in. squares). Melt butter in saucepan or chafing dish. Add cheese, beer mixed with egg yolk, Worcestershire and Tabasco sauces and all the spices. Stir constantly, and when the mixture begins to coat the spoon, secure toast pieces on fork, and dip the pieces into the bubbling mixture. Eat "alfresco."

PRESBYTERIAN

COOK BOOK

PRESBYTERIAN

COOK BOOK,

COMPILED BY

THE LADIES

OF THE

FIRST PRESBYTERIAN CHURCH,

DAYTON, OHIO.

" He had not din'd.
The veins unfilled, our blood is cold, and then
We pout upon the morning, are unapt
To give or to forgive; but when we have stuffed
These pipes and these conveyances of our blood
With wine and feeding, we have suppler souls
Than in our priest-like fasts."

CORIOLANUS, V. 1.

FIFTH THOUSAND.

DAYTON, OHIO:
JOHN H. THOMAS & CO.
1875.

"Please convey my acknowledgments for the Presbyterian Cook Book to the compilers.

"I have examined it carefully, and take pleasure in pronouncing the recipes it contains, as a whole, practical, economical, and good. I only regret the brevity of some and the small size of the book itself. I shall make use of the work in my own family, having a sort of passion for trying new recipes that promise well; and these are certainly tempting. Wishing the ladies of the First Presbyterian Church much success in their enterprise, I am,

"Very respectfully,

"MARION HARLAND.

"MARCH 16, 1874."

JOHN H. THOMAS & Co. will mail this book, postpaid, on receipt of $1.50. Agents are wanted everywhere. Those who have sold it have found it one of the best selling books. Liberal terms.

Address

JOHN H. THOMAS & CO.,
Dayton, O.

FIRST PRESBYTERIAN CHURCH.
Erected 1839.   Taken down in 1867.
CORNER SECOND AND LUDLOW STS., DAYTON, O.

FIRST PRESBYTERIAN CHURCH.
Erected 1867–8.
CORNER SECOND AND LUDLOW STS., DAYTON, O.

PREFACE.

In March last, the Ladies' Society of the First Presbyterian Church of Dayton hastily compiled and published a "Cook Book," or a small collection of recipes for plain household cooking. Five hundred copies were published, and, notwithstanding the book contained some errors and the arrangement was very imperfect (necessarily so from the haste with which it was prepared for publication), it met with such gratifying and unexpected success that its authors felt it to be their duty to revise and republish it.

The present book is much larger than its predecessor, and the recipes it contains have been selected with great care. Many of them were sent voluntarily by parties who were willing to hold themselves responsible for their excellence, while others were solicited, often at the cost of much time and pains,—a corn-bread here, a pudding there, a salad from some one else,—from ladies who had gained a reputation for preparing this or that particular dish.

Our subject is an inexhaustible one, and this book does not venture into the mystical realm of fancy cookery; but is a collection of safe and reliable recipes for the preparation of plain food.

The matter of the book, we claim, is all right; for the manner of it, we beg indulgence. The phraseology is often

7

peculiar, and may provoke a smile; but it must be remembered that the recipes were written by ladies unaccustomed to writing for publication; and, in most cases, they have been inserted precisely as written, and, whenever no objection was made, the name of the author has been given.

Persons familiar with Dayton names will recognize many who do not belong to the Presbyterian sisterhood. We feel ourselves under great obligations to the ladies who have assisted us, but we hope our book will prove so useful as to amply repay them for their trouble.

DAYTON, OHIO, July 1, 1873.

CONTENTS.

SOUP.

PUDDINGS.

SAUCES.

CUSTARDS, CREAMS, Etc.

LAYER CAKES.

SMALL CAKES.

PICKLES AND RELISHES.

CANNED FRUIT AND VEGETABLES.

DRINKS FOR FAMILY USE.

FOOD FOR THE SICK.

MISCELLANEOUS.

PRESBYTERIAN COOK BOOK.

SOUP.

A FEW points are essential in making good soup. Beef is the best meat for the purpose, as it contains the most nourishment. A shank bone should be well cracked (that the marrow may be extracted), put on to cook in cold water, allowing a full quart for every pound of beef, and by very gradual heat come to a slow simmer, which should be kept up five or six hours. Soup on no account should be allowed to boil, except for the last fifteen minutes, to cook the vegetables in finishing. For the first hour of simmering it should be frequently skimmed. Salt, pepper, and savory should be cooked in it from the first; rice, tapioca, macaroni or dumplings added at the last to thicken. If vegetables are desired, they should be nicely sliced. Soup is much better to be made and allowed to cool, and used the second day, as then all grease can be removed. It should be strained before putting away.

BEEF SOUP.

MRS. JOHN G. LOWE.

Put on a shin of beef early in the morning. An hour before dinner put in the vegetables,—corn, tomatoes, potatoes, or any other the season affords. Half an hour before dinner add pearl barley, vermicelli, or dumplings, as you prefer. Season with salt, pepper, and catsup to taste.

2

BEAN SOUP.

MRS. ACHSAH GREEN.

To a quart of beans, a teaspoonful of soda.   Cover well with water, and set them on to boil until the hulls will easily slip off; throw them into cold water; rub well with the hands; the hulls will rise to the top.   Drain carefully, and repeat until the hulls are wholly removed.   To a quart of beans, two quarts of water. Boil until the beans mash perfectly smooth.   It seasons the soup to boil a piece of meat (mutton, beef, or pork) with it.   If you have not meat, add butter and flour rubbed together.   Break into tureen well-toasted bread, pour over it the soup, and add plenty of salt and pepper.

CORN SOUP.

MRS. S. B. SMITH.

Clean and scrape twelve ears of corn.   Boil the cobs for fifteen or twenty minutes in one quart of water; remove them and put in the corn.   Let it boil a short time, then add two quarts of rich milk.   Season with pepper, salt, and butter that has been melted enough to rub flour into it (two tablespoonfuls of flour).   Let the whole boil ten minutes, and then turn the soup into a tureen into which the yolks of three eggs have been beaten.

TOMATO SOUP.

MRS. SIMON GEBHART.

One quart of tomatoes, one quart of milk, and one quart of water.   Boil the water and tomatoes together about twenty minutes, and then add the milk; then one teaspoonful of soda. Let it just boil up.   Season as you do oyster soup, with butter, pepper, and salt; add crackers if desired.

OKRA GUMBO.

MRS. S. CRAIGHEAD.

Cut up one chicken (an old one is preferable); wash and dry it; flour it well; salt and pepper; have ready in a skillet a lump of lard as large as an egg ; let it get hot ; put in your chicken ; fry very brown all over, but do not let it burn. Put it in your vessel in which you make soup ; pour on it five quarts of water ; let it boil two hours ; then cut up about two dozen okra pods and add to it ; be sure they are tender and pretty well grown ; then let it boil another hour. When you first put on your soup, cut up an onion in it ; salt and pepper to taste. To be served with rice, either boiled or steamed dry. Dried okra can be used by being put to soak the night previous ; pour off most of the water.

PLAIN GUMBO SOUP.

Take a piece of ham half the size of your hand, and a knuckle of veal ; put them in a pot with two quarts of cold water, simmer slowly two or three hours, then add two quarts of boiling water. Twenty minutes before serving, put in one small can of okra and as many oysters as you please. Season to taste.

PLAIN CALF'S-HEAD SOUP.

MRS. S. CRAIGHEAD.

Take a calf's head well cleaned, and a knuckle of veal ; put them into a large porcelain vessel ; put a large tablespoonful of sweet marjoram, and one of sweet basil, in a clean rag ; also a large onion, cut up, in a cloth ; take at least four quarts of water (it must be started as early as eight o'clock, if you wish it for a one o'clock dinner) ; let it boil steadily but not too rapidly ; salt and pepper well. About twelve o'clock take off the soup, pour it through a cullender, pick out all the meat carefully, chop very fine and return it to the soup, placing again upon the fire. Boil four eggs very hard ; chop them fine ; and slice one lemon very thin ; and at last add a wineglass of wine.

CORN AND TOMATO SOUP.

MRS. S. CRAIGHEAD.

Take a good soup-bone ; wash it nicely ; pour over it sufficient water to cover it well ; cut up an onion in it ; salt and pepper; cut down about one dozen ears of corn and as many tomatoes in it, and let it boil slowly for at least three hours. For dumplings, take one egg and beat it a little, one coffee-cup sour milk, small teaspoonful of soda, a little salt, and flour enough to make a stiff batter; drop it into the boiling soup, from a spoon, twenty minutes before serving. These dumplings are good in bean soup also.

GREEN PEA SOUP.

MRS. ELIZA PIERCE.

One peck green peas; four tablespoonsful of lard heated in the kettle; put in the peas and stir them till perfectly green; add pepper and salt, and pour in as much water as you want soup; boil three-fourths of an hour, then add one teacupful of milk thickened with a tablespoonful of flour; put in the soup three or four young onions cut fine and fried a light brown in butter. Just as you take it up, add yolks of two eggs, beaten in a little cream.

PEA SOUP.

MRS. ROBERT BUCHANAN.

Boil the hulls with a chicken or knuckle of veal, then strain the liquid; throw in a handful of peas, and boil to thicken the soup; when done, put in some peas cooked separately; pepper and salt, cream and butter to taste.

MACARONI SOUP.

Take six pounds of beef, and put into four quarts of water, with two onions, one carrot, one turnip, and a head of celery; boil it down three or four hours slowly, till there is about two quarts of water; then let it cool. Next day, half an hour before dinner, take off the grease and pour the soup into the kettle (leaving the sediment out), and add salt to suit the taste; a pint of macaroni broken into inch pieces, and a tablespoonful and a half of tomato catsup.

NOODLES FOR SOUP.

Beat up one egg; add a pinch of salt and flour enough to make a stiff dough; roll out in a very thin sheet; dredge with flour to keep from sticking; then roll up tightly; begin at one end and shave down fine like cabbage for slaw.

MEAT BALLS.

Half a pound of lean veal and a pound of fat beef chopped fine; a tablespoonful of thyme, one of parsley, a little less marjoram and a little more onion, a pinch of mace, cloves, and nutmeg, the yolks of two eggs, a little crumbled bread, pepper, and salt; mix with the hand in a large bowl; mould into balls the size of a walnut, and fry in lard. After frying the balls, make a browning of the lard they are fried in (put flour in and stir until well cooked) and brown the soup with it; put the balls in the soup whole.

DUMPLINGS.

Take a small teacupful of flour, a pinch of salt, and butter the size of a walnut; rub well with the flour; sprinkle in a little pepper; add sweet milk enough to form a stiff dough; flour the board and roll very thin; cut in small squares; drop into the soup, and let them boil ten minutes.

FISH.

BOILED FISH.

ALL large fish, with the skin whole, should be wrapped in a cloth, wound with twine, and covered with more than two inches of cold water. In the water put a little flour, a small lump of butter, a chopped onion, and parsley. Be careful not to have too much water. After the fish has boiled sufficiently, take the yolks of four eggs, the juice of one lemon, a little mace, and about a gill of the water in which the fish has been boiled; put all into a stew-pan and let boil until it thickens, stirring all the time; then pour over the fish.

FRIED FISH.

Having cleaned the fish thoroughly, wipe dry; sprinkle with salt; dust thick with flour. Take yolks of four eggs; beat tolerably light. Put a little sweet oil in the frying-pan, and let it be boiling. Dip the fish in the batter; put them in the pan, and fry slowly. Fish should not be put in to fry until the fat gets boiling hot. It is very necessary to observe this rule.

BAKED FISH.

MRS. GEO. L. PHILLIPS.

After cleaning, salt the fish for about an hour, then wash it. Make a dressing of bread-crumbs, salt and pepper, summer savory, and a piece of butter the size of a walnut. Then put in a pan and sprinkle with flour; put on a little butter, pepper, salt, and about half a pint of water. Bake an hour and a half.

BAKED CODFISH.

Soak the codfish over night; clean it off with a brush kept for that purpose; then put it into a stone crock and cover with water. Let it simmer until quite tender, then take it out, pick it over, and mash it fine. Take two-thirds mashed potatoes, seasoned with butter and salt, and one-third codfish; mix well together, and bake in a dish until brown; then make a sauce of drawn butter, and cut up two hard-boiled eggs into it.

STEWED CODFISH.

MRS. ISAAC VAN AUSDAL.

Pick the codfish into small pieces; cover it with cold water, and let it remain over night. In the morning pour that off, and put on some boiling water. Let it stand a few minutes, then drain, and stir it up with two tablespoonfuls of cream and a lump of butter the size of an egg. Let it come to the boil, and serve with fresh-boiled potatoes.

FISH FRITTERS.

MRS. J. A. MCMAHON.

Take the remains of any fish which has been served the preceding day; remove all the bones, and pound in a mortar; add bread-crumbs and mashed potatoes in equal quantities. Mix half a teacupful of cream with two well-beaten eggs, cayenne pepper, and anchovy sauce; beat all up to a proper consistency; cut it into small cakes, and fry them in boiling lard.

CLAM FRITTERS.

Twelve clams minced fine; one pint of milk; three eggs. Add the liquor from the clams to the milk; beat up the eggs, and put to this salt, pepper, and flour enough for a thin batter; lastly the chopped clams. Fry in hot lard. A tablespoonful makes a fritter, or you can dip the whole clam in batter and cook in like manner.

FISH SAUCE.

Stir in one cup of drawn butter the yolks of two eggs well beaten, pepper and salt, and a few sprigs of parsley; let it boil, and pour over the fish when ready for the table.

ANOTHER SAUCE FOR FISH.

MRS. R. P. BROWN.

Piece of butter size of two eggs; melt, and mix with it one-half teacupful of vinegar, two mustardspoonfuls of made mustard, a little salt, one well-beaten egg. Stir all the time or it will thicken in lumps. It is best made over boiling water, as the heat from the stove is apt to harden the sauce.

TURBOT A LA CREME.

MRS. SARAH CRANE.

Boil a nice fresh fish; pick out all the bones, and season highly with white pepper and salt. Mix one-quarter pound of flour smoothly with one quart of milk; put in five very small onions, a bunch of parsley, a sprig of thyme, one teaspoonful of salt, and one-half teaspoonful of white pepper. Place over a quick fire, and stir all the time until it forms a thick paste; then take off, and put in one-half pound of butter and the yolks of two eggs. Mix all together and pass through a sieve. Pour some of this sauce into a baking-dish, and add a layer of fish and sauce alternately until it is all used. The sauce must be on top, with bread-crumbs and cheese. Bake in a moderate oven half an hour.

PICKLED SALMON.

MRS. GEO. W. HOGLEN.

Soak salt salmon twenty-four hours, changing the water several times; afterward put boiling water around it (not over it), and let it remain fifteen minutes; then pour on boiling vinegar, with cloves and mace added.

LOBSTER CROQUETTES.

MRS. JONATHAN HARSHMAN.

Chop the lobster very fine, and mix with it a little parsley, black pepper, salt, and bread-crumbs; moisten with a little cream. Butter added makes them less dry. Shape them with your hands; roll in bread-crumbs; dip in egg and fry.

OYSTERS.

OYSTER SOUP.

MRS. E. F. STODDARD.

To three pints of oysters put three pints of water; when thoroughly cooked add one pint of cream or milk, the yolks of four eggs, three tablespoonfuls of butter, and three of flour.

OYSTER SOUP.

MRS. J. J. PATTERSON.

To two half-cans of oysters add three quarts of good milk; let the whole come to a boil. Put into a soup-tureen seven crackers rolled fine, salt and pepper to taste, and half-pound of butter; when the oysters have cooked, pour the soup over the crackers and serve.

STEAMED OYSTERS.

Drain the oysters well, and turn them into a steamer over a pot of boiling water; let steam for half an hour, stirring occasionally; season with plenty of butter, pepper, and salt.

ESCOLLOPED OYSTERS.

MRS. HARVEY CONOVER.

Roll crackers very fine, and cover with them the bottom of a baking-dish previously buttered; spread a layer of oysters over these crumbs; pepper and salt them, and drop on bits of butter; cover with a layer of crumbs, and thus alternate the layers until the dish is full, having the crumbs cover the top; place in a very hot oven that it may brown nicely. It takes three-quarters of an hour. No liquid is put in the dish, not even the liquor of the oysters, for the butter moistens it sufficiently.

ESCOLLOPED OYSTERS.

MRS. J. F. E.

Take two half-cans of oysters; look them over carefully to see that there are no pieces of shell among them. Take equal quantities of rolled cracker and bread-crumbs; cover the bottom of a well-buttered dish with them; then a layer of oysters sprinkled with pepper and salt; add a generous supply of butter, then another layer of crumbs, and so on, making the top layer crumbs, with bits of butter through it. Pour over one pint of milk or water; bake three-quarters of an hour; cover with a plate; when nearly done, take it off and let them brown.

OYSTER PIE.

MRS. J. A. MCMAHON.

Take a large dish, butter it, and spread a rich paste over the sides and around the edge, but not on the bottom. The oysters should be fresh and as large and fine as possible; drain off part of the liquor from the oysters; put them into a pan, and season them with pepper, salt, and spice. Have ready the yolks of three eggs, chopped fine, and grated bread-crumbs; pour the oysters, with as much of their liquor as you please, into the dish that has the paste in it; strew over them the chopped egg and grated bread; roll out the lid of the pie and put it on, crimping the edges; bake in a quick oven.

OYSTER PATTIES.

MRS. G. W. R.

Line small, deep tins with puff paste, and bake; when cold, put into each three or four oysters, and season with pepper, salt, and a little butter; bake about ten minutes. Have ready equal parts of water and butter, and pour over each as you dish them up.

BROILED OYSTERS.

Drain the oysters well, and dry them with a napkin. Have ready a griddle, hot and well buttered; season the oysters; lay them on the griddle, and brown them on both sides. Serve them on a hot plate with plenty of butter.

OYSTER FRITTERS.

MRS. D. A. BRADFORD.

One quart of oysters; half-pint of milk; two eggs. Open the oysters; strain the liquor into a pan, and add to it half-pint of milk and the eggs well beaten; stir in flour enough to make a smooth but rather thin batter; when perfectly free from lumps, put in the oysters. Have some beef drippings or butter made hot in a frying-pan; when boiling, drop in the batter, one or more oysters in each spoonful. Brown on both sides, and serve in a hot dish.

FRIED OYSTERS.

MRS. D. W. STEWART.

Take large oysters; wash and drain them; lay on a napkin to dry. Have cracker-flour well seasoned with salt and cayenne pepper; roll the oysters in the cracker, and fry in hot butter and lard in equal quantities. When there is a large quantity needed it is best to put them, as soon as done, into a tin vessel tightly covered, and place in the heater till all are cooked, as but few can be attended to at a time.

OYSTER CROQUETTES.

Take a can of the best oysters; pick them over and dry in a napkin; season well with pepper and salt. Have ready the whites of two eggs well beaten, and some fine corn meal. Take one oyster at a time, dip it first into the egg, then the meal, and drop in a deep skillet of boiling lard. Cook a light brown. Serve on a hot dish.

OYSTER CHOWDER.

LEWIS G. EVANS.

Fry out three rashers of pickled pork in the pot you make the chowder; add to it three potatoes and two onions, both sliced; cover with water; boil until they are nearly cooked; soak two or three dozen crackers in cold water a few minutes, then put into the pot a half-can of best oysters, one quart of milk, and the soaked crackers. Boil all together for a few minutes; season with salt, pepper, and butter. Fish chowder can be made in the same way by using fresh fish instead of oysters.

COVE OYSTERS.

One heaping tablespoonful of butter; one even tablespoonful of flour; put in a skillet and stir till a dark brown; pour on the liquor of the oysters; stir till it thickens; then put in oysters and let them get hot. Season with pepper and fine herbs; keep well covered.

MEATS.

RULES FOR BOILING MEAT.

ALL fresh meat should be put to cook in boiling water, then the outer part contracts and the internal juices are preserved.

For making soup, where you want all the juices extracted, put on in cold water.

All salt meat should be put on in cold water, that the salt may be extracted in cooking.

In boiling meats, it is important to keep the water constantly boiling, otherwise the meat will absorb the water. Be careful to add boiling water if more is needed.

Remove the scum when it first begins to boil.

Allow about twenty minutes for boiling for each pound of fresh meat. The more gently meat boils the more tender it will be.

To broil meat well, have your gridiron hot before you put it on.

In roasting beef it is necessary to have a brisk fire. Baste often. Season well with pepper and salt. Twenty minutes is required for every pound of beef.

BOILED TURKEY.

Stuff the turkey as for roasting. A very nice dressing is made by chopping half a pint of oysters and mixing them with bread-crumbs, butter, pepper and salt, thyme or sweet marjoram, and wet with milk or water. Baste about the turkey a thin cloth, the inside of which has been dredged with flour, and put it to boil in cold water with a spoonful of salt in it. Let a large turkey simmer for two and a half or three hours. Skim it while boiling. Serve with oyster sauce made by adding to a cupful of the liquor in which the turkey was boiled the same quantity of milk and eight oysters chopped fine. Season with minced parsley; stir in a spoonful of rice or wheat flour wet with cold milk; a tablespoonful of butter. Boil up once and pour into a tureen.

TO ROAST A TURKEY.

MRS. S. CRAIGHEAD.

A turkey a year old is considered best. See that it is well cleansed and washed. Salt and pepper it inside. Take a loaf and a half of bakers' stale bread for a good-sized turkey; rub it quite fine with your hands; have in your skillet a lump of butter as large as an egg (or a little more); cut into it one large white onion; let it cook a few minutes, but not get brown; then stir in your bread, one teaspoonful of salt, one of pepper; let it get thoroughly heated. Put the turkey into a dripping-pan; salt and pepper the outside, and sprinkle a little flour over it. Put about one coffee-cup of water in the pan; baste very frequently; use a good, moderate oven; roast about three hours, or three and a half. Be sure to keep up an even fire.

PLAIN, EXCELLENT STUFFING.

MRS. R. P. BROWN.

Take stale bread; cut off all the crust; rub very fine, and pour over it as much melted butter as will make it crumble in your hand; salt and pepper to taste.

TURKEY DRESSED WITH OYSTERS.

MRS. W. A. B.

For a ten-pound turkey take two pints of bread-crumbs, half a teacupful of butter cut in bits (not melted), one teaspoonful of sweet basil, pepper and salt, and mix thoroughly. Rub the turkey well, inside and out, with salt and pepper; then fill with first a spoonful of crumbs, then a few well-drained oysters, using half a can for the turkey. Strain the oyster liquor, and use to baste the turkey.   Cook the giblets in the pan, and chop fine in the gravy.   A fowl of this size will require three hours' cooking in a moderate oven.

POTATO STUFFING.

MRS. J. HARRIS.

Take two-thirds bread and one-third boiled potatoes grated, butter the size of an egg, pepper, salt, one egg, and a little ground sage.   Mix thoroughly.

APPLE STUFFING.

Take half a pound of the pulp of tart apples which have been baked or scalded ; add ·two ounces of bread-crumbs, some powdered sage, a finely-shred onion ; and season well with cayenne pepper.   This is a delicious stuffing for roast geese, ducks, etc.

CHESTNUT STUFFING.

Boil the chestnuts and shell them ; then blanch them and boil until soft ; mash them fine, and mix with a little sweet cream, some bread-crumbs, pepper and salt.   Excellent for roast turkey.

BOILED CHICKEN POT PIE.

MRS. JAMES STOCKSTILL.

Cut up a good-sized chicken in all the joints ; make a rich crust or like soda biscuit ; have ready a smooth pot ; put in a layer of the chicken at the bottom ; pepper and salt ; then small, square pieces of dough, and then a layer of potatoes (quartered if large) and small pieces of butter ; then another layer of chicken, and so on.   Put a crust over the top with a slit cut each way, so that you can turn back and add more water if necessary.   Before putting it on fill the pot with boiling water and cover closely ; boil with a good fire one hour and a half.

CHICKEN PIE.

MRS. W. R. S. AYRES.

Boil a chicken until it is tender (one a year old is best); peel half-dozen potatoes while it is stewing. To make the crust, take one quart of flour, one tablespoonful of baking-powder, a little salt, half a teacupful of lard, and sufficient water to make a stiff dough. Roll half the dough to the thickness of half an inch; cut in strips and line the dish. Then put in half the chicken and half the potatoes; season with butter, pepper, and salt; dredge well with flour, and put in some of the crust cut in small pieces. The other half of the chicken and potatoes put in with butter, salt, and pepper, and dredge with flour as before; roll out the remainder of the dough for upper crust. Before putting on the cover, fill the dish with boiling water; put in the oven immediately, and bake one hour.

CHICKEN PIE.

MRS. JUDGE HOLT.

Stew chicken till tender; season with one-quarter of a pound of butter, salt, and pepper; line the sides of pie-dish with a rich crust; pour in the stewed chicken, and cover loosely with a crust, first cutting a hole in the centre, size of a small teacup. Have ready a can of oysters; heat the liquor; thicken with a little flour and water, and season with salt, pepper, and butter size of an egg. When it comes to a boil pour it over the oysters, and about twenty minutes before the pie is done lift the top crust and put them in.

FRICASSEED CHICKEN.

MRS. JOHN A. MCMAHON.

Stuff two chickens as if to boil; put in a pot; don't quite cover with water; put them on two hours before dinner. Chop an onion, some parsley, and a little mace; rub a piece of butter

3

twice as large as an egg with flour, and stir all in.   Before dish-
ing, beat the yolks of six eggs and stir in carefully ; cook five
minutes.

TURKEY SCALLOP.

Pick the meat from the bones of a cold turkey (without any
of the skin) ; chop it fine.   Put a layer of bread-crumbs on the
bottom of a buttered dish ; moisten them with a little milk ;
then put in a layer of turkey with some of the filling, and cut
small pieces of butter over the top ; sprinkle with pepper and
salt ; then another layer of crumbs, and so on until the dish is
nearly full ; add a little hot water to the gravy that was left from
the turkey, and pour over it.   Then take two eggs, two tablespoonfuls of milk, one of melted butter, a little salt, and
cracker-crumbs as much as will make it thick enough to spread
on top with a knife ; put bits of butter over it, and cover with
a plate ; bake three-quarters of an hour.   About ten minutes
before serving, remove the plate and let the crust brown nicely.

TURKEY OR CHICKEN CROQUETTES.

MRS. S. GEBHART.

Mince turkey or chicken as fine as possible ; season with
pepper, salt, a little nutmeg, and a very little onion.   Take a
large tablespoonful of butter, two of flour, one-half glass of
cream ; mix, boil, and stir the meat in.   When cold, take a
spoonful of the mixture and dip into the yolk of an egg ; then
in bread-crumbs ; roll lightly in your hand into the proper
shape, and fry in boiling lard deep enough to cover them.

CROQUETTES.

MRS. J. R. YOUNG.

One sweet-bread ; one pound of chopped chicken ; half-pound
bread-crumbs ; pour on of boiling water enough to moisten
them ; add the yolks of two eggs ; stir over the fire till quite
stiff, and set away to cool.   Chop three teaspoonfuls of parsley,

three of thyme, three of onions, one of mace, one of nutmeg; salt and cayenne pepper to taste; add half-pound of butter; then beat in the mixture two eggs; mix well with hand; shape as pears; dip in bread-crumbs and egg, and fry, in hot lard, a light brown.

CROQUETTES.

Take the breast of two chickens, or as much cold, cooked veal; beat in a mortar; add as much ham. Add parsley, thyme, salt, and pepper to taste. Boil a pint of new milk, and thicken it with a little flour. Put in the meat; boil it a short time; take it out, and set it away to cool. Roll in grated cracker, then in the yolk of an egg, and fry.

CURRIED CHICKEN.

LEWIS G. EVANS.

Fry out, in the pot you make the curry, three large rashers of pickled pork, and three onions sliced; fry until the onions are brown; cut the chicken into small pieces, and slice three potatoes thin; add them to the pork and onions; cover well with water; cook until the chicken is done and the potatoes have thickened the water; salt to taste. Slice two or three more potatoes very thin; put two tablespoonfuls of curry powder in a tumbler, and mix with water; add the potatoes, and mix curry powder to the stew, and boil until the potatoes are cooked, but not broken. Serve with rice. Green peas and corn are a valuable addition. The above is for one extra large chicken, or two of ordinary size.

STEWED CHICKEN WITH OYSTERS.

MRS. J. F. E.

Season and stew a chicken in a quart of water until very tender, but not to fall from the bones. Take it out on a hot dish and keep it warm; then put into the liquor in which it was stewed a lump of butter the size of an egg; mix a little flour and water, smooth, and make thick gravy; season well with pepper and salt, and let it come to a boil. Have ready a quart of oysters picked over, and put them in without any of the liquor; stir them around, and as soon as they are cooked pour all over the chicken.

TOMATO STEWED BEEF.

Scald the tomatoes; skin and quarter them, and sprinkle with salt and pepper. Bury the meat in a stew-pan with tomatoes, and add bits of butter rolled in flour, a little sugar, and an onion minced fine; let cook until the meat is done and the tomatoes dissolved into a pulp.

BEEFSTEAK SMOTHERED IN ONIONS.

MRS. SARAH S. CRANE.

Put in the skillet a little lard and the steak; peel the onions; slice and lay them over the meat till the skillet is full; season with salt and pepper; cover it tightly and put it over the fire. After the juice of the onions has boiled away and the meat begins to fry, remove the onions, turn the meat to brown on the other side, then replace the onions as before. Be very careful that they do not burn.

STUFFED BEEF-STEAK.

Take a flank or round steak; pound it and sprinkle with pepper and salt; then make a plain filling and spread it on the meat; roll it up and tie closely. Put in a pot with a quart of boiling water, and a lump of butter the size of an egg. Boil slowly one hour, then put in a pan with the water in which it was boiled, and bake until nicely browned, basting it frequently. Dredge a little flour into the gravy, boil, and pour over the meat.

POUNDED BEEF.

Boil a shin of twelve pounds of meat until it falls readily from the bone; pick it to pieces; mash gristle and all very fine; pick out all the hard bits. Set the liquor away, and when cool take off all the fat; boil the liquor down to a pint and a half; then return the meat to it while it is hot; add what salt and pepper is needed, and any spice you choose. Let it boil up a few times, stirring all the while. Put it into a mould or deep dish to cool. Use cold, and cut in thin slices for tea, or warm it for breakfast.

PRESSED BEEF.

MRS. G. ARNOLD.

Corn a bit of brisket (thin part of the flank or the top of the ribs) with salt and pulverized saltpetre five days, then boil it gently until quite tender. Put it under a heavy weight or a press till perfectly cold. It is very nice for sandwiches.

CORNED BEEF PICKLE.

MRS. J. F. SCHENCK.

Ten pounds of salt; three of sugar; one-fourth of ginger; one-half of pulverized saltpetre; one ounce cayenne pepper; nine gallons of water.

CORNED BEEF.

MRS. J. F. EDGAR.

Take your beef, be it much or little, rub it over lightly with salt, and put it in either an earthen or wooden vessel; let it stand two or three days, then take it out; throw away the liquor; cleanse the vessel, and put it back again. Make a pickle of good salt that will bear up an egg; to about every four gallons of liquor add two pounds of sugar and two ounces of pulverized saltpetre; mix well together, and pour over the meat until it is covered; it must be kept under the brine.

SPICED BEEF.

MRS. J. A. MCMAHON.

For a twenty-five pound round take one and a half ounces of pulverized saltpetre and a handful of brown sugar; pound and mix thoroughly; then rub the beef well with the mixture. Put it into a tub as near the size of the round as you can get, and let it remain forty-eight hours, during which time turn and rub the beef twice. Then have prepared one and a half ounces of ground pepper, two ounces of allspice, one of cloves, and three or four good handfuls of fine salt; pound and mix the spice and salt, and rub the beef with it; turn and rub it every day for a week, taking care to preserve the pickle. It will be ready for use in three or four weeks.

SPICED BEEF.

MISS BLOSSOM BROWN.

To twenty pounds of round beef take two and a half pounds of suet, chopped very fine, and mixed with black pepper until it is almost black. Mix with this one handful whole allspice, and one of whole cloves; punch holes through the meat and stuff with suet; sew up in a bag very tight, and cover well with a brine made of four gallons of water, one and a half pounds of sugar, two ounces of pulverized saltpetre, and six pounds of common salt. It is ready for use in three weeks. Boil well, and when cold remove the bag, and slice from the cut end.

VEAL OMELET.

Three pounds of finely-chopped veal; six rolled crackers; three eggs well beaten; two large spoonfuls of cream; one of salt; one teaspoonful of white pepper; use powdered sage, thyme, or sweet marjoram if you like; mix all well together; form into one or two loaves; baste with butter and water while baking. Bake one hour and a half. Fresh beef can be used in the same way.

VEAL ROLL.

MRS. A. C. CLARK.

Two pounds of pork-steak; three pounds of veal chopped fine; ten crackers, rolled; one tablespoonful of thyme, summer savory, or parsley; six eggs; salt and butter. Mix thoroughly. Bake one hour; then spread eggs and cracker over it and put in to brown.

VEAL CUTLETS.

MRS. S. CRAIGHEAD.

Have a steak of first cut; pound and season it well; cut the outer edges; then beat it into a good shape. Take one egg, beat it a little; roll the cutlet in it; then cover thoroughly with rolled crackers. Have a lump of butter and lard mixed hot in your skillet; put in the meat and let cook slowly; when nicely browned on both sides, stir in one spoonful of flour for the gravy; add a half-pint of sweet milk, and let it come to a boil; salt and pepper, and grate a little nutmeg on it.

VEAL CROQUETTES.

MRS. S. GEBHART.

Mince veal very fine; add one onion chopped; mix half a cup of milk with one teaspoonful of flour; piece of butter size of a walnut; cook until thickened, and stir into the meat; roll into balls; dip into a beaten egg and roll in bread-crumbs; fry in plenty of hot lard.

SCOLLOPED VEAL.

Take three veal-steaks; boil until very tender; take them out; save the water in which they were boiled; chop the meat up very fine; put into a deep dish alternate layers of the meat and bread-crumbs; salt and pepper each layer; use small lumps of butter. When the bowl is pretty full, add the liquor, of which there should be about a pint, and a teacup of milk; a pint of bread-crumbs will be about enough. Cold roast veal, with the stuffing and gravy, can be used in the same way.

MARBLED VEAL.

MRS. D. A. BRADFORD.

Take some cold roasted veal; season with spice; beat in a mortar. Skin a cold boiled tongue; cut up and pound it to a paste, adding to it nearly its weight of butter; put some of the veal into a pot, then strew in lumps of the pounded tongue; put in another layer of the veal, and again more tongue; press it down and pour clarified butter on top. This cuts very prettily, like veined marble. The dressed white meat of fowls may be used instead of veal.

IRISH STEW.

WINNIE.

Take mutton-chops (one for each person); cover well with water, and let come to a boil. Pour off this and add more water. Take a lump of butter the size of an egg, two table-spoonfuls of flour, a teacupful of milk, with pepper and salt to taste; also potatoes and a small onion or two, if liked. Boil all till the potatoes are done.

SWEET-BREADS.

Parboil the sweet-breads as soon as you get them. Remove the tough parts carefully. Let them lie in cold water a short time before using them, then have rolled crackers to rub them in, and broil or fry as you choose.

SWEET-BREADS WITH TOMATOES.

MRS. JOHN A. MCMAHON.

Take two large parboiled sweet-breads; put them into a stew-pan with one and a half gills of water, and season with salt, cayenne and black pepper to taste. Place them over a slow fire. Mix one large teaspoonful of browned flour with a small piece of butter, to which add a leaf of mace. Stir the butter and gravy well together. After letting them stew slowly for half an hour, set the stew-pan into a quick oven, and when the sweet-breads are nicely browned, place them on a dish. Pour the gravy into half a pint of stewed tomatoes thickened with one dessert-spoonful of flour and a small piece of butter, and seasoned with salt and pepper; strain it through a small wire sieve into the stewpan; let it come to a boil and stir until done, then pour it over the sweet-breads and send it to the table hot.

SWEET-BREADS WITH MUSHROOMS.

Parboil sweet-breads, allowing eight medium ones to a can of mushrooms. Cut the sweet-breads about half an inch square; stew until tender. Slice mushrooms and stew in the liquor for one hour, then add to the sweet-breads a coffee-cup of cream, pepper and salt, and a tablespoonful of butter. Just before serving, throw quickly in two tablespoonfuls of Madeira wine.

Sweet-breads broiled, and served with a dressing of green peas, make a very nice dish.

FRIED LIVER.

MRS. G.

Cut the liver in pieces an inch thick; steam fifteen minutes; have frying some slices of pickled pork; when done take out the pork and fry the liver in the hot grease a nice brown; add a little flour and water to the gravy, cooking a few minutes; pour over the meat, and serve; pepper and salt to taste.

MOCK TERRAPIN.

Half a calf's-liver, seasoned and fried brown; hash it, not very fine, and dredge it thickly with flour. Take one teaspoonful of mixed mustard; a pinch of cayenne pepper; two hard-boiled eggs, chopped fine; a piece of butter the size of an egg; one teacupful of water; and boil together a minute or two.

DRIED LIVER.

MRS. W. A. B.

Allow a beef's-liver to remain in corned-beef brine for ten days. Hang it up ten days to dry. Slice thin and broil, or fry in butter

BOILED HAM.

MRS. P. P. LOWE.

Scrape off the outside gently; soak in cold water for three hours, if the ham is small, or over night if it is large. Take the ham from the water; wipe it dry, and place it in a boiler large enough to hold it without bending, and cover with cold water. Throw in six cloves, four small onions, and a handful of parsley; boil gently four hours for a medium-sized ham. When boiled, take out and trim; removing the rind and the small bone at the large end, by breaking it off carefully without tearing the meat. After the ham is trimmed, put it in the oven for from one-half to one hour, basting it frequently.

BAKED HAM.

A ham of sixteen pounds to be boiled three hours slowly; then skin, and in the fat rub half a pound of brown sugar; pour over it a gill of wine, and cover with bread-crumbs. Bake for two hours, basting with wine.

HAM SANDWICHES.

MRS. J. W. S.

Chop fine some cold dressed ham, and mix with it a teaspoonful of chopped pickle, one of mustard, and a little pepper. Beat about half a pound of butter to a cream, and then add the ham and seasoning. Spread on thin slices of bread, and place between them bits of cold roast beef, mutton, chicken, or quail.

TRAVELING LUNCH.

MISS HATTIE BROWN.

Sardines chopped fine; also a little ham; a small quantity of chopped pickles; mix with mustard, pepper, catsup, salt, and vinegar; spread between bread nicely buttered. To be like jelly-cake, cut in slices crossways. Will keep fresh some time.

SANDWICHES.

MRS. REBECCA BUCK.

Rub one tablespoonful of mustard into one-half pound of sweet butter; spread on thin slices of bread; cut boiled ham very thin, and place in between two pieces of the bread.

HASH.

Take cold beef of any kind; cut very fine; then take about one-third mashed potatoes; warm, season, and pound all together in a stone crock; cut in slices and brown in butter.

CRACKER HASH.

MRS. D. W. S.

To one pound of cooked beef chopped fine take seven crackers (rolled). First cook the meat in a little water a few minutes, seasoning with salt and pepper; then stir into the crackers and pour all into a pudding-dish; if too dry, add a little water. Take a piece of butter size of a walnut, and cut in small pieces over the top of the dish. Bake about twenty minutes, or until quite brown. Serve in the same dish.

HAM BALLS.

Beat together two eggs and half a cupful of bread-crumbs; chop fine some bits of boiled ham, and mix with them; make into balls, and fry a nice brown.

FRIED PATTIES.

Mince a little cold veal and ham, allowing one-third ham to two-thirds veal; add an egg boiled hard and chopped fine, and a seasoning of pounded mace, salt, pepper, and lemon-peel; moisten with a little gravy or cream. Make a good puff paste; roll rather thin and cut into round or square pieces; put the mince between two of them, pinch the edges to keep in the gravy, and fry a light brown. They may also be baked in patty-pans; in that case they should be brushed over with the yolk of an egg before they are put in the oven.

SCRAMBLED EGGS WITH BEEF.

Chip dried beef very fine; put equal parts of lard and butter in a skillet; when hot put in the beef; heat up a few minutes, stirring to keep from burning; break up some eggs in a bowl; season and stir in. It will require but a few minutes' cooking.

OMELET, OR FRENCH EGG CAKE.

E. C.

Beat up thoroughly six eggs, a teaspoonful of sweet cream or milk, and a little salt. Fry in a pan in which there is one-half ounce of melted butter, over a quick fire. In order that the omelet may remain soft and juicy, it is necessary that the pan should be hot before the eggs are poured in. During the frying move the pan continually to and fro, so that what is below may always come on top again. Continue this until there is a cake formed, then let it remain still a moment to give it color. Turn out on a dish, and serve immediately.

FRENCH OMELET.

One quart of milk; one pint of bread-crumbs; five eggs; one tablespoonful of flour; one onion, chopped fine; chopped parsley; season with pepper and salt. Have butter melted in a frying-pan; when the omelet is brown, turn it over. Double it when served.

SAUCES AND CATSUPS.

DRAWN BUTTER (FOR SAUCE).

MRS. R. P. BROWN.

One-quarter pound of butter; rub with it two teaspoonfuls of flour. When well mixed, put in a sauce-pan, with one table-spoonful of water and a little salt. Cover it, and set the sauce-pan in a larger one of boiling water. Shake it constantly till completely melted and beginning to boil. If the pan containing the butter be set on coals, it will oil the butter and spoil it. A great variety of sauces, which are excellent to eat with fish, poultry, or boiled meats, can be made by adding different herbs to melted butter.

CURRY POWDER,

FOR GRAVIES FOR DUCKS AND OTHER MEATS.

MRS. D. W. S.

Mix an ounce of ginger; one of mustard; one of black pepper; three of coriander seed; three of tumeric; quarter of an ounce of cayenne pepper; half an ounce of cardamom; half an ounce of cumin seed and cinnamon. Pound the whole very fine; sift, and keep it in a bottle corked tight.

CELERY SAUCE.

As this sauce is to be used for boiled chicken or turkey, put a good handful of celery, tied up in a bunch, into the pot with the fowl. When quite soft take it out, chop it fine, and mix with rich drawn butter and some of the water in which it was boiled. Season with pepper and salt, and stew all together.

TOMATO CATSUP.

MISS PERRINE.

Take one gallon of strained tomatoes; four tablespoonfuls of salt; one and a half of allspice; three of mustard; eight pods of red pepper. Grind the articles fine. Simmer slowly in strong vinegar three or four hours, then strain through a hair sieve, and bottle. Enough vinegar should be used to have half a gallon of liquor when the process is over.

TOMATO CATSUP.

MRS. H. L. BROWN.

Cut up ripe tomatoes; boil soft and strain; put them on again and boil half down. Then to every three and a half gallons of juice put twelve tablespoonfuls of salt, six of pepper, one of allspice, one of mustard, one of mace, one-half of cloves, one of ginger, six small pods of red pepper chopped fine; boil hard one hour.

TOMATO CATSUP.

MRS. E. F. S.

To one and a half bushels of tomatoes use the following spices: Three papers of cloves, two of allspice, a little cayenne pepper, and plenty of black pepper and salt, and a pint of vinegar to each gallon. Tie up a few onions in a bag, and boil with the catsup. Boil half down.

COLD TOMATO CATSUP.

MRS. BIERCE.

One-half peck tomatoes, run through a sieve; one teacupful of salt; one of mustard-seed; six red peppers; three table-spoonfuls of pepper; one-half gallon of vinegar; piece of horse-radish; one teacupful of nasturtions; half a cup of celery-seed. Do not cook, but seal tight in bottles.

TOMATO MUSTARD.

Take one peck of tomatoes; cut them into a porcelain kettle; boil until soft; rub through a sieve; put the pulp back in the kettle, and boil until quite thick. Take one teaspoonful of cayenne pepper, one of white, half a one of cloves, two of mustard, one tablespoonful of salt. Let all boil together a few minutes, then stir in half a pint of vinegar. When cool, bottle and cork tightly.

FOR MIXING MUSTARD.

MRS. L. MOORE.

Three teaspoonfuls good mustard; one teaspoonful salt; half teaspoonful pepper; two tablespoonfuls brown sugar, rolled; mix with hot vinegar. Better after the first day.

MIXED MUSTARD.

Two tablespoonfuls of dry mustard; one teaspoonful of salt; one teaspoonful of brown sugar. Mix to a thick paste with oil, and then to a proper consistency with vinegar. Let stand twenty-four hours before using.

CUCUMBER CATSUP.

MRS. WILLIAM BOMBERGER.

Take three dozen large cucumbers, three white onions; grate all to a pulp; drain through a sieve several hours; add to the pulp salt, pepper, and good vinegar. Seal up in bottles.

WALNUT CATSUP.

MRS. E.

Take young, tender walnuts; prick them and place in a jar with sufficient water to cover them; add a handful of salt to every twenty-five walnuts. Stir them twice a day for fourteen days; drain off the liquor into a kettle; cover the walnuts with boiling vinegar; crush them to a pulp, and strain through a cullender into the juice. For every quart, take two ounces each of white pepper and ginger and one each of cloves and grated nutmeg, a pinch of cayenne pepper, a small onion minced fine, and a teaspoonful of celery seed tied in muslin. Boil all together for one hour. When cold, bottle.

MUSHROOM CATSUP.

Put the mushrooms in layers, with salt sprinkled over each layer. Let them stand four days. Then mash them fine, and to every quart add two-thirds of a teaspoonful of black pepper, and boil in a stone jar, set in boiling water, two hours. Strain without squeezing; boil the liquor; let it stand to cool and settle. Then bottle and cork tight, and set in a cool place.

WILD PLUM CATSUP.

MRS. ADMIRAL SCHENCK.

To ten pounds of plums take five pounds sugar. Boil, mash, and strain the fruit; and to every quart of juice add rather more than one-half pint of vinegar; add cinnamon, cloves, and nut-megs; boil fifteen minutes, and put into bottles.

GOOSEBERRY CATSUP.

MRS. E. ROHRER.

To five pounds of berries put two and a half pounds of sugar; boil down as thick as apple-butter; add cinnamon and cloves to taste; a pinch of salt; one pint of vinegar; strain through a hair sieve.

CURRANT CATSUP.

MRS. JOHN DAY.

Two quarts of currant-juice; three pounds of sugar; one pint of vinegar; one tablespoonful each of cinnamon, cloves, pepper, allspice, and nutmeg; boil twenty minutes.

GRAPE CATSUP.

MRS. J. D. LOOMIS.

Ten pints of grapes; two pounds of sugar; one pint of vine-gar; one ounce cloves; one ounce cinnamon. Put the vinegar and sugar together; boil fifteen minutes; then squeeze the pulps of the grapes out of the skin and boil a few minutes; then warm the pulps and rub the seeds out in a cullender; put the skins and pulps together and add them to the vinegar and sugar; boil the whole twenty minutes.

CHILI SAUCE.

MRS. R. P. BROWN.

Six good-sized onions; twelve green peppers; three dozen ripe tomatoes peeled and chopped; three or four tablespoonfuls of fine salt. Stew all together gently several hours, until soft and beginning to thicken; seal hot.

CELERY VINEGAR.

Pound two large spoonfuls of celery-seed fine; put it in a quart bottle and fill up with sharp vinegar; it must be closely corked. The same steeped in brandy is nice for flavoring soups.

CELERY SOY.

MRS. J. MOREHEAD.

One peck of tomatoes boiled; one teacup of salt; one-half teacup of fine white pepper; one teaspoonful cayenne pepper; four onions chopped fine; one pound sugar. Boil one hour, and just before removing from the fire add a quart of good, sharp vinegar. When cold, add a half cup of celery-seed, rolled; two tablespoonfuls ground cloves and allspice. Let stand one night; then press through a sieve, and bottle closely.

TO KEEP HORSE-RADISH ALL WINTER.

Have a quantity grated while the root is in perfection; put in bottles; fill up with strong vinegar and keep tightly corked.

4

VEGETABLES.

ENDEAVOR to have your vegetables as fresh as possible. Wash them thoroughly, and cut out all the decayed parts. Lay them in cold water until you are ready to use them.

Vegetables should be put on to cook in boiling water and salt. Never let them stand after coming off the fire; put them instantly into a cullender, over a pot of boiling water, if you have to keep them back for dinner.

Peas, beans, and asparagus, if young, will cook in twenty-five or thirty minutes. They should be boiled in a good deal of salt water.

Cauliflower should be wrapped in a cloth, when boiled, and served with rich drawn butter.

Potato-water is thought to be unhealthy; therefore do not boil potatoes in soup, but in another vessel, and add them to it when nearly cooked.

BAKED TOMATOES.

Fill a deep pan with ripe tomatoes (as many as will lie on the bottom); round out a hole in the centre of each, and fill up with bread-crumbs, butter, salt, pepper, and a little sugar. Put a teacupful of water in the pan to prevent them from burning. Bake brown, and send to the table hot.

BROILED TOMATOES.

Take smooth, flat tomatoes; wipe and set them on a gridiron, with the stem-side down, over live coals. When this is brown, turn them and let cook until quite hot through; place them on a hot dish. To be dressed, when eaten, with butter, pepper, and salt.

SCOLLOPED TOMATOES.

Put alternate layers of sliced tomatoes and bread-crumbs into a bread-pan. Season with sliced onion, butter, pepper, and salt; and bake for one hour.

FRIED TOMATOES.

Slice tomatoes quite thick; pepper and salt them; roll in flour; and fry in equal parts of butter and lard. Put them in a dish to be served; keeping very hot. A little flour and butter mixed; stir into the skillet with a cup of milk; boil until well thickened; pour over the tomatoes.

SLICED TOMATOES.

Scald ripe tomatoes; let them stand in cold water fifteen minutes; then take off the skin, and slice in a dish garnished with sweet peppers.

TOMATO SALAD.

Slice tomatoes, and serve with mayonnaise salad-dressing.

STEWED CORN.
KATE P. BROWN.

Cut the corn from the cobs; boil the cobs ten or fifteen minutes; then take them out and put the corn into the same water. When it is tender, put in some milk; season with butter, pepper, and salt. Just before serving, stir in beaten eggs, allowing three eggs to a dozen ears of corn; one pint of milk to a quart of corn.

SUCCOTASH.
KATE P. BROWN.

Put Lima beans on to boil soon after breakfast; let them get well done. Have the corn boiling in a separate pot. When done, cut the corn off the cobs, and have twice as much corn as beans; put the corn with the beans, and let them boil. Just before serving, put in a little butter, pepper, and salt.

GREEN CORN PUDDING.

MRS. JAMES STOCKSTILL.

Four ears of green corn cut down fine; two eggs; one pint of milk; butter size of an egg; three tablespoonfuls of flour; salt and pepper; beat well together; bake one hour. To be served as a vegetable.

CORN OYSTERS.

To one quart of grated corn add three eggs and three or four grated crackers; beat well, and season with salt and pepper; fry in butter or lard. If the corn is young and juicy, more crackers may be needed; drop in the pan with a spoon.

CORN FRITTERS.

MRS. P. P. LOWE.

One dozen ears of corn when it first comes, or a half-dozen ears after it is grown. Cut the grains down the middle of each row, and cut carefully off the cob. If the grains are large, chop them a little with the chopping-knife after they are cut off. Add to the corn and mix well the yolks of two eggs, half a cup of sweet milk, a lump of butter the size of a walnut, a pinch of salt, pepper, and a small cup of flour; lastly, beat to a stiff froth the whites of the eggs. Fry a nice brown on both sides in a skillet with fresh lard, and serve hot.

BOILED ONIONS.

Boil in four waters and drain off; pick to pieces with a fork as they cook. Mix a little flour and butter together, and put in two tablespoonfuls of warm milk; boil and pour over the onions; season well.

BOILED TURNIPS.

MRS. MCM.

Boil turnips in a good deal of salt water; when soft, drain off the water and put them in a skillet with cream and butter, and let them simmer.

GREEN PEAS.

KATE P. BROWN.

Put the hulls in a pot; cover them with water and boil thoroughly; then strain and put the peas in the same water, and let boil until tender. When ready to serve, put in some butter and pepper, a pinch of salt, and the least bit of sugar.

FRICASSEED PEAS.

MRS. ELIZA PIERCE.

Put the peas in a pot; boil till soft; season with salt, pepper; add a cup of milk and a small cup of butter; a tablespoonful of flour in the milk. When ready to serve, add the yolks of two eggs in a cup of milk or cream.

STRING BEANS.

Get them young and crispy; break off both ends, and string them; break in halves, and boil in water with a little salt until tender; drain free from water, and season with pepper; add butter and a spoonful of cream or milk, and boil a few minutes.

COOKING BEANS.

FROM MOORE'S "RURAL NEW YORKER."

If, my dear Rural, you should ever wish
For breakfast or dinner a tempting dish
Of the beans so famous in Boston town,
You must read the rules I here lay down.
When the sun has set in golden light,
And around you fall the shades of night,
A large, deep dish you first prepare;
A quart of beans select with care;
And pick them over, until you find
Not a speck or a mote is left behind.
A lot of cold water on them pour
Till every bean is covered o'er,

And they seem to your poetic eye
Like pearls in the depth of the sea to lie ;
Here, if you please, you may let them stay
Till just after breakfast the very next day,
When a parboiling process must be gone through
(I mean for the beans, and not for you) ;
Then if, in the pantry, there still should be
That bean-pot, so famous in history,
With all due deference bring it out,
And, if there's a skimmer lying about,
Skim half of the beans from the boiling pan
Into the bean pot as fast as you can ;
Then turn to Biddy and calmly tell her
To take a huge knife and go to the cellar ;
For you must have, like Shylock of old,
"A pound of flesh," ere your beans grow cold ;
But, very unlike that ancient Jew,
Nothing but pork will do for you.
Then tell once more your maiden fair,
In the choice of the piece to take great care,
For a streak of fat and a streak of lean
Will give the right flavor to every bean !
This you must wash, and rinse, and score,
Put into the pot, and round it pour
The rest, till the view presented seems
Like an island of pork in an ocean of beans ;
Pour on boiling hot water enough to cover
The tops of the beans completely over,
Shove into the oven and bake till done,
And the triumph of Yankee cookery's won !

BAKED BEANS.

MRS. A. C. COBURN.

Three pints of beans and half a pound of salt pork ; put beans
to soak over night ; next morning put them in a vessel with a
gallon of soft water and half a teaspoonful of soda ; let simmer

TO COOK ASPARAGUS.

Cut off all the tough parts and lay the bunches in a pan; cover
with boiling water and let them cook slowly half an hour.   Ten
minutes before they are done, add a little salt.   Have ready two
or three slices of toasted bread.   Butter well, and put a tablespoonful or two of liquor over it; take the asparagus up carefully
and lay it on the toast; mix a piece of butter thoroughly with a
little flour; add pepper and salt, and stir into the liquor and
pour over the asparagus.

NEW POTATOES.

Scrape and wash new potatoes; put in a sauce-pan with hot
water; when done, pour off the water; set them on top of the
stove a few minutes to steam; put in a lump of butter size of an
egg, two tablespoonfuls of cream; season with salt and pepper;
boil a few minutes.   Shake the pan to keep them from burning.

STEWED POTATOES.

Boil the potatoes, and cut into thin slices; make a dressing by
mixing one tablespoonful of melted butter with a little flour and
a cupful of cream; add the yolk of an egg and a little chopped
parsley.   Stir up with potatoes, and serve immediately.

POTATO BALLS.

MRS. R. P. BROWN.

Mix mashed potatoes with the yolk of an egg; roll into balls,
and flour them; or cover with egg and bread-crumbs.   Fry them
in clean drippings, or brown in a Dutch oven.

POTATO PUFFS.
MRS. W. A. PHELPS.

Take two cupfuls of mashed potatoes, and stir in two table-spoonfuls of melted butter; beating to a white cream before adding anything else. Then put with this two eggs whipped very light, and a teacupful of cream or milk; salting to taste. Beat all well; pour into a deep dish; and bake in a quick oven until brown.

POTATO FRITTERS.

One cupful of mashed potatoes; two eggs; one-half pint of milk; one tablespoonful of flour, and lump of butter. Drop in boiling lard.

POTATO CROQUETTES.
MISS HOTCHKISS.

Take six potatoes; peel, and cut in small pieces; cover with boiling water; when soft, strain off the water, and pass through a cullender; mix three eggs (one at a time) with the potatoes; add two tablespoonfuls of bread-crumbs and a little salt; place all over the fire, and stir constantly. When thoroughly mixed, take off the fire, and set to cool. Roll into balls, and fry in hot lard.

SARATOGA POTATOES.
MRS. D. W. S.

Take four large potatoes (new ones are best); pare, and cut into thin slices on a slaw-cutter; put them into salt water, and let stand while breakfast is preparing. Then have ready a skillet of boiling lard. Take a handful of the potatoes, squeeze the water from them, and dry in a napkin; separate the slices and drop into the lard, being careful that the pieces do not adhere to each other. Stir with a fork till they are a light brown color. Take them out with a wire spoon, and drain well before putting into the dish. Do not put more than a handful into the lard at a time. Do not cover the dish when served.

CABBAGE A LA CAULIFLOWER.

MRS. R. P. BROWN.

Cut the cabbage fine, as for slaw; put it into a stew-pan; cover with water, and keep closely covered; when tender, drain off the water; put in a small piece of butter with a little salt; half a cup of cream, or one cup of milk. Leave on the stove a few minutes before serving.

CREAM CABBAGE.

MRS. CHARLES SPINNING.

Beat together the yolks of two eggs; one-half cup of sugar; one-half cup of vinegar; a piece of butter the size of an egg; salt, and a little cayenne pepper. Put the mixture in a sauce-pan, and stir until it boils; then stir in one cup of cream. Let it boil. Pour it over the cabbage while hot.

STEAMED RICE.

One large cup of rice; pick it over and wash thoroughly, and drain; put it in a bucket and cover closely; set in boiling water; don't stir while cooking. Steam till soft. Season, and eat while warm, with cream.

BOILED RICE.

MRS. W. R. S. AYRES.

Take one cup of rice in half a pint of water, and put on to boil; when the rice has absorbed the water, put in one pint of sweet milk, and let boil three-quarters of an hour; don't stir while cooking.

RICE CROQUETTES.

Take cold boiled rice; add three eggs, with sugar and lemon-peel to your taste. Make into oval balls; rub with bread-crumbs, and dip them in beaten egg. Fry in butter; when done, sprinkle sugar over them.

FRIED EGG–PLANT.

Cut in slices, and lay in salt and water for one or two hours ; wipe dry, and season with pepper and salt ; dip the slices into yolk of egg and grated bread-crumbs.   Fry in butter till brown.

TO COOK EGG–PLANTS.

HATTIE B. BROWN.

Slice, pare, and parboil ; mash, and season with butter, salt, and pepper ; one egg to a plant ; about two tablespoonfuls of flour ; milk enough to make a batter.   Drop a spoonful at a time into hot lard, and fry like fritters.

STUFFED EGG–PLANT.

MRS. S. CRAIGHEAD.

Take a full-grown egg-plant ; cut it in two lengthwise ; take all the inside out (leaving the skin about half an inch thick) ; chop it quite fine ; mix with it about as much bread-crumbs as you have of egg-plant ; salt and pepper to taste ; one teaspoonful of sugar.   Have ready a tablespoonful of butter in a skillet, and, when hot, put in the mixture, and let it cook about ten minutes, stirring it occasionally.   Then return it to the shells ; put in the oven, and bake about half an hour.   Serve in the shells.

OYSTER-PLANT.

MRS. GEO. L. PHILLIPS.

Wash and scrape ; cover with water and a little salt.   When tender, pour off the water ; chop them up immediately, or they will turn black ; put into a kettle ; add half a pint of cream, one teaspoonful of flour, a lump of butter.   Pour over, and let come to a boil.

FRIED OYSTER-PLANT.

Parboil oyster-plant ; scrape off the outside ; cut it in slices ; dip it into beaten egg and fine bread-crumbs ; fry in hot lard.

FRIED OYSTER-PLANT, No. 2.

Scrape the roots, and boil in water, with a little salt, until tender; drain and mash them; put in a small lump of butter and one egg; season with pepper and salt; add flour enough to make them stick together. Make into cakes, and fry in butter.

BOILED HUBBARD SQUASH.

MRS. EVANS.

Skin, and cut up in long slices; put in a pot, with points down; boil till tender; pour off water, and drain; mash, with butter and salt.

BAKED SQUASH.

Cut in squares, leaving on the rind, and bake in the oven like sweet potatoes.

SPINACH.

E. C. B.

After being carefully washed, stuff it into a sauce-pan, without any water; sprinkle over a little salt, and cover closely; shake occasionally while cooking. When tender, drain it, and serve with drawn butter.

GREENS.

Boil beet-tops, turnip-tops, spinach, cabbage-sprouts, poke-sprouts, dandelion, and lamb's quarters in salted water until they are tender; drain in a cullender, pressing hard. Serve them, garnished with hard-boiled eggs cut in slices.

BROILED MUSHROOMS.

Cut off the stems and peel off the skins of the mushrooms; put them on the gridiron, hollow side up; put a little butter, pepper, and salt on each; cook over hot coals a few minutes; do not turn. Serve hot, with a little more butter.

STEWED MUSHROOMS.

Prepare as above; put them in a stew-pan, with a little water and salt; simmer slowly half an hour; add butter, a little flour, pepper, and two tablespoonfuls of cream. Boil up once, and serve on toast.

MACARONI AS A VEGETABLE.

MRS. R. P. BROWN.

Simmer one-half pound of macaroni in plenty of water till tender, but not broken; strain off the water. Take the yolks of five and the whites of two eggs; one-half pint of cream; white meat and ham, chopped very fine; three spoonfuls of grated cheese; season with salt and pepper; heat all together, stirring constantly. Mix with the macaroni; put in a buttered mould, and steam one hour. It is quite as good baked.

BAKED MACARONI.

Boil half a pound of macaroni until quite soft; put it into a vegetable-dish with a little mustard, pepper, and salt, a small piece of butter, and some grated cheese. Bake ten or fifteen minutes.

SALADS.

CHICKEN SALAD.
MISS L.

EIGHT eggs; one pint of vinegar; one-half pound of butter; three tablespoonfuls of olive oil; sixteen teaspoonfuls of made mustard; one teaspoonful, each, of red and black pepper. Beat the eggs very light; stir in a tablespoonful of salt; add one-half pint of vinegar, one-half pound of melted butter; set the jar in a pot of boiling water; stir well till cooked to a good thickness; take off the fire, and stir in the rest of the vinegar; then add the pepper, mustard, and oil. This quantity is sufficient for three chickens or one turkey. After boiling the chickens, chop up, not too fine; take equal quantities of celery and chicken; put in cabbage, if you like it.

CHICKEN SALAD.
MRS. G. L. PHILLIPS.

For one chicken use six eggs, and twice as much celery as chicken. Beat the eggs separately; one heaping teaspoonful of mustard in yolks; one and a half cups of vinegar; one large spoonful of sugar; lump of butter the size of an egg; a little cayenne pepper. Cook the dressing same as custard. Save a little for the top.

MAYONNAISE SALAD DRESSING.
MRS. E. F. STODDARD.

Into the yolk of one raw egg stir all the olive oil it will hold; if dropped in very slowly, half a pint of oil can be used; season with cayenne pepper, salt, and mustard.

CHICKEN SALAD.

MRS. R. R. DICKEY.

To one pint of chopped chicken take one pint of chopped celery; a heaping teaspoonful of mustard; one and a half tea-cupfuls of vinegar, one tablespoonful of sugar, and one of melted butter; five eggs beaten separately; a pinch of cayenne pepper. Salt to taste. Mix sugar, vinegar, mustard, and eggs together, and scald the dressing as you would float. One large chicken will fill a pint cup.

SALAD DRESSING.

MRS. G. L. PHILLIPS.

One teacupful of vinegar; put it on to boil; yolks of three eggs beaten with a dessert-spoonful of flour; six mustard-spoon-fuls of mixed mustard, a pinch of cayenne pepper, three tablespoonfuls of white sugar and three of salad oil. Two tea-spoonfuls of salt. Beat all together, and let cook until it thickens, stirring all the time.

SALAD DRESSING.

MRS. J. H. PIERCE.

Rub till smooth the yolks of five hard-boiled eggs; add five tablespoonfuls of rich, sour cream, thick enough to heap upon the spoon; season with salt, pepper, plenty of mustard, and but little vinegar. Serve upon lettuce alone; or add cold chicken, or any delicate meat or fish cut small.

MUSTARD CABBAGE.

MRS. A. F. PAYNE.

Beat one egg with a tablespoonful of sugar; mix one tea-spoonful of mustard in one-half teacupful of vinegar; add this to the egg and sugar, and boil until it is quite thick, stirring all the time; pour while hot over finely-cut cabbage, previously salted.

LETTUCE SALAD.

MRS. A. L. STOUT.

Cut two bunches of lettuce; mix two tablespoonfuls of mustard, two of catsup, one of horseradish, with yolks of two eggs, and butter the size of an egg; a little vinegar; chop the whites of the eggs, and mix all together.

CELERY SALAD.

MRS. J. R. YOUNG.

One head of cabbage; three bunches of celery; chopped very fine. Take one teacupful of vinegar; a lump of butter the size of an egg; yolks of two eggs; one teaspoonful mustard; one of salt; a pinch of cayenne pepper.; two teaspoonfuls of sugar. Mix these well; put the mixture on the stove and heat it until it thickens; stir it all the time; when cold, add two tablespoonfuls of rich, sweet cream. Pour this over your salad; and if it does not make it moist enough, add a little cold vinegar.

POTATO SALAD.

MRS. A. L. STOUT.

Take two large potatoes; boil with the skins on; boil two onions. When all is cold, cut the potatoes about half an inch square; cut the onions very fine; mix with them a handful of parsley, cut into little pieces; also one large bunch of celery, chopped. Put all together; then add pepper and salt, and wet with about half a teacupful of vinegar.

POTATO SALAD.

MRS. CADY, INDIANAPOLIS.

Boil four potatoes; peel and slice; add half of a small onion, cut fine; two small bunches of celery, chopped fine; also whites of two hard-boiled eggs. The yolks mixed with mustard, oil, vinegar, pepper, and salt to taste.

CELERY SLAW.

MISS DRYDEN.

One-half head of cabbage; one bunch of celery; two hard-boiled eggs, all chopped fine. Mix with it two teaspoonfuls of sugar, two of mustard, one-half of pepper and salt. Moisten with vinegar.

COLE-SLAW.

MRS. DR. MCDERMONT.

Put two large spoonfuls of cream on to boil, with a wineglass of vinegar; beat the yolks of three eggs, and stir in the cream; let it boil a moment, then set away to cool. Chop fine a small-sized head of cabbage, and sprinkle it with salt, pepper, and mustard. Add the egg-mixture just before serving.

COLE-SLAW.

MRS. WM. CRAIGHEAD.

Beat the yolks of two eggs; and half a pint of cream or rich milk; two tablespoonfuls of sugar; one of mustard; four of vinegar; one teaspoonful celery seed; two teaspoonfuls salt; a little cayenne pepper; a piece of butter size of a walnut. Pour the mixture into a sauce-pan; stir constantly, until it boils. Chop your cabbage fine, and pour the mixture over while hot. Let it stand until cold, before sending to the table.

DRESSING FOR HOT SLAW.

MRS. D. W. IDDINGS.

Yolks of two eggs, well beaten; one teaspoonful of salt and pepper; one tablespoonful of sugar; three of melted butter; four of vinegar; two of water. Let come to a boil. Then put in the cabbage and boil.

PIES.

PASTRY.

MRS. ELIZA PIERCE.

ONE and a quarter pounds of flour; one pound of shortening (two-thirds butter and one-third lard); wet sufficiently with cold water and mix with a knife, stirring as little as possible. This quantity will make five pies.

CELEBRATED PUFF PASTE.

MRS. JEROME BUCKINGHAM.

One pound of flour; one pound butter and one egg. Mix the flour with an egg and a lump of butter the size of an egg to a very stiff paste with cold water; knead well for ten or fifteen minutes; divide the butter into six equal parts; squeeze the buttermilk all out of the butter; roll the paste, on which spread one part of the butter, dredging it with flour; repeat until all the butter is rolled in.

PASTRY.

MRS. JAMES TURPIN.

One pound of flour; one-half pound of lard; one-quarter pound of butter. Rub lard and flour well together; add water sufficient to make a dough; and roll out into a thin sheet. Spread all the butter over it. Roll up the paste into close folds as you would a sheet of music; fold over once, and roll lightly. This quantity will make three pies.

PLAIN PIE CRUST.

MRS. H. STRONG.

Three cups of flour; one cup of shortening; rub lightly through the flour; wet with cold water; mould it as little as possible. This makes crust for two pies.

5

TO ICE PIES.

White of one egg to one pie ; beat up and spread on top crust with a feather, after the pie is a little cool. Then spread sugar on with a knife dipped in hot water ; repeat several times. Set in a cool oven to dry.

PLAIN PASTRY.

MRS. JAMES STOCKSTILL.

To one quart of flour, one-half teaspoonful of salt, and two tablespoonfuls of butter or lard. Rub lightly through the flour (it is better to use a spoon) ; then add only enough water to moisten. Take out on the board and roll very thin without kneading it ; spread with butter in bits ; sprinkle with flour, and fold evenly and square. If you desire, it can be rolled a second time. Before putting the top crust on the pie, wet with milk ; it improves the appearance.

POTATO PASTE.

Boil and mash ten potatoes ; add a teaspoonful of salt, a large spoonful of butter, and one-half cup of milk or cream ; then stiffen with flour until it can be rolled out. This is nice for pot-pie or apple-dumplings.

BAKED APPLE-DUMPLINGS.

Pare, quarter, and core the apples ; put one tablespoonful of baking-powder in one quart of flour ; one teacupful of butter. Mix with milk ; make stiffer than for biscuits ; roll and cut in strips, and put around the pieces of apple. Put in a pudding-dish one quart of water, one teacupful of sugar, and a small lump of butter ; set it on top of the stove, and let it come to a boil ; then put in the dumplings. Bake in a brisk oven.

BOILED APPLE-DUMPLINGS.

MRS. ISAAC VAN AUSDAL.

On one quart of flour pour enough boiling water to make a stiff paste ; one teaspoonful of salt in the flour. Roll the paste half an inch thick. Cover the apple, and tie up separately. Boil until tender.

STRAWBERRY SHORT-CAKE.
MRS. H. WYATT.

Make a short pie-crust; roll two thicknesses, and sprinkle flour between them. Bake together in a quick oven. Have the berries sprinkled with sugar. As soon as the cake is done, split open and spread the berries over it, and replace the cover.

STRAWBERRY SHORT-CAKE.
MRS. W. R. S. AYRES.

In one quart of flour mix one tablespoonful of baking-powder and one teacupful of butter; roll, and cut out with a bucket-lid the size of a breakfast-plate. Bake in a quick oven. Sugar the berries well, and mash them; spread between the cakes, and over the outside, after they are put together.

PEACH PIE.

Line your pans with paste; pare and cut the peaches; lay them in thickly, with pits upward; sprinkle sugar over them, and bake without upper crust. When fresh fruit cannot be obtained, canned will answer.

CREAM PIE.

One quart of milk; two tablespoonfuls of flour, three of sugar, two of butter; three eggs; vanilla to taste; bake with lower crust; beat whites to a froth, and put in a little sugar; spread on, and let it brown.

LEMON CREAM PIE.
MISS M. J. DICKSON.

One teacupful powdered sugar; one tablespoonful butter; one egg; the juice and grated rind of one lemon; one teacupful of boiling water; one tablespoonful of corn-starch mixed in a little cold water; cream the butter and sugar together, and pour the hot mixture over them; when cool, add the lemon and beaten egg; take the inner rind of the lemon, and mince very small. Bake in an open shell.

LEMON PIE.
MRS. A. DEGRAFF.

Grate the outside of three lemons, and squeeze the juice separately; take two cups of white sugar; one-half cup of butter; six eggs, beaten separately; beat to a cream the butter, sugar, and outsides of the lemons; add one cup of sweet milk and the juice of the lemons. Put whites of the eggs in last. This will make three pies.

LEMON PIE.
MRS. J. W. S.

Four ounces of butter; one pint of cream; nine eggs; juice and rind of two lemons; three-quarters of a pound of sugar.

IOWA LEMON PIE.
MRS. J. BALDWIN.

The juice and grated rind of two lemons; two cups of water; two cups of sugar; one small teacup of butter; two eggs; two tablespoonfuls of corn-starch. Boil the water; wet the corn-starch with a little cold water and stir in; when it boils, pour it on the sugar and butter; when cool, add the eggs and lemon. Bake with two crusts.

LEMON PIE.
MRS. A. A. BUTTERFIELD.

To the grated rind and juice of two lemons add one cup and a half of sugar; two tablespoonfuls of flour; lump of butter the size of an egg; four eggs, beaten separately; one pint of milk. Stir all together, and bake.

SCOTCH PIE.
MISS HANNAH C. STRONG.

Mince enough ripe apples to fill a deep dish; then make a stiff batter of one pint of sweet milk, two teaspoonfuls of baking-powder, and flour enough to make a batter; lastly, a tablespoon-ful of melted butter. With a knife spread the batter over the apples, and cook well. When done, turn into a plate, leaving apples uppermost; season with sugar and butter.

COCOANUT PIE.

MRS. T. A. PHILLIPS.

One large cup of grated cocoanut; one quart of milk; the yolks of five eggs; a lump of butter size of a hickory-nut; sweeten to the taste; beat the whites of the eggs, and bake over the top, after the pie is done.

COCOANUT CUSTARD.

MRS. ARMSTRONG.

One cocoanut; one quart of milk; three eggs; one nutmeg; a little cinnamon; a little wine, brandy, and rose-water; a piece of butter size of an egg. Sweeten to taste; make like a custard; stir the cocoanut in; bake in a crust.

CUSTARD PIE.

Take three tablespoonfuls of butter; one egg beaten; grated lemon or nutmeg to your taste; three tablespoonfuls of flour; a quart of sweet milk. Put in part of the milk, and mix until smooth; then add the rest of the milk; bake it on a crust. Beat the whites of two or three eggs with sugar, as for icing; with a little tartaric acid in it. When the pies are baked, spread the icing over them and put them back in the oven to brown, being careful not to have it too hot. The above will make three pies. Pies you intend for the second day, do not put on the icing until the morning before you use them.

A GOOD SUGGESTION.

A bowl containing two quarts of hot water set in the oven of the stove prevents any article such as cakes, pies, etc., from being scorched.

PUMPKIN PIE.

To one pint of stewed pumpkin take one quart of milk, a pinch of salt, six eggs. Ginger and grated lemon or nutmeg are good spices for the pies.

HASTY PUMPKIN PIE.

One pint of grated pumpkin (raw); one quart of milk; six eggs; sugar and spice to taste. Boil the pumpkin in the milk until it swells; then let it get cold; add eggs and sugar, with any spice you choose.

SQUASH PIE.

MRS. EVANS.

Four pounds of squash; one quart of milk; four eggs; a pinch of salt; nutmeg and sugar to taste.

ORANGE PIE.

The juice and part of the rind of one orange; two table-spoonfuls of corn-starch; one teacupful of hot water with one-quarter box of gelatine dissolved in it; mix, and bake in one or two pies; to be eaten cold.

PINE-APPLE PIE.

To one teacupful of grated pine-apple add one-half teacupful of sugar. Bake with paste top and bottom thirty minutes.

POTATO PIE.

MRS. LUCY GREEN.

Scald one quart of milk; grate in four large potatoes and add four ounces of butter, while the milk is hot. When cold, add four eggs well beaten; spice and sweeten to your taste; bake with under crust.

SWEET-POTATO PIE.

MRS. J. STOCKSTILL.

One pound of sweet potatoes, boiled and rubbed through a sieve; one-half pound of butter; one-half pound of sugar; quart of milk; seven eggs beaten separately. Warm the butter and milk, and add other ingredients; nutmeg and brandy to taste.

MOCK APPLE PIE.

One teaspoonful tartaric acid; two cupfuls pounded crackers; two eggs; one and a half cups of sugar; five cupfuls of water. Bake with two crusts.

APPLE CUSTARD PIE.

Grate the apples; then make a custard of one pint of milk, three eggs, a pinch of salt, small lump of butter, and a little grated cracker, nutmeg, or cinnamon. This will make two pies.

APPLE JONATHAN.

Take a small piece of bread-dough; work in butter until quite short; then line the sides of a pie-dish; fill with good cooking-apples, and cover with a pretty thick paste. When baked, lift off the crust; turn it bottom up on another dish; then put sugar and a small lump of butter with the apples, mix, and spread on the crust; add spice if you like. To be eaten warm, with cream.

MINCE MEAT.

MRS. E. F. STODDARD.

Two pounds of beef, cooked and minced; one and one-half pounds of beef suet; two pounds of currants; two pounds of raisins; one-half pound of citron; two and one-half pounds of apples, chopped fine; two pounds of sugar; juice of three lemons; one tablespoonful, each, of cloves, cinnamon, and nutmeg; cider to thin; use brandy and sherry wine to taste, when making up the pies.

MINCE MEAT.

MRS. L. A. TENNEY.

Seven pounds of lean beef (a neck is best); boil until very tender, without salt, in a little water, adding more if needed to prevent burning; save one-half pint of the liquor. When the meat is cold, chop it fine ; add to it six quarts of tart apples, two quarts of cider or juice of spiced fruit, two quarts of brown sugar, one and one-half pints New Orleans molasses, two cups of strong green tea, two pounds of chopped suet, the juice of the meat, one and one-half dessert-spoonfuls of cloves, two of cinnamon, four nutmegs, a little mace, four dessert-spoonfuls of salt, and three pounds of raisins. Boil slowly one hour and a half, stirring occasionally to prevent burning. This will keep, in a covered stone jar, without fermenting. If too thick, when you make the pies, warm and thin with a little cider or fruit juice. A tablespoonful of wine or brandy poured into the pie, with nutmeg grated over it just before covering, is an improvement.

MINCE MEAT.

MRS. J. J. PATTERSON.

Take two pounds of finely-chopped beef of the best quality ; four pounds of raisins, after they are stoned ; two of currants, picked and dried ; two and one-half pounds of beef suet ; two pounds of apples, after they are chopped ; two pounds of sugar ; one pint of wine and one of brandy ; nutmeg, cloves, mace, and cinnamon, and one large piece of citron, cut up fine.

APPLE MINCE PIE.

MISS B. PEASE.

Twelve apples (part sweet), chopped fine ; six eggs, well beaten ; half a pint of cream ; raisins, and spice.

MOCK MINCE PIE.

One cup of vinegar ; two cups of water ; one cup of sugar ; one of molasses ; one of chopped raisins ; two of bread-crumbs ; one-half cup of butter, and two eggs. Spice to suit taste. Bake with upper and lower crust.

PUDDINGS.

BOILING PUDDINGS.

In boiling puddings, have plenty of water in the pot boiling when the pudding goes in, and do not let it stop. Have a tea-kettle of boiling water at hand to add to it as it evaporates. The pudding should be frequently turned. When it is done, dip it in a pan of cold water to prevent its adhering to the cloth. In using pudding-moulds, grease well with butter; tie lid on closely, and set in a pot with very little water, and add more as it is needed.

PICCOLOMINI PUDDING.

One pint of grated bread-crumbs; one quart of sweet milk; the yolks of four eggs; one teacupful of sugar; lump of butter the size of an egg; rind of one lemon. Bake in a dish, and let cool; spread fruit over; add the beaten whites of the eggs, five tablespoonfuls of sugar, juice of one lemon. Bake a few minutes.

BOILED BREAD PUDDING.

Three-fourths of a pound of bread-crumbs; eight eggs, beaten to a froth; three or four spoonfuls of sugar; one nutmeg, grated; and one quart of milk. Boil, and pour on the bread. Let it remain until one-half of the milk is soaked up; then stir in two tablespoonfuls of flour; one teaspoonful of salt. Put in a mould, and boil one hour. To be eaten with rich sauce.

CLEVELAND BISCUIT PUDDING.

Grate stale bread, or light biscuit, till you have six heaping tablespoonfuls of crumbs; sift them; beat six eggs very light;

stir into a pint of cream or rich sweet milk alternately with the crumbs, a little at a time. Beat the mixture very hard and light; then butter some large breakfast-cups; fill with the batter, and set immediately into an oven, and bake half an hour. To be eaten with wine sauce.

CRACKER PUDDING.

Mix ten ounces of finely-powdered crackers with a wine-glass of wine, a little salt, half a nutmeg, three or four tablespoonfuls of sugar and two of butter. Beat eight eggs to a froth; mix with three pints of milk. Pour over the crackers, and let stand till soft; then bake.

MINUTE PUDDING.

MRS. E. E. B.

Eight tablespoonfuls of flour; one pint of milk (cold); a small quantity of saleratus, dissolved in the milk; sift in flour to the consistency of thin starch; add four eggs, well beaten. Bake in a quick oven, and eat with cream sauce.

VIRGINIA PUDDING.

One teacupful of butter; one teacupful of sugar; one teacupful of molasses; two and one-half cups of flour; four eggs; two teaspoonfuls of soda; add spice to taste. Bake one hour. To be eaten with wine sauce.

CREAM PUDDING.

MISS MARY E. MITCHELL.

One pint of flour; same of sweet milk; seven eggs; three tablespoonfuls of white sugar, and one of melted butter; one pint of sweet cream. Mix milk and flour together until smooth. Beat eggs and sugar together to a froth; then add to the batter; then the butter and a pinch of salt; lastly add the cream, and bake from three-quarters to one hour. Serve hot with sauce. It is best baked in cups.

GELATINE PUDDING.

Two tablespoonfuls of gelatine ; pour over it one pint of boil-ing water, and sweeten to taste. Prepare this at night, and keep in a cool place. In the morning make a custard of pint of milk and three eggs, using yolks only and sugar. Beat the whites to a stiff froth ; and just before serving cut the jelly in small squares ; pour over the whites of the eggs first, and then the custard. It is better to let the jelly form in the dish in which it is to be served.

SNOW PUDDING.

MISS HATTIE BROWN.

One quart of milk ; three tablespoonfuls of flour ; four eggs ; boil the milk, leaving out sufficient to moisten the flour ; beat the eggs, leaving out the whites of three for the top ; mix the moistened flour and eggs thoroughly together ; add a little salt ; pour the boiling milk over it (stirring gently at the same time) ; pour into pudding-dish ; bake about fifteen minutes, not too fast ; then beat the three whites ; add a teacupful powdered sugar and a little lemon or vanilla extract, and pour over the pudding as it comes from the oven. To be served warm.

TAPIOCA SNOW PUDDING.

MRS. A. A. BUTTERFIELD.

Three tablespoonfuls tapioca soaked four hours, or over night ; a quart of milk ; boil half an hour ; one-half teaspoonful of salt ; one-half teacupful sugar ; and the beaten yolks of three eggs ; flavor to taste. As soon as this thickens like custard, remove from the fire and stir in the whites, beaten stiff ; then pour into the dish for the table, and set away to cool.

GELATINE SNOW PUDDING.

One-quarter of a box of Cox's gelatine ; one heaping cup of sugar ; one large lemon ; the whites of five eggs. Pour over the gelatine one-fourth of a pint of cold water ; let it soak until it is soft; then pour over half a pint of boiling water; let it thoroughly dissolve and stand until cold but not stiff; when it begins to stiffen, add the whites of the eggs beaten to a stiff froth. Whip well together and turn into a mould and set on the ice; make a boiled custard, flavored with vanilla, and pour over it.

FULLER PUDDING.
MRS. DR. CRAIGHEAD.

One cup of molasses; two-thirds cup of butter; one of water; one teaspoonful soda; two of cloves; one of salt; four even cups of flour; steam two or three hours; fruit if you like.

DORRIT PUDDING.
MRS. T. A. PHILLIPS.

Three cups of flour; one cup of milk; one cup of molasses; one of chopped suet; one of raisins; two teaspoonfuls cinnamon; one of cloves; two teaspoonfuls soda.   Boil three hours.

PLUM PUDDING.

One pound of raisins; one of currants; one of suet; one-quarter pound of citron; four eggs; one teaspoonful of cloves; two of cinnamon; one-half of nutmeg, grated; wine-glass of brandy; one teaspoonful of salt; one cup of sugar; one of milk; flour enough to make a thick batter.   Butter a pudding-mould, and boil four hours.   Pour a little spirits over the pudding, and bring to the table burning.

ENGLISH PLUM PUDDING.
MRS. DR. GUNDRY.

Two and one-half pounds of raisins; two of currants; two of fine moist sugar; two of bread-crumbs; two of suet; six ounces of candied lemon-peel; one of ground nutmeg; one of cinnamon; one-half ounce of almonds; one-half pint of brandy; rind of two lemons; sixteen eggs.   Well butter and flour the pudding-cloth. The water should be boiling when the pudding is put in. Boil eight or nine hours, or divide it and boil six hours.

BAKED INDIAN PUDDING.

Boil one pint of milk; while boiling stir in one large teacupful of Indian meal; cool a little, and add three eggs, well beaten; one pint of cold milk; one tablespoonful of flour; one-half cup sugar; one-half cup molasses; one teaspoonful of ginger; one of cinnamon; a little salt. Bake one hour and a half.

BOILED INDIAN PUDDING.

MRS. EVANS.

One pint of corn-meal, scalded; two-thirds of a cup of molasses; a little cinnamon, and salt; two eggs beaten together (if not eggs, one teaspoonful of soda); make a thick batter. Put in a mould, and boil several hours.

TAPIOCA PUDDING.

MISS ARMSTRONG.

One cup of tapioca soaked several hours in water; drain, and rub fine; one quart of milk; let come to a boil; add a little salt; then stir the yolks of six eggs, well beaten, with one and a half cupfuls of sugar; stir in the milk; let it boil to the consistency of custard; then add the tapioca, and let it boil ten minutes, stirring all the time; it must not be too thick; flavor with vanilla. When the pudding is cool, cover it with the whites of the eggs beaten, with a cupful of white sugar; put in the oven and bake to a light brown. This can be made the day before using.

BAKED TAPIOCA.

MISS MARY GEBHART.

Soak six tablespoonfuls of tapioca over night, in about one quart of water. In the morning stand it over the fire until it becomes like starch; then add the juice and rind of one lemon, and one cup of sugar. Pare apples, put them in the pudding-dish, and pour the tapioca over them. Bake until the apples are soft. Serve with cream.

APPLE TAPIOCA PUDDING.

MRS. HENRY STODDARD.

Put a teacupful of tapioca in a quart of cold water; let it stand from three to five hours; put it into a stew-pan, on a hot stove, and let it boil thoroughly for fifteen minutes, or until it looks perfectly clear; stir constantly, thinning it from time to time with boiling water, so that when done it will run from a spoon; then season well with salt, and add four tablespoonfuls of white sugar. Half fill a glass dish in which the pudding is to be served with coddled apples, sprinkling ground cinnamon over the top; then pour over it the tapioca while still hot. When cold, serve with cream.

TAPIOCA PUDDING.

MISS DRUSIE HARRIS.

One large cup of tapioca soaked over night; six large apples, peeled·and cored; fill the apples with butter and sugar. After arranging them in a pan, pour tapioca over them, with an additional cup of water. Bake.

BOILED TAPIOCA.

MRS. W. A. B.

One teacupful of tapioca soaked over night in one pint of water; six large tart apples sliced thin. Put them in layers in a milk-boiler, and boil two hours. Serve with cream, sugar, and nutmeg.

RICE PUDDING.

Put one-half cupful of rice into a dish; cover up with water, and soak over night. In the morning drain off the water; add two quarts of milk, a pinch of salt, two tablespoonfuls of sugar, one tablespoonful vanilla, a few lumps of butter. Stir this well, and place in the oven. To be eaten cold.

LEMON RICE PUDDING.

Boil one teacupful of rice in one pint of water till dry; add one quart of new milk, and boil till thick; then add the yolks of three eggs well beaten, six tablespoonfuls of sugar, the rind of one lemon; beat together, and put in a pudding-dish; beat the whites to a stiff froth; then add six tablespoonfuls of sugar and the juice of the lemon; spread it on the pudding, and put in the oven to brown.

RICE MERINGUES.

MISS B. PEASE.

One teacupful of rice boiled soft; when cold, add one quart of milk, the yolks of three eggs, three tablespoonfuls of sugar, and a little nutmeg. Pour in a dish and bake half an hour; when partly baked, stir a few large raisins through it. When cold, beat the whites of the eggs with two tablespoonfuls of sugar; spread over the rice, and bake a light brown.

FRUIT RICE PUDDING.

Put a teacupful of rice in a quart of milk, and boil slowly till soft; add a little salt, a teacupful of cream, and sugar enough to sweeten it. Have ready, in a deep dish, any kind of fruit,— cherries, blackberries, apricots, apples or peaches, cut up and well sweetened (uncooked). Spread the rice roughly over, and bake slowly two hours.

FARINA PUDDING.

KATE P. BROWN.

To one quart of milk, three tablespoonfuls of farina and two eggs. Put the eggs, milk, and raisins on together, and let them scald; then add the farina, and let it cook twenty minutes; sweeten, and flavor to taste.

FLORENTINE PUDDING.

MRS. J. W. STODDARD.

One quart of milk; five eggs; three tablespoonfuls of corn-starch; three tablespoonfuls of white sugar. Boil the milk; dissolve the starch in a little milk, and stir in the boiling milk, with the yolks and sugar. Bake twenty minutes. Spread with the whites of the eggs.

CORN-STARCH PUDDING.

Heat one quart of milk to boiling, then stir in slowly one cupful of corn-starch; mix with this about six good apples, pared and sliced; add two tablespoonfuls of sugar, one of butter, and a little spice. Pour the whole in a dish, and bake forty minutes.

VALISE PUDDING.

Make a light biscuit dough; roll out, and spread on one quart of seeded cherries; fold over, and fasten the edges closely to secure the syrup. Sew up in a pudding-cloth, previously wrung out of hot water and dredged with flour. Put in boiling water, and boil one hour and a half. Any other fresh fruit may be used in the same way. Serve with butter and sugar.

WAPSIE PUDDING.

Take one pint of sour cream, with a little soda, and flour enough stirred in to form a batter. Fill a pan with nice baking-apples, not packed too closely; pour the batter over, and bake till brown. Eat with cream and sugar.

SPONGE PUDDING.

Six eggs; the weight of five in sugar; the weight of three in flour; one teaspoonful of baking-powder. Steam in a pudding-mould one and one-half hours.

BATTER FRUIT PUDDING.

Butter thickly a pudding-dish that will hold a pint and one half; fill it nearly full of good baking-apples, cut up fine. Pour over them a batter made with four tablespoonfuls of flour, three eggs, and one-half pint of milk. Tie a buttered and floured cloth over the dish (which ought to be quite full), and boil the pudding one and one-quarter hours; turn it out into a hot dish, and strew sugar thickly over it.

HUCKLEBERRY PUDDING.

One pint of best Orleans molasses; a pinch of salt; one teaspoonful of cloves, one of cinnamon, and one of soda dissolved in a teacupful of sweet milk; flour enough to make it the consistency of pound-cake; one quart of huckleberries; boil two and a half hours in a pudding-mould. Eat with cream and sugar, or pudding-sauce.

SEVEN–CENT PUDDING.

One pint of flour; one teacupful of sugar, one of sweet milk; one egg; butter size of an egg; one teacupful currants, and one-half teaspoonful baking-powder; spread over with melted butter; sprinkle with cinnamon. To be eaten warm, with sauce.

DRIED FRUIT PUDDING.

Take half-pound of suet chopped fine, four teacupfuls of flour, and five eggs. Beat these very light; then add a quart of milk and one-half teaspoonful of salt. Rub three teacupfuls of raisins in flour, and stir in; scald the pudding-bag and flour it; allow room for the pudding to swell. Boil three hours. Dried cherries or pared dried peaches can be used instead of raisins.

DRIED FRUIT PUDDING.

One pint of flour, one pint of milk, made into a batter; then add one pint of suet, one of cut peaches, one of raisins,
6

one of currants or dried cherries. Tie up well in a floured cloth; put in boiling water, and boil three hours.

EVE'S PUDDING.

Six large apples pared and chopped; six tablespoonfuls of grated bread; six tablespoonfuls of sugar; six of currants; six eggs; citron to taste; a wine-glass of wine; a tablespoonful of mixed nutmeg, cinnamon, and cloves; a quarter of a pound of butter, and three tablespoonfuls of flour. Put in a pudding-mould. and boil three hours; use cold sauce.

MERINGUE PUDDING.
MISS CARRIE BROWN.

Bake a sponge-cake in jelly-cake pans; spread with strawberry jam or other fruit; make the layers of the fruit as thick as the layers of cake; spread over the top and sides the whites of three eggs beaten to a froth; and mix with them at the moment of using three tablespoonfuls of powdered sugar; place in the oven a moment or two to brown.

YOUNG AMERICA PUDDING.
MRS. WM. HEISLEY.

One tea upful of sugar; three eggs; one tablespoonful of butter; three tablespoonfuls of sweet milk; one tablespoonful of baking-powder; flour enough to make it the consistency of sponge-cake. Divide in three parts, and bake quickly in jelly-cake pans; spread fruit or jelly between each layer; serve with warm sauce.

JELLY-CAKE PUDDING.
MRS. E. F. STODDARD.

One cup of butter; two cups of sugar; three and a half cups of flour; four eggs; one cup of sour cream; one teaspoonful of soda; bake in two pans. For the jelly, make a custard of one pint of milk, three eggs, two tablespoonfuls of white sugar, one tablespoonful of flour; flavor with vanilla or fine brandy. After the milk boils, stir in the other ingredients and let it get very thick. Open the cake when hot, and put half the custard into each. To be eaten cold with cream.

SAVOY PUDDING.

Stale sponge or other plain cake may be made into a nice pudding by crumbling it into a little more than a pint of milk, with two or three beaten eggs, and baking it. Sauce,—sugar and butter beaten together.

SPANISH CHARLOTTE.

Place crumbs of stale cake or rolled crackers on the bottom of a pudding-dish, and put a layer of any kind of jelly or fruit over them. Continue them alternately until the dish is nearly full, making the crumbs form the top. Pour a custard over it, and bake. Serve with sauce.

TIPSY CHARLOTTE.

MISS DRUSIE HARRIS.

One large stale sponge-cake; one pint of rich sweet cream; one cup of sherry wine; one-fourth of a box of Cox's gelatine, soaked in a cup of cold water two hours; one teaspoonful of vanilla or bitter almond; three eggs, the whites and yolks beaten together very light; one pint of milk; and one cup of sugar. Heat the cream almost to boiling; put in the soaked gelatine and one-half cup of sugar, and stew until dissolved. Remove from the fire; flavor; and, when cool, beat to a standing froth. Cut off the top of the cake in one piece, and remove the middle, leaving the sides and bottom three-quarters of an inch thick. Over the inside pour the wine in spoonfuls, that all may be evenly moistened; fill with the whipped cream; replace the top, which should also be moistened with the wine, and set in a cold place. Serve with it, or pour around it, a custard made of the eggs, milk, and the other half-cup of sugar.

LEMON PUDDING.

MRS. J. R. YOUNG.

One-half of a pound of flour ; one-half of a pound of suet, cut very fine ; one-half of a pound of sugar ; the rind of two lemons, and the yolks of two eggs. Boil it four hours in a mould. Serve without sauce.

ORANGE PUDDING.

Grate the rind and squeeze the juice of two large oranges ; stir to a cream one-half pound of butter with one-half pound of powdered sugar ; add a wine-glass of mixed rum and brandy ; beat very lightly six eggs ; stir them gradually into the mixture. Put into a buttered dish with broad edge, around which lay a border of puff paste. Bake half an hour ; and, when cold, grate sugar over it.

COCOANUT PUDDING.

MRS. MUNGER.

Nearly two quarts of milk ; six eggs ; one cocoanut, grated ; sugar to taste ; one teacupful of butter ; add nutmeg after it is placed in the oven. Stir once or twice as soon as it commences to form.

RICH COCOANUT PUDDING.

MRS. J. W. STODDARD.

One-quarter of a pound of butter ; the yolks of five eggs ; one-quarter of a pound of sugar ; beat the butter and sugar together ; add a little of the cocoanut at a time, and one-half teacupful of cream. Don't bake too long, or it will destroy the flavor. After it is baked, beat the whites of the eggs with four or five tablespoonfuls of sugar ; spread over the pudding, and bake a light brown.

GERMAN CHOCOLATE PUDDING.

MRS. S. B. SMITH.

Two ounces of grated chocolate ; two ounces or four tablespoonfuls of flour ; the yolks of four eggs ; one pint of milk ; two ounces of butter. Put the butter over the fire to melt ; when hot add the other ingredients, and stir till it thickens; when cool add the yolks of four more eggs; beat the whites of the eight eggs, and add them. Butter a pan, and, after putting in the pudding, sift sugar over the top, and bake for one-half hour. It rises like a batter pudding, and must be sent to the table hot as soon as it is taken from the oven. Put more sugar in the milk, and use more chocolate if desired.

CHOCOLATE PUDDING.

MRS. JAMES STOCKSTILL.

Not quite one-quarter of a pound of Baker's chocolate, scraped and dissolved slowly in one quart of milk; sweeten to taste, and flavor with vanilla. Beat the yolks of three eggs with one-half tablespoonful of corn-starch. When the chocolate boils, stir in and boil up once; pour in a dish (to be brought to the table). Beat the whites, and spread on the top with cracked almonds and coarse sugar sprinkled over; brown slightly.

CHOCOLATE PUDDING.

H. MAILLARD.

Scrape very fine two ounces of Maillard's single, double, or triple vanilla chocolate, and add to it half a teaspoonful of powdered cinnamon. Put it into a pan; pouring over it one quart of new milk, stirring it until it boils, and adding by degrees four ounces of sugar; milling the chocolate until it is smooth and light; then pour it out to cool. Beat eight eggs to a froth; mix them with the chocolate; pour into a buttered dish, and bake three-quarters of an hour. Serve cold, with sifted sugar over it.

LEMON SAUCE.

MRS. J. J. P.

One large coffee-cup of white sugar; half the rind of one lemon; one teaspoonful of juice; a lump of butter the size of an egg; one-half pint of water; add a teaspoonful of corn-starch mixed with a little water; let all simmer, but not boil.

ORANGE CHEESE-CAKE.

MRS. CRANE.

One-third of a pound of butter; one-third of a pound of sugar; three eggs; wine-glass of milk or cream; the rind of an orange grated; one-half of a nutmeg grated; one tablespoonful of brandy; two of rose-water; two ounces of sponge-cake. Pour the cream or milk over the cake to moisten it; then stir this with sugar and butter; beat your eggs; mash the cake very fine, and mix all together with the brandy and spice. Lemons can be used in the same way; only add the juice of half a lemon. Serve with sauce.

CREAM SAUCE.

One cup of milk; one of sugar; three tablespoonfuls of corn-starch; boil it a few minutes; then add one tablespoonful of butter and two of brandy.

PUDDING SAUCE.

.One cup of sugar; a little less than one-half cup of butter; work together until smooth; add a wine-glass of wine; flavor with nutmeg, and stir in boiling milk until the whole is of the consistency of thick cream. Send to the table, and stir well when served. Don't put the wine in until perfectly cold.

PUDDING SAUCE.

One-fourth of a cup of butter; one cup of sugar; yolk of one egg; one-half glass of wine; one-half teaspoonful of flour; beat well together; then pour on a teacupful of boiling water. Let it simmer.

FOAM SAUCE.

One cup of sugar; two eggs; three tablespoonfuls of cold water; set over a teakettle of boiling water; stir all the time, till well cooked. Then put a piece of butter size of an egg in a bowl, and pour the mixture over it. Flavor to taste.

SNOW SAUCE.

One cup of sugar; one-half cup of butter; yolk of one egg; one glass of wine or brandy. Heat the wine before mixing, and, when ready to send to the table, beat the white of the egg very light, and put on top of the sauce.

SAUCE FOR MINUTE PUDDING.

Four heaping tablespoonfuls of sugar; one of flour; two of butter. Beat all together until like cream. Just before using, stir in boiling water to make it the consistency of starch. Flavor with vanilla, the last thing.

HARD SAUCE.

MRS. C. WIGHT.

Stir to a cream one cup of butter and three cups of sugar; add one-half cup of wine, one teaspoonful of lemon essence, cinnamon and nutmeg to suit the taste. Beat till light and creamy; smooth into shape, and put upon the ice until the pudding is served.

WHITE SAUCE.

Make a rich syrup of white sugar; boil it; and put in ground cinnamon and nutmeg while boiling. Serve hot.

SAUCE FOR MERINGUE PUDDING.

One-half pint of water; one-quarter pound of white sugar; one-quarter pound of butter rubbed into a tablespoonful of flour; boil a short time; adding a sliced lemon just before taking from fire.

PUDDING SAUCE.

MRS. HENRY STODDARD.

One pint of wine, the yolks of six eggs and the whites of three; a sufficient quantity of lemon; ground cinnamon and sugar to taste. Heat the whole over the fire, but don't let it boil. Serve hot.

VINEGAR SAUCE FOR PUDDINGS.

One cup of brown sugar; one of water; pinch of salt; one spoonful of butter; a few drops of essence of lemon; one spoonful of vinegar. Beat butter, sugar, lemon, vinegar, and flour well together; pour the water boiling on them, and let it scald up.

CUSTARDS, CREAMS, Etc.

FLOAT.

MRS. J. T. WOLF.

ONE quart of milk; let it come to a boil; the yolks of three eggs; one and a half tablespoonfuls of corn-starch; beat together with a little cold milk. When the milk boils, stir in the starch and eggs. When done, sweeten and flavor to taste. Beat the whites of the eggs; pour boiling water over them in a bowl; then lift off, on the custard.

APPLE FLOAT.

MRS. G. W. ROGERS.

One quart of apples slightly stewed and well mashed; whites of three eggs, well beaten; four heaping tablespoonfuls of sugar. Beat together for twenty minutes. To be eaten with cream soon after made.

APPLE CODDLE.

MISS LOUIE PHILLIPS.

Pare and quarter tart apples, and boil them gently, with one lemon for every six apples, till a straw will pass through them. Make a syrup of half a pound of white sugar to each pound of apples; put the apples and lemons sliced into the syrup, and boil gently until the apples look clear; then take them up carefully so as not to break them, and add an ounce or more of gelatine to the syrup and let it boil up; then lay a slice of lemon on each apple, and strain the syrup and pour over them.

APPLE OMELET.

MRS. C. WIGHT.

Eight large apples; four eggs; one cup of sugar; one table-spoonful of butter; nutmeg or cinnamon to taste. Stew the apples, and mash fine; add the butter and sugar. When cold, add the eggs, well beaten. Bake until brown, and eat while warm.

OMELET SOUFFLE.

Take two ounces of sugar, two ounces of butter, three ounces of flour, and one pint of milk. Mix all together well; set on a slow fire; keep stirring until it gets the thickness of soft butter; then take it from the fire, and add the beaten yolks of five eggs; then beat the whites of five eggs to a stiff froth; mix well the above. Add any flavoring you prefer. Pour into buttered pudding-cups, and bake in a moderate oven.

BLANC MANGE.

Mix one tablespoonful of Sea-Moss Farina with a little cold milk; then add one quart of milk, and half a teacupful of powdered white sugar. Heat slowly; let it boil fifteen minutes, stirring all the time. When taken off, flavor to taste. Pour into moulds, and serve with cream.

RICE BLANC MANGE.

One quart of new milk; six tablespoonfuls of coarse-ground rice. Wash the rice very well, and drain the water off. Just as the milk begins to boil, add the rice, one tablespoonful at a time, stirring constantly; boil for twenty minutes, or until it becomes quite thick; sweeten to taste; add two tablespoonfuls of water, and one teaspoonful of rose-water.

GELATINE BLANC MANGE.

MRS. C. G. G.

Two and a half sheets of gelatine dissolved in cold water to one quart of milk. Sweeten and flavor to taste.

CORN-STARCH BLANC MANGE.

Four tablespoonfuls of corn-starch dissolved in a little milk. Put one quart of milk on the stove, and, when boiling, stir the starch into it; add a lump of butter the size of a hickory-nut; flavor to taste.

PEACH BLANC MANGE.

MRS. L. G. EVANS.

Boil in one quart of sweet milk about ten fresh peach-leaves, with four ounces of sugar, and one teacupful of corn-starch dissolved in a quarter of a pint of cold milk; stir all the time; boil a few minutes, and turn out into a mould.

CHOCOLATE BLANC MANGE.

MRS. M. EELLS.

One ounce of Cox's gelatine dissolved in as much water as will cover it; four ounces of grated chocolate; one quart of milk; three-quarters of a pound of sugar. Boil the eggs, milk, and chocolate together five minutes; then put in the gelatine, and let the whole boil five minutes longer, stirring constantly. Add one teaspoonful of vanilla extract, and put in moulds to cool.

NEAPOLITAN BLANC MANGE.

Heat one quart of milk to boiling; stir in one ounce of gelatine that has been soaked in one cup of the milk for an hour, and three-fourths of a cup of sugar. When the gelatine is dissolved, strain it through a thin muslin bag. Divide into four portions, allowing one cupful for each. Wet one large tablespoonful of chocolate with a little boiling water; rub it up very smooth. Put this in one portion, and set on the fire, stirring until very hot, but do not let it boil. Mix with the second portion the yolk of one egg, beaten very light, and heat as above. Color the third with cochineal or cranberry juice. Wet a mould, and put the white in ; and, when cold, put in the pink, then the yellow, then the chocolate. Set in a cold place. Loosen by dipping the mould in warm water for a second.

CUSTARD.

The general rule to observe in making custard is to take five eggs to one quart of milk, and a tablespoonful of sugar to every egg. Beat the eggs separately. Always boil milk, custard, rice, and cracked wheat in a vessel set within another of boiling water. Stir in the yolks of the eggs before the milk boils, to prevent its curdling.

CREAM CUSTARDS.

MRS. DR. STEWART.

One quart of cream ; four tablespoonfuls of white sugar ; whites of four eggs. Stir the sugar into the cream ; then add the whites of the eggs without beating them ; stir all well, and flavor with bitter almonds or vanilla. Bake in cups, set in a pan half filled with water ; put in the oven, and bake till it thickens.

ALMOND CUSTARD.

One pint of new milk ; one cup of pulverized sugar ; one-quarter pound of almonds, blanched and pounded ; two teaspoonfuls of rose-water ; the yolks of four eggs. Stir this over a slow fire until it is of the consistency of cream ; then remove it quickly, and put in a dish. Beat the whites with a little sugar added to a stiff froth, and lay on the top.

INDIAN CUSTARD.

MRS. E. P. FILLEO.

Heat two quarts of milk ; then stir in one cup of molasses, a small cup of fine corn-meal, two beaten eggs, and a little salt. Cook slowly one hour. If it seems too thick, thin it with a little cold water.

LEMON CREAM.

Take one lemon, and grate it up fine; one cup of sugar; three-fourths of a cup of water, one cup of butter, and three eggs. Take the lemon, sugar, butter, and water, and put them in a pan, and let it come to a boil. Have the eggs well beaten, and stir in while boiling; let it thicken, then take off to cool. Is nice for traveling-lunch.

WINE CREAM.

One-half ounce of gelatine dissolved in one and one-half cups of white wine, to which is added the rind and juice of one lemon, and three-quarters of a pound of white sugar. Let it simmer till mixed; then strain. When cool, but not congealed, add one and one-half pints of cream, stirring gently, that it may not separate. A little orange-juice and peel is an improvement.

HAMBURG CREAM.

MRS. ARMSTRONG.

Take the rind and juice of two large lemons; eight eggs; with one cup of sugar. Stir together the yolks of the eggs, lemons, and sugar. Put in a tin bucket set within another of boiling water; place over the fire; stir well for three minutes; take from the fire and add the whites of the eggs, which must be beaten to a froth. Put in custard-cups or small glasses. To be eaten before quite cold, with cake.

ITALIAN CREAM.

NELLIE ANDREWS.

One quart of milk; three eggs; six tablespoonfuls of sugar; three tablespoonfuls of corn-starch. Boil like custard. Make a meringue with the whites, and a little sugar. Flavor with vanilla.

RUSSIAN CREAM.

NELLIE ANDREWS.

Five eggs; one-quarter of a pound of sugar; one lemon, grated. The yolks, sugar, and lemon to be beaten together very light; then boil; stir in the whites while cooking.

SPANISH CREAM.

MISS DRUSIE HARRIS.

One box of gelatine soaked in a large cup of milk or water; one quart of milk boiled and poured into it; then beat the yolks of eight eggs and add to the gelatine, with one and a half cups of sugar. Let it thicken as for custard. Beat the whites of the eggs in a dish, and pour in the custard; mix well; flavor with lemon or vanilla, and let cool in the mould.

TAPIOCA CREAM.

MRS. A. BUTTERFIELD.

Soak two tablespoonfuls of tapioca in a cupful of milk or water over night. In the morning place a quart of milk over the fire; let it come to a boil. Beat the yolks of three eggs, and mix with the tapioca; sweeten and flavor to taste. Pour in the milk, and cook the same as boiled custard; when done, pour in cups. Beat the whites to a froth with two tablespoonfuls of sugar, and put over the top.

WINE JELLY.

MRS. JOHN G. LOWE.

One box of Cox's gelatine; pour on it a pint of cold water, and let it stand ten minutes; then pour on four pints of boiling water one pint of wine, two pounds of sugar, the juice of three lemons and the grated rind of one. Strain immediately through a jelly-bag, and let stand to cool.

WINE JELLY.

Two ounces of Cox's gelatine dissolved in one pint of cold water; soak one hour; half-pint of wine; wine-glass of brandy; juice of two lemons; grated rind of one; one and three-fourths pounds of sugar. Over this pour three pints of boiling water; strain into moulds.

CHOCOLATE JELLY.

MRS. ADMIRAL SCHENCK.

One cup of sugar; one cup of molasses; three-fourths of a cup of milk; one-half cake of chocolate dissolved in water; a piece of butter size of a hickory-nut; one tablespoonful of flour mixed with a little milk to thicken; one-half teaspoonful of soda. Boil one-quarter of an hour.

FROST JELLY.

MISS FANNIE CLARKE.

One-half box of gelatine; one-half pint of cold water poured over to dissolve it; one-half pint of boiling water; two cupfuls of sugar; juice of two lemons. When cool, and just beginning to form, add the beaten whites of two eggs, and beat the whole together until it is thoroughly mixed. Set in a cool place.

ORANGE OR LEMON GELATINE.

HATTIE B. BROWN.

One-half box of gelatine dissolved in one-half pint of cold water; one-half cupful of sugar; juice of six and grated rind of one orange; and one-half pint of boiling water. For lemon gelatine, after dissolving, add one and a half pints of boiling water; one cup of sugar; the juice of three and rind of one lemon; then strain and set to cool.

CHARLOTTE RUSSE.

MRS. J. J. PATTERSON.

Beat the yolks of seven eggs and stir them into one pint of scalding milk with a little sugar; boil like custard, and set away to cool. Pour a large cup of warm water over a half-box of gelatine; set it on the stove, but don't let it get hot. Beat the whites of the eggs very light, and add enough pulverized sugar to make it stiff; then whip one quart of cream and stir into the custard; then the whites flavored with vanilla; then the gelatine well dissolved; mix thoroughly and set away to cool (about two hours). Line your dish with either sponge-cake or lady fingers, and fill with the mixture; let stand five or six hours.

CHARLOTTE RUSSE.

MRS. J. R. YOUNG.

One quart of cream whipped to a stiff froth; one-third of a box of Cox's gelatine dissolved in one-half pint of boiling water; sweeten and flavor to taste; stir in a little cream, not whipped, to cool it; then stir in the whipped cream. Line a dish with sponge-cake, and pour on the cream, and set it away to congeal. Let the gelatine stand in warm water until it is almost dissolved; then set the cup in a pan of boiling water, and, when it is scalding hot, pour it over the egg and sugar.

CHARLOTTE RUSSE.

MRS. F. W. GRIMES.

One quart of cold cream; two ounces of gelatine; two eggs (if the cream is thick, omit the eggs); one-half of a pound of sugar. Dissolve the gelatine in a little milk very slowly; beat the eggs and sugar together; whip the cream to a stiff froth; line the mould with sponge-cake; mix the ingredients together, and put into the mould; set it on ice.

CHOCOLATE CHARLOTTE RUSSE.

MRS. D. W. STEWART.

Soak in cold water one ounce of isinglass; take three ounces of best chocolate; mix in a pint of cream, adding the soaked isinglass. Put all over the fire, and boil slowly until the whole is melted; then take off the fire, and let it cool. Take the yolks of eight and whites of four eggs; beat very light, and stir gradually in the mixture in turn with one-half pound of sugar. Simmer the whole over the fire, but do not let it boil; then take it off, and whip to a strong froth; line the moulds with sponge-cake, and set it on the ice.

SOUFFLE DE RUSSE.

MRS. A. BROWN.

Three pints of milk; four eggs; one-half box of gelatine; sweeten and flavor to taste. Boil as custard. As it is taken from the fire, stir in the whites beaten to a stiff froth. Pour into moulds, and when cold eat with cream.

LEMON SPONGE.

MRS. J. L. BRENNER.

To one-half box Cox's gelatine take one and a half pints of cold water; dissolve over the fire; then add one pound of white sugar, rinds of two and juice of three lemons. Boil all together for a few minutes. When nearly cold, add the whites of three eggs beaten to a froth. Beat all well together; then set in a cool place. When it begins to thicken, stir thoroughly; let stand again and beat as before. The oftener this is repeated the whiter it will become. Pour into moulds; serve with cream. One-half this recipe is enough for five or six persons.

ICE CREAM.

One quart of cream; two eggs; two cups of sugar; eggs beaten separately, sugar in the yolks, then beaten very hard together; stir the eggs into the cream; flavor to taste.

ICE CREAM.

MRS. JOHN W. STODDARD.

Two quarts of pure cream; one pound of powdered sugar; whites of four eggs.   Flavor to taste.

CHOCOLATE ICE CREAM.

Use five ounces of chocolate, dissolved in warm milk, to one gallon of cream.

CHOCOLATE CREAM.

H. MAILLARD.

One quart of cream; eleven ounces powdered sugar; yolks of six eggs; white of one egg; zest of lemon, a piece as large as a nickel cent; one bar of chocolate (Maillard's single, double, or triple vanilla).   Scrape the chocolate very fine, and put it with the eggs and sugar; stir or beat until the mixture is complete, and add the cream by degrees.   Pour into a milk-boiler, and stir until the cream is thick enough to stick to the spatula; then pour the contents into an earthen dish or freezer, and set in a very cold place.   The boiling of the cream is of great import-ance, and requires particular attention, especially when no milk-boiler is at hand, and the cream is boiled on an open fire. In this case, as soon as the cream begins to stick to the spatula, the pan must be immediately withdrawn.   The flavoring should be added after the cream is boiled.   Before freezing, it is advisable to pass it through a hair sieve.

BISCUIT GLACÉ.

MRS. HENRY STODDARD.

One and one-half pints of cream; four ounces of macaroons; six ounces of white sugar; the yellow rind of one orange, grated, and the juice of two.   If oranges cannot be had, use one ounce of orgeat.   Beat the cream on ice until it hangs to the beater; then add the sugar, oranges, and the macaroons (grated and put through a sieve).   Freeze like ice cream, and afterward put into moulds.

LEMON ICE.

Make a rich lemonade; add a little arrow-root. Be careful to stir steadily while freezing.

ORANGE ICE.

Juice of six oranges, and grated rind of three; juice of two lemons; one pint of sugar dissolved in one pint of cold water. Mix, and freeze same as lemon ice.

ORANGE ICE.

One and one-half pints of water; one pint of sugar; juice of eight oranges and two lemons; whites of four eggs beaten very light; rub some of the sugar on the orange to extract the flavor. Boil the sugar and water together for ten or fifteen minutes, and pour it over the eggs boiling hot, stirring all the time; then add the juice, which must be strained. When cool, freeze.

FROZEN PEACHES.

Take two quarts of rich milk, and two teacupfuls of sugar; mix well together, and put into a freezer, with ice and salt packed around it. Have ready one quart of peaches, mashed and sweetened. When the milk is very cold, stir them in, and freeze all together. Strawberries can be used in the same way, but will require more sugar.

FROZEN STRAWBERRIES.

Take nice ripe strawberries; put them into a bowl and mash them; make them rather sweeter than for the table. Let them stand until the juice is drawn out, then freeze. Serve with cream or ice cream.

CONFECTIONERY.

TAFFY.

MELT in a stew-pan three ounces of butter and one pound of moist sugar; stir well over a slow fire; boil one-quarter of an hour; pour out on a buttered dish, and mark in squares.

MOLASSES CANDY.

LILLIE.

One-half pound of sugar; one-quarter pound of butter; one quart of molasses; boil until it will crack in cold water.   When cool, it can be pulled until white.

CREAM CANDY.

MISS M. A. CUMMIN.

One pound of loaf sugar; one cupful of water; one-half teaspoonful of cream tartar, two of vanilla, two of vinegar; butter size of an egg.   Boil until it hardens when dropped into water. When nearly cold, pull as you would other candy.

CHOCOLATE CARAMELS.

MRS. ASHLEY BROWN.

Take of grated chocolate, milk, molasses, and sugar, one cupful each; piece of butter size of an egg; boil until it drops hard; put in a buttered pan, and, before it cools, mark off in square blocks.

CANDY DROPS.

MRS. ASHLEY BROWN.

One pint of sugar; half-pint of water; boil till it cracks when dropped in water; flavor with lemon or peppermint; drop in small drops on buttered paper.

COCOANUT CANDY.

Two pounds of coffee sugar to one cocoanut; dissolve sugar in the milk of the nut; then let it come to a boil and add the grated meat. Boil until tender; then pour out and let cool on buttered pans; cut in squares.

BUTTER SCOTCH.

MATTIE.

One cupful of Orleans molasses; one cupful of sugar; one-half cupful of butter; boil until it snaps in water.

BREAD.

YEAST.

Pour three pints and a half of cold water on one handful of hops; grate three large potatoes; boil the hops fifteen minutes; then mix together one-half cup of sugar, a large kitchen-spoon-ful of flour, one tablespoonful of ginger and one of salt, a lump of alum the size of a hazel-nut. After straining the water off the hops, pour it over the mixture and let it boil five minutes; stir all the time. When cool, add one pint of sponge, and let stand twenty-four hours, stirring it frequently; then jug and cork tight. Put in a cool place. It will keep three weeks.

DRY YEAST.

Take three pints of flour and put it in a crock; boil and skin six common-sized potatoes; press them through a cullender into the flour; add three pints of water in which a handful of hops has boiled five minutes. Mix well together and let stand fifteen minutes, or until about milk-warm; then pour in enough cold water to make it of the consistency of sponge. Soak half a pint of dry yeast and add to it. Let it rise very light, stirring it down three or four times; then put three quarts of sifted corn-meal into a bread-bowl, and pour the raised yeast into the middle of it. Mix until quite stiff; spread out thin, and dry it in the shade, turning occasionally. It will dry in a couple of days.

BREAD.

In the evening, pare and cut six or eight potatoes ; boil and mash them ; add one quart of boiling water ; while hot, stir in flour to make a batter ; when cool enough, add one teacup of dry yeast that has been soaked in a little tepid water. The next morning, stir up the sponge to a thick batter with one quart of water and two tablespoonfuls of salt, and add the yeast. When light, mix in flour and knead well ; then let it rise again ; mould, and put into pans. When light, bake one hour. This will make four small loaves.

BREAD.

MRS. W. R. S. AYRES.

Four pints of good sour milk ; let it come to a boil ; pour it over two large tablespoonfuls of flour ; let it stand till cool. Then make a thin batter by adding flour and one-half teacupful of jug yeast ; let stand till morning, then mix in flour enough to make it stiff ; knead well ; let it rise in the bowl until very light. Mould into four loaves ; let it rise again before baking. Bake in a quick oven three-quarters of an hour.

BREAD, WITH DRY YEAST.

In the evening, take four medium-sized potatoes ; pare and boil them ; when soft, drain off the water, and mash, with a teacupful of flour ; then rub the lumps out with your hands ; if too hot, add a little cold water. Add a cake of dry yeast soaked in a little tepid water ; mix well, and let stand till morning. Then stir into the sponge a quart of milk, two tablespoonfuls of salt, and flour enough to make a dough. Knead well, and let it rise ; then make into loaves, and, when light, bake one hour.

BROWN LOAF.

MRS. A. D. WILT.

One coffee-cup of molasses ; nearly one teaspoonful of soda, dissolved in one-half teacupful of boiling water, stirred into the molasses till it foams; then mix three parts of Graham flour and one part corn-meal, to make a thick batter, and add one dessert-spoonful of lard. Pour the mixture into a well-greased mould, and steam four hours. To be eaten hot. Very nice as a pudding, with rich sauce.

BROWN BREAD.
MRS. D. W. STEWART.

Take a quart of bread-sponge that has been raised over night; a small teacupful of Orleans molasses; one teaspoonful of soda, dissolved in a little water; a piece of alum the size of a pea, dissolved in water. Have the molasses, alum, and soda well mixed into the sponge, then add unbolted flour enough to make a soft dough,—not quite as stiff as white bread. Make into small loaves; let stand until light, and bake. Never use sugar-house molasses or syrup.

BROWN BREAD.
LENA VIGNOS.

For six loaves of bread take three pints of warm water, one cent's worth of brewer's yeast; set it in the evening. In the morning add one teacupful of Orleans molasses and a little salt; mix stiff; let rise again; knead and bake as other bread.

RYE BROWN BREAD.
MRS. C. E. CORP.

One pint of corn-meal, scalded; when cool, add one pint of sponge, one teaspoonful of soda, two-thirds cupful of Orleans molasses, wheat or rye flour to make a stiff batter. Place in a pan; let stand until very light. Bake one and one-quarter hours.

RICE BREAD.

Take a plate of boiled rice warm enough to melt a lump of butter the size of a walnut; beat two eggs separately. Mix with them one and one-half teacupfuls of flour, and milk enough to make a thick batter, adding a little salt. Grease the pans, and bake like bread or muffins.

CORN BREAD.

One pint of sour milk; one teaspoonful of saleratus; one pint of corn-meal; three eggs; two tablespoonfuls of sugar, and one of melted butter. Bake in shallow pans.

CORN BREAD.

PIQUA, OHIO.

Three eggs beaten separately; put the yolks in last; one-fourth cupful of lard and butter mixed together; one teacupful of buttermilk; one teaspoonful of soda, and a little salt; corn-meal enough to make it stiff as pound-cake.

CORN BREAD.

MRS. DR. STEELE.

One quart of corn-meal; one pint of flour; one pint of thick, sour milk; one egg; two tablespoonfuls of molasses; one tea-spoonful of soda. Mix together, putting the white of the egg in last. Steam one hour in a two-quart tin pan; then bake ten minutes to brown.

MISSISSIPPI CORN BREAD.

MRS. ADMIRAL SCHENCK.

Same quantity of soft-boiled rice and sifted corn-meal; add a little lard or butter; mix with sour milk sweetened with soda. Bake in a deep tin pan in a quick oven. Bring it to the table in the pan hot.

CORN DODGERS.

MRS. A. GRIMES.

Two pints of corn-meal; one tablespoonful of lard; two eggs, and one teaspoonful of salt. Scald the meal with the lard in it; cool with a very little milk; add the eggs, and beat hard for ten minutes. If too thick, add a little more milk. They must be just thick enough to retain their shape when dropped from a spoon. Grease the pan, and have it hot before putting them in.

RUSKS.

MRS. J. F. EDGAR.

One quart of milk; six eggs; three-fourths pound of butter; two cups of sugar; one pint of potato-yeast; mix with flour to a batter. When light, make into a soft dough; let rise again; then roll out, cut, and put into pans to rise. When light, bake.

RUSK.

MRS. A. M. WOODHULL.

Piece of bread-dough large enough to fill a quart bowl; one teacupful of melted butter; one egg; one teaspoonful of saleratus. Knead quite hard; roll out thin; lap together, cut with a mould; and set them to rise in a warm place.

ENGLISH ROLLS.

MRS. D. A. BRADFORD.

Take two pounds of flour, two ounces of butter, three table-spoonfuls of yeast, and a pint of warm milk. Stir well together, and set before the fire to rise; knead, and make into twelve rolls. Bake in a moderate oven twenty minutes.

SARATOGA ROLLS.

One pint of sweet milk; two pints of flour; two tablespoon-fuls of butter; four tablespoonfuls of yeast. Beat thoroughly, and let rise five or six hours, or all night. Before baking, add one-half teaspoonful saleratus dissolved in a little warm water. Pour into a shallow pan, and bake half an hour.

PARKER HOUSE ROLLS

MRS. WM. CLARK.

At night take two quarts of flour; rub in two tablespoonfuls of lard; make a hole in the middle, and put in one pint of cold boiled milk, one-half cup of yeast, three tablespoonfuls of sugar, and a little salt. Let this stand until morning without mixing;

then beat hard and let it stand until noon. Then roll, and cut round; spread a little butter on each one, and fold over; put them into pans, and let stand until ready to bake.

GRAHAM BREAKFAST ROLLS.

Two pounds of potatoes boiled and pressed through a cullender; one pint of water; one-half cupful of sugar; one teaspoonful of salt, and one-half cupful of yeast. Mix into a stiff dough with Graham flour; let it rise over night. In the morning mould into small cakes, and, when light, bake.

POUNDED BISCUIT.

One quart of flour; a pinch of salt; one-half teacupful of butter; make a stiff dough with milk; knead it a little; then beat hard with a rolling-pin fifteen or twenty minutes. Roll out, and cut into small biscuits. Stick with a fork, and bake in a hot oven.

HUNTER'S BISCUIT.

MRS. J. H. PIERCE.

Into five pints of sifted flour mix three teaspoonfuls of cream tartar; stir in one-half pint of sweet milk and one-half pint of melted butter or fresh lard. Into this stir one-half pint of sweet milk with a saltspoonful of salt and one teaspoonful of soda thoroughly dissolved in it. The dough should be very stiff, rolled in thin sheets, and cut upon the baking-pan with a knife or notched wheel.

SODA BISCUIT.

MRS. DAVID RENCH.

One pint of sweet milk; one teaspoonful of cream tartar; one-half teaspoonful of soda with the milk; one teaspoonful of lard mixed with the flour; a little salt Cut one-quarter of an inch thick. Bake ten minutes.

DROP BISCUITS.

One quart of flour; three teaspoonfuls of baking-powder; one small teaspoonful of salt; piece of butter the size of an egg rubbed thoroughly in the flour; one pint of milk. Drop from a spoon into buttered pans. Bake in a quick oven.

RYE DROP CAKES.

To one pint of sour milk or buttermilk add three eggs, a small teaspoonful of soda, a little salt, and rye-meal sufficient to make a stiff batter; add the soda to the milk before the meal; then the yolks, and lastly the whites, well beaten. Bake in muffin-rings, or drop on a griddle.

WHIGS.

One quart of flour; one pint of milk; three eggs; one large spoonful of melted butter; three teaspoonfuls of baking-powder. Bake in muffin-rings or cups.

MUFFINS.

MRS. G. W. H.

One pint of warm milk; three or four eggs; a piece of lard the size of an egg; one teaspoonful of salt, and one-half cup of yeast. Mix the flour stiff enough to drop from a spoon; let rise three hours in a warm place.

CORN MUFFINS.

MRS. S. GEBHART.

One large cupful of sweet milk; one of buttermilk or sour cream, in which dissolve one-half teaspoonful of soda; one large tablespoonful of lard, one cup of boiled rice, one cup of corn-meal, one tablespoonful of sugar, and two eggs. Beat the milk, rice, lard, sour cream, and yolks of the eggs well together; then add the whites, beaten very light; lastly, the flour. Bake in muffin-pans.

RICE MUFFINS.

MRS. S. G.

One pint of boiled rice; one of sweet milk; five eggs; one-half cup of butter and lard mixed; one pint of sponge, and a pinch of salt. Beat the yolks of the eggs, rice, and butter together; then add the sponge and milk; stir in sufficient flour to make a batter. Let it rise very light; beat the whites of the eggs, and stir in just before baking.

GRAHAM GEMS.
MRS. J. F. E.

Two eggs; two cups of sweet milk; one cup of Graham flour, one of wheat flour, and a little salt. Grease the pans with lard; heat them very hot; fill almost full, and bake about half an hour.

POTATO CAKES.

Two pounds of mashed potatoes; two tablespoonfuls of butter, and a little salt; two pounds of flour; stir in milk enough to make a batter; put in one-half teacupful of yeast. Set before the fire to rise; when light, bake in cakes the size of a muffin.

SALLY LUNN.
MRS. G. W. LOOMIS, SUFFIELD.

One pint of milk; three eggs, beaten separately; one table spoonful of sugar, one teaspoonful of salt, and three pints of flour; one-half teacupful of yeast, and a piece of butter the size of an egg, warmed in milk. Mix it up in the morning if wanted for tea. When light, stir down, and pour into pans, and let Sally rise again. Bake from three-quarters to one hour.

SALLY LUNN, WITHOUT YEAST.

One quart of flour; one-half pint of milk; two eggs; a piece of butter the size of an egg; three tablespoonfuls of sugar, one teaspoonful of soda, and two of cream tartar. Bake twenty minutes.

SALLY LUNN.
MRS. DR. STEWART.

One-half teacupful of butter, warmed in a pint of milk, with a little salt; three well-beaten eggs; seven cups of sifted flour, and one-half teacup of yeast.   Pour into pans, and bake when light.

BREAKFAST PUFFS.

MRS. F. W. GRIMES.

One cup of milk ; one cup of flour ; two eggs, beaten separately ; a pinch of salt, and a little cream.   Half fill the cups, and bake three-quarters of an hour.

PUFFETS.

MISS SIDNEY SIMMS.

One quart of flour ; one-half teaspoonful of salt ; a piece of butter the size of an egg ; two eggs ; two tablespoonfuls of white sugar ; one pint of sweet milk, and three teaspoonfuls of baking-powder.   [In all such recipes, sift the baking-powder into the flour.]   Rub the butter in the flour ; beat the eggs separately, adding the whites last.   Bake in gem-pans, in a hot oven.

ROSETTES.

MRS. E. F. STODDARD.

To three eggs, the yolks beaten very light, add one quart of milk ; a piece of butter the size of an egg, cut in little pieces into the milk and eggs ; three coffee-cups of flour, or enough to make a batter of the consistency of waffles ; a little salt ; two teaspoonfuls of cream tartar, one of soda, and last of all the whites of the eggs, beaten very light and stirred quickly into the mixture.   To be baked in a quick oven.

POP OVERS.

One cupful of milk ; one cupful of flour ; one egg, and one teaspoonful of salt.   Bake in gem-pans ; let them get hot before putting in the batter ; bake quickly.   Serve immediately.

YEAST WAFFLES.

MRS. JNO. G. LOWE.

Take three pints of milk and one tablespoonful of butter ; put them into a pan on the stove until the butter melts ; add five eggs, well beaten; one teaspoonful of salt; one and one-half tablespoonfuls of yeast, and about three pints of flour. Make up, and let rise three or four hours before baking.

RICE WAFFLES.

One teacupful of boiled rice (if cold, warm it on the stove); a piece of butter the size of an egg; three eggs; add the yolks, well beaten; stir in gradually one and one-half cupfuls of flour, one cupful of milk, a little salt, one teaspoonful of soda, two of cream tartar, and, lastly, just before baking, stir in the whites of the eggs, well beaten.

SOUR MILK WAFFLES.

One quart of sour milk; one teaspoonful of soda, and a little salt; two tablespoonfuls of melted butter; five eggs, beaten separately, and flour enough to make a stiff batter; add the whites of the eggs.

BUCKWHEAT CAKES.

Put in a jar two quarts of tepid water, one pint of milk, and a little salt; stir in buckwheat flour to a smooth but not very thick batter; add one handful of corn-meal, and a teacup of potato yeast. Cover the jar and keep in a warm place; let rise very light; bake on a griddle.

CORN BATTER CAKES.

MRS. B. C. R.

One pint of corn-meal; a small teaspoonful of soda and salt. Pour on enough boiling water to make it like mush; let stand a few minutes to cool; then take four eggs; put the yolks in with the meal; a handful of flour, with two teaspoonfuls of cream tartar; stir in enough milk or water (either will answer) to make the batter suitable to bake; beat the whites last, and put in just before baking.

CORN BATTER CAKES.

Mix two parts buttermilk with one of sweet milk; one egg; one handful of wheat flour; a little salt; one teaspoonful of soda, and as much corn-meal as is needed to make a batter.

HOMINY FRITTERS.

To one quart of well-boiled hominy, seasoned with pepper and salt, add one egg, two tablespoonfuls of milk, and one of flour. Stir all together; mould into small cakes, and fry in a skillet with a little butter or lard.

PANCAKES OF RICE.

MRS. GORTON ARNOLD.

Boil half a pound of rice to a jelly in a small quantity of water; when cool, mix with it a pint of cream, eight eggs, a pinch of salt, nutmeg, eight ounces of melted butter, and flour enough to stiffen. Fry in as little lard as possible.

FRIED MUSH.

MRS. W. A. B.

Into two quarts of boiling water stir corn-meal until it makes a smooth mush; boil half an hour; add salt, and stir briskly. Have hot, in a skillet, one tablespoonful each of lard and butter; drop the boiling mush into the skillet in little pats; fry a light crisp brown on both sides.

CRUMB CAKES.

Put pieces of stale, light bread in a dish; pour some milk (or buttermilk) over them, and let stand until soft. Rub and press through a cullender; beat up three eggs and stir in; add a little salt and a teaspoonful of saleratus. Stir in flour enough to make it of the proper consistency to bake on a griddle.

PENNSYLVANIA FLANNEL CAKES.

The yolks of five eggs well beaten ; one quart of milk slightly warmed ; a little salt, and flour enough to make a batter ; add one cup of yeast. They will take several hours to rise, and must be kept warm. Just before baking, add two tablespoonfuls of melted butter, and the whites of the eggs beaten to a froth. Bake on a griddle.

LEMON TURNOVERS.

MRS. D. A. BRADFORD.

Four dessert-spoonfuls of flour ; one of powdered sugar ; the rind of one lemon ; two ounces of melted butter ; two eggs, and a little milk. Mix the flour, sugar, and the grated rind of the lemon with a little milk to the consistency of batter ; then add the butter and eggs, well beaten. Fry, and turn·over.

PEACH FRITTERS.

Make a batter with eight eggs, eight tablespoonfuls of flour, and one quart of milk. Have ready in a frying-pan some hot butter. To each tablespoonful of batter add one-half of a peach, and fry.

SPANISH FRITTERS.

Cut baker's bread into strips thick as a lady-finger, and any shape desired. Take one pint of cream ; sweeten ; add ground cloves, cinnamon, nutmeg, pepper, and a pinch of salt. Stir in the whites of two or three eggs, well beaten ; dip the bread in the cream, and fry in butter quickly. Serve very hot.

8

CAKE.

IN cake-baking much of the success depends on the oven, which should be well and evenly heated before baking, and not allowed to cool.

Do not remove the cake until it is thoroughly baked, or it will fall. Try it by piercing with a broom-splinter; if nothing adheres, it is done.

Flour should never be used without sifting.

BUCKEYE CAKE.

One cup of butter; two cups of white sugar; four cups of flour; one cup of sweet milk; six eggs; two teaspoonfuls of cream tartar, and one of soda.

POUND CAKE.

MISS P.

One pound of sugar; three-quarters of a pound of butter; one of flour; nine eggs; a piece of sal volatile the size of a pea, dissolved in a teaspoonful of water. Beat butter and sugar to a cream; then add the eggs, beaten separately; lastly, the flour.

CORN–STARCH CAKE.

MISS M. J. DICKSON.

Two cups of powdered sugar; one of butter; three-fourths of a cup of milk; the whites of six eggs; three-fourths of a cup of corn-starch; two full cups of flour; three teaspoonfuls of baking-powder mixed in the flour. Flavor with lemon.

DELICATE CAKE.

MRS. J. R. REYNOLDS.

Two teacupfuls of white sugar; three-quarters of a cupful of butter; one cupful of sweet milk; four of flour; the whites of four eggs, beaten to a stiff froth; three teaspoonfuls of baking-powder. Flavor with vanilla, lemon, or nutmeg.

DELICATE CAKE.

MRS. R.

One-half pound of flour; one-half pound of sugar; one-quarter of a pound of butter; one teaspoonful cream tartar; one-half teaspoonful of soda, and whites of eight eggs. Flavor to taste.

SNOW CAKE.

Whites of ten eggs; one and one-half glasses of sugar; one of flour; one teaspoonful of cream tartar, and one-half teaspoonful of salt. Put the cream tartar and salt in the flour; stir in the sugar; beat the whites of the eggs very light, and stir all together. Flavor with lemon.

SILVER CAKE.

The whites of five eggs; one cup of sugar; two and one-half cups of flour; one-half cup of butter; one-half cup of milk; one teaspoonful of cream tartar, and one-half teaspoonful of soda. Mix the butter and sugar together; add the milk; then the flour, in which has been mixed the cream tartar; then the whites of the eggs; then the soda, dissolved in a little boiling water.

GOLD CAKE.

One cup of butter; two cups of sugar; three cups of flour; one-half cup of milk; the yolks of five eggs; one teaspoonful of cream tartar; one-half a teaspoonful of soda; flavor to taste.

FRENCH BUNN.

MRS. G. W. ROGERS.

One pound of sugar; one pound of flour; one-half pound of butter; two wine-glasses of new milk; one teaspoonful of soda, two of cream tartar, and eight eggs. Beat butter and sugar to a cream.

LIVERPOOL CAKE.

MISS MARY A. CUMMIN.

One pound of flour; one pound of sugar; one-half pound of butter; four eggs; one cupful of sweet milk; two teaspoonfuls of cream tartar, and one teaspoonful of soda, in the milk. Flavor to taste. Beat the sugar and butter together; then the eggs, without separating; add milk, flour, and soda last.

SOCIAL CAKE.

MRS. L. MOORE.

One cup of butter; two of sugar; three and one-half cups of flour; five eggs, beaten separately; three-quarters of a cup of milk; one teaspoonful of cream tartar, and half a teaspoonful of soda. Flavor with lemon.

QUEEN CAKE.

MISS LUCY CHAMBERS.

One pound of sugar; one pound of flour, light weight; ten eggs, leaving out four whites. Beat the yolks and sugar together; then add the whites and flour. Spice to suit taste.

SIMPLE SPONGE CAKE.

MISS S. M.

Three eggs; one cup of sugar, and one of flour. Beat the eggs very light; then add the sugar; stir in the flour, and one teaspoonful of water. Flavor to taste.

SPONGE CAKE.

MISS ARMSTRONG.

Take twelve eggs and weigh them; take their weight in sugar, and one-half their weight in flour; two small lemons, or one very large one, grated. Bake in a hot oven.

SPONGE CAKE.

MRS. A. F. PAYNE.

One pound of powdered sugar; one-half pound of flour; ten eggs; the juice of one lemon, and a little salt. Beat the yolks until very light; then stir in the sugar, lemon-juice, and salt; then add part of the flour, and part of the whites, beaten stiffly; then the remainder of the flour, and, lastly, the remaining whites.

COCOANUT SPONGE CAKE.

MISS MARY GEBHART.

Beat the yolks of six eggs with one-half pound of sugar; one-quarter pound of flour; add one teaspoonful of lemon essence. Stir in the whites of eggs beaten to a froth; add the grated pulp of one cocoanut.

COCOANUT POUND CAKE.

MRS. J. A. MCMAHON.

One pound of butter, one of flour, one of sugar, one of cocoanut, grated, and ten eggs. Beat the butter and sugar to a cream; put the cocoanut in before the flour; beat the eggs separately, and mix like other cake. Bake three hours in a moderate oven.

COCOANUT CAKE.

MISS MAGGIE CONNELLY.

One cupful of butter, three of sugar, and four of flour; whites of eight eggs; one cupful and three tablespoonfuls of milk; one teaspoonful of soda, two and one-half of cream tartar, one and one-quarter of grated cocoanut in the cake; mix the butter and sugar with your hand; then add the milk (use that of the cocoanut); mix the cocoanut with the flour, and add the eggs last. Bake in square pans. Use the following

ICING.

Whites of three eggs; two cups of sugar; three-fourths of a cup of grated cocoanut. Spread thickly all over the top and sides; set in the oven with the door open for a few minutes.

ALMOND CAKE.
MISS MARY BRADY.

One cupful of butter, two of sugar, three of flour, one of sweet milk; the whites of eight eggs; one teaspoonful of cream tartar; one-half teaspoonful of soda; two pounds of almonds, blanched and powdered fine in rose-water. Best when several days old.

HICKORY-NUT CAKE.
MRS. MUNGER.

Two cupfuls of sugar; three-fourths of a cupful of butter; three cupfuls of flour, mixed with three teaspoonfuls of baking-powder; three-fourths of a cupful of sweet milk; whites of six eggs; one pint of nuts, rolled fine.

HICKORY-NUT CAKE.
MRS. DR. SMITH.

Three tumblerfuls of sugar, one of butter, a little more than one of milk, four of flour; one teaspoonful of soda; three eggs, beaten separately; essence of lemon; one and one-half pints of kernels, chopped fine, and two tablespoonfuls of raisins, chopped.

WATERMELON CAKE.
MRS. GRAHAM.

WHITE PART.—Two cups of sugar; one-half cup of butter, one of sweet milk; two teaspoonfuls of baking-powder; two and one-half cups of flour, and one lemon.

PINK PART.—Made the same as the white, except use pink

sugar (which can be bought at the confectioner's), and one-half pound of raisins. Put the raisins in the sugar. Put the pink part all in the centre of the pan, and the white on the outside.

COFFEE CAKE.

MRS. J. D. DUBOIS.

One cup of butter, one of sugar, one of molasses, one of raisins, one of cold coffee, three of flour; two eggs; a piece of citron, cut small; nutmeg and cinnamon.

"ERIE" COFFEE CAKE.

Three cups brown sugar, one of butter, one of cold coffee; three eggs; three teaspoonfuls of soda, two of cinnamon, one of cloves, one of nutmeg, and three and one-half cups of flour.

CITRON CAKE.

MRS. H. CONOVER.

Whites of twelve eggs; two cups of butter; two cups of sugar; four and one-half cups of flour; one-half cup of milk; one teaspoonful of soda, two of cream tartar, and one pound of citron.

CURRANT CAKE.

MRS. H. C.

Two cups of butter; two cups of sugar; one cup of milk; four cups of flour; one teaspoonful of soda, two of cream tartar; one pound of currants, and seven eggs.

BREAD CAKE.

MRS. J. F. EDGAR.

Three cups of light dough, before it is kneaded; three cups of sugar; one cup of butter; four eggs; spice, cinnamon, and cloves. Mix together thoroughly; let it rise until very light; then mix pretty stiff with flour; add what fruit may be desired, and one teaspoonful of soda. Divide into two cakes, and let it rise again. Bake three hours.

FRUIT CAKE.

MRS. G. A. BLACK.

One cup of butter, one of sugar, one of molasses, one of sweet milk, three of flour; four eggs; cinnamon, cloves, and allspice to taste; one teaspoonful of soda, two of cream tartar, and two pounds of raisins.

FINE FRUIT CAKE.

MRS. A. F. PAYNE.

One pound of powdered sugar, one of butter, one of flour; twelve eggs; two pounds of raisins, two of currants; one-half pound of citron; one tablespoonful of powdered mace, one of cinnamon; two nutmegs, grated; mix a large wine-glass of Madeira wine and one of brandy together, and steep the spices in it over night. Flour the fruit before adding it to the cake. Bake in two loaves.

BLACK FRUIT CAKE.

MRS. T. M. MCCORMICK.

Four cups of sugar, two of butter, one of molasses, one of brandy, eight of flour; one-half pint of sour cream; eight eggs; two pounds of raisins, two of currants, and two of almonds; one-half pound of citron; one tablespoonful of cloves, one of saleratus; one lemon; two nutmegs, grated.

BLACK CAKE.

MRS. JOHN W. GREEN.

One and one-quarter pounds of butter; one pound of brown sugar; one of flour; three of raisins, seeded and chopped; two of currants; one of citron, cut thin and small; one of figs, chopped; thirteen eggs; one wine-glass of Madeira wine and two of brandy; one teacupful of molasses; one large nutmeg, grated; two teaspoonfuls of cinnamon, one of mace, and one of cloves. Beat the butter and sugar until very light; then stir in one-fourth of the flour; whisk the eggs very stiff, and add them gradually; then the remainder of the flour, one-half at a time; after beating well, add the wine, brandy, and spices; then mix all the fruit together, and add one-third at a time. Beat well; butter the pan, and line it with white paper; put in the mixture, and smooth with a knife. Bake in a moderate oven about four hours.

FRUIT CAKE.

MRS. MARY C. KING.

Two cups of butter; two and one-half cups of sugar; two and one-half cups of molasses, eight of flour, two of sour milk; eight eggs; two teaspoonfuls of soda; three pounds of raisins, three of currants, one of figs, one of citron; two lemons, grated; two tumblers of currant-jelly; one-half pint of brandy; cloves, mace, cinnamon, and nutmegs. Mix flour and fruit alternately. Bake three and one-half hours.

GINGER FRUIT CAKE.

MRS. S. CRAIGHEAD.

One-half pound of butter; one-half pound of sugar; six eggs, beaten separately; one pint of molasses; one pint of sour milk, in which put one tablespoonful of soda; three pints of sifted flour; one wine-glass of brandy; three tablespoonfuls of ginger; one of cinnamon; one of nutmeg, grated; one teaspoonful of cloves; one pound of raisins, mashed with the seeds in; one pound of currants; one-half pound of citron; put the whites of the eggs in last. To be baked in a slow oven. This will make two cakes, and will keep several weeks.

DRIED-APPLE FRUIT CAKE.

MRS. LUCY GREEN.

Two cupfuls of dried apples soaked over night; chop fine, and simmer slowly in two cups of New Orleans molasses until it looks dark. When cool, add one cupful of butter, one-half cupful of sugar, three cupfuls of flour, one cupful of sweet milk, two teaspoonfuls of cinnamon, two of cloves, two of allspice, three of baking-powder, one-half pound of raisins, and three eggs. If you wish, add one cupful of currants and one-quarter cupful of citron. Bake in a slow oven two and one-half hours.

FRENCH LOAF CAKE.

Two and one-half cupfuls of powdered sugar; one and one-half cupfuls of butter, five of flour, one of milk; one-half glass of wine; one-half glass of brandy; one-half pound of raisins; two ounces of citron, cut in small pieces; one nutmeg, grated; and one tablespoonful of baking-powder. Stir the sugar and butter to a cream; then add part of the flour, with the milk (slightly warmed), and the beaten yolks of the eggs; then the remainder of the flour, and the whites of the eggs well beaten; add the spice, wine, brandy, and baking-powder. Mix thoroughly together; put the fruit in last. This will make two loaves. Bake one and one-quarter hours.

SPONGE GINGERBREAD.

One cup of sour milk, one of molasses; one-half cup of butter; two eggs; one and one-half teaspoonfuls of soda; one quart of flour, and one large tablespoonful of ginger.

BLACK GINGERBREAD.

Three cupfuls of molasses, one of butter, one of sour cream; five cupfuls of flour; four eggs; one ounce of ginger; one teaspoonful of soda in the cream; fruit if you like.

GINGERBREAD.

MRS. D. W. IDDINGS.

One pint of molasses; one glass of sour milk or cream; one tablespoonful of soda; one-half pint of melted lard. Put the soda into the molasses and milk, and beat to a foam. Make the dough very soft.

MARBLE CAKE.

MISS J. A. E.

Whites of seven eggs; three cups of white sugar, one of butter, one of milk, four of flour; one and one-half teaspoonfuls of baking-powder. Dark part.—Yolks of seven eggs; two cupfuls of brown sugar, one of butter, one of milk, one of Orleans molasses, and four of flour; one tablespoonful of baking-powder, one of cinnamon, one of allspice, and one-half tablespoonful of cloves. Put some of the white mixture first into the pan, then with a large spoon drop in some of the dark, alternating until all is used. This will make one large and one small cake.

CHOCOLATE MARBLE CAKE.

MISS SALLIE C. WIGHT.

One cupful of butter; two cupfuls of sugar, one of sweet milk, three of flour; whites of five eggs; two teaspoonfuls of cream tartar, and one of soda. Take one teacupful of the batter, and stir into it one large spoonful of grated chocolate; wet with a small tablespoonful of milk; fill cake-dish about one inch deep with the white batter; then drop in two or three places a spoonful of the dark mixture; continue this until the batter is all used.

LAYER CAKES.

CHOCOLATE CAKE.

MISS LINA MILLER.

The yolks of three eggs; one and one-half cupfuls of sugar; three-quarters of a cupful of butter; one cupful of milk; three teaspoonfuls of baking-powder; flour enough to stiffen. Bake in jelly-cake pans.

ICING.

Whites of three eggs, beaten stiff; add white sugar enough to sweeten; nine tablespoonfuls of sweet chocolate, grated. Mix well, and spread on each layer while a little warm.

CHOCOLATE CAKE.

BLOSSOM BROWN.

One cupful of sugar; one-half cupful of butter; one-half cupful of milk; two eggs; one and one-half teaspoonfuls of baking-powder; two cupfuls of flour. Bake in thin layers. For filling, take one-half cake of sweet chocolate, grated; one-half cup of sweet milk; one-half cupful of sugar; yolk of one egg; one tablespoonful of vanilla. Boil in a pan set in a kettle of boiling water, until stiff, like jelly. When cool, spread it between layers.

SPRINGFIELD ALMOND CAKE.

Two cupfuls of sugar, one of butter, one of milk, four of flour; five eggs; two teaspoonfuls of cream tartar, and one of soda. Bake in jelly-cake pans. Make a custard of one cupful of sour cream; one egg; one-half pound of almonds, blanched and chopped fine; one tablespoonful of sugar. Flavor it with vanilla. Do not spread the custard on until the cake is cold. If you cannot procure sour cream, take jelly; flavor, and mix almonds with it, and spread between layers.

ORANGE CAKE.

MRS. G. W. ROGERS.

One cupful of butter, two of sugar, one of milk, and three and one-fourth cupfuls of flour; five eggs, leaving out the whites of three; one and one-half teaspoonfuls of baking-powder; juice of one orange. Bake in jelly-cake tins, and spread between the layers an icing made of the whites of three eggs and enough sugar to make it stiff; juice of one and grated rind of two oranges.

LEMON CAKE.

One cupful of butter, four of flour, three of sugar, one of sweet milk; five eggs; one tablespoonful of baking-powder; juice and rind of one lemon. Bake in flat tins.

AMBROSIA CAKE.

MISS LOUIE MYERS.

One-half cupful of milk; three-fourths cupful of butter; two cupfuls of sugar; three of flour; four eggs; three teaspoonfuls of baking-powder. Bake in jelly-cake pans. When cold, spread with one pint of cream, whipped, one grated cocoanut, two eggs, one cupful of sugar, two oranges, and the grated rind of one.

JELLY CAKE.

MISS ELLEN P. DICKSON.

Five eggs; four cupfuls of flour; three cupfuls of sugar; one cupful of butter; one cupful of sour cream; three-fourths teaspoonful of soda.

WASHINGTON CAKE.

MRS. J. T. WOLF.

Two cupfuls of sugar; one-half cupful of butter; three cupfuls of flour; three teaspoonfuls of baking-powder; seven eggs; one-half cupful of sweet milk.

FILLING.

Three tart apples, grated; one cupful of white sugar; one egg; the grated rind and juice of one lemon. Boil about two minutes; then let it stand to cool before spreading on the cake.

RAILROAD CAKE.

One cup of sugar, one of sweet milk, two of flour; one teaspoonful of butter; two of baking-powder, and three eggs, beaten separately. Mix, and bake immediately; use shallow pans. While hot, spread on jelly, and roll up. This will make two cakes.

ROLLED SPONGE CAKE.

Two eggs; two cupfuls of sugar, two of flour; essence of lemon or brandy to taste. Bake in thin sheets; spread the jelly on while warm, and roll up. Use it while fresh. It makes a nice pudding with wine-sauce.

SPONGE CUSTARD CAKE.
MISS LOUIE MYERS.

Six eggs; two cupfuls of sugar, three of flour; three teaspoonfuls of baking powder, and four tablespoonfuls of water.

CUSTARD.

One pint of milk; put one-half cupful of butter into the milk and let come to a boil; then stir in two eggs; one cupful of sugar; two small teaspoonfuls of corn-starch; spread this between the layers of cake.

SPONGE COCOANUT CAKE.
MISS MARY GEBHART.

Take one pint of sugar, one of flour, eight eggs, beaten separately, and one tablespoonful of water; mix, and bake in jelly-cake pans.

FILLING.

One cocoanut, grated; one cupful of sugar; one of cream; butter the size of an egg; warm it a little; mix thoroughly, and spread it between the layers.   The cake is nicest when fresh.

COCOANUT CAKE.
MRS. W. A. B.

One cupful of butter; three of sugar; three of flour; one-half cupful of sweet milk; whites of ten eggs, well beaten; three teaspoonfuls of baking-powder.   Beat butter and sugar to a cream; add flour, milk, and baking powder; and last, stir in the eggs very lightly.   Bake, in a moderate oven, in pans one inch deep.   Make three cakes.

ICING.

Three eggs; one pound of sugar; two cocoanuts, grated; one lemon.   Beat the eggs to a stiff froth; then add the sugar and lemon-juice. Put one cake on a stand; while warm, spread on the icing; then sprinkle thick with cocoanut. Lay on another cake and do the same. At the last, spread icing all over the top and edges, and put on as much cocoanut as will adhere.

WHITE MOUNTAIN CAKE.

MRS. I. VAN AUSDAL.

One pound of flour; one of sugar; one-half pound of butter; one teacupful of sweet milk; six eggs, beaten separately; one teaspoonful of soda; two of cream tartar; the grated rind and juice of one lemon. Bake in jelly-cake pans; put icing between the layers. Previous to icing, dredge with flour.

ICING.

One-half teacupful of water; three of sugar, and the whites of three eggs. Boil the sugar and water until quite thick; pour it on the whites of the eggs (previously beaten), and beat all together until cool.

SMALL CAKES.

GOOD COOKIES.

MRS. DR. MCDERMONT.

Five eggs, beaten light; four tablespoonfuls of cream; one-half pound of butter; two cups of white sugar; two teaspoonfuls of cream tartar, one of soda. When rolled out, sprinkle with sugar, and roll again; cut into small cakes.

AUNT BETSEY'S COOKIES.

Twenty ounces of sugar; ten of butter; two teaspoonfuls of saleratus; two teacupfuls of milk; caraway seed, and flour to make it stiff enough to roll.

CANADA COOKIES.

MRS. MUNGER.

One-half pound of butter; one-half pound of sugar; one pound of flour; two eggs; rub the butter and sugar to a cream; beat the eggs well together; add flour, and roll out very thin; sprinkle with white sugar, and bake quickly.

COOKIES.

MRS. FRED. LANGE.

Two coffee-cups of brown sugar; one of butter; five of sifted flour; one egg; one-half cupful of milk; one-half teaspoonful cream tartar; one-fourth teaspoonful soda, in the milk. Roll thin; bake in a quick oven.

SAND TARTS.

Two cups of sugar; one of butter; four eggs, leaving out the yolk of one. Beat the butter and part of the sugar together, and the remainder with the eggs; flour enough to make a very stiff dough. Roll thin; wet the top with white of egg; sprinkle with sugar and cinnamon, and put blanched almonds over the top.

GINGER–NUTS.

MRS. GIBBS.

Three pounds of flour; one of butter; one pint of molasses; two teaspoonfuls of saleratus; ginger to the taste.

GINGER–SNAPS.

MISS MARY E. MITCHELL.

One pint of molasses; one and one-half coffee-cups of butter; two and one-half cups of sugar; one-half cup of water; two eggs; one tablespoonful of ginger; one heaping teaspoonful of soda. Mix all together with flour to make a soft dough; roll very thin, and bake in a quick oven.

GERMAN CRACK CAKE.

AMELIA.

One cupful of sugar; one cupful of butter; three-quarters pound of flour; four eggs, leaving out the whites of two; beat all together, and bake in a biscuit-pan. Sprinkle sugar and cinnamon over the top. Bake in a quick oven; while warm (before taking out of the pans), cut in squares.

NANCY'S DOUGHNUTS.

Two small cupfuls of sugar; one cupful of sweet milk; three eggs; one tablespoonful of melted butter; one small teaspoonful of soda, and two of cream tartar. Mix with flour as soft as they can be rolled out. Fry in hot lard.

RAISED DOUGHNUTS.

Two cupfuls of sweet milk; one of lard; one and one-half cupfuls of white sugar; one cupful of yeast; two eggs; a little grated nutmeg, and salt; add flour enough to make a thick batter. Let it rise until very light; knead well, roll out and cut with a biscuit-cutter, and cut the centre out with a canister top; put them on a floured board to rise again. When light, fry in hot lard.

THE QUEEN OF DOUGHNUTS.

MRS. MARY SPINNING.

One-half pound of butter; one tablespoonful of lard; three quarters of a pound of sugar; five eggs; one and one-half pints of milk, and one coffee-cupful of home-made yeast. Heat the milk and sugar together; mix with them flour enough to make a stiff dough; heat the butter and lard; pour over the dough when very hot, and work in well with the hands; add the eggs beaten separately, cinnamon or nutmeg, and then the yeast; let stand until light; pinch off pieces about as large as a walnut; roll into balls, and fry in hot lard. When done, and while warm, sift powdered sugar over them.

9

EXCELLENT CRULLERS.

MRS. J. LANGDON.

One egg; four tablespoonfuls of sugar; one pint of sweet buttermilk; one tablespoonful of butter or lard; flour enough to make a soft dough.

CRULLERS.

MRS. H. L. BROWN.

To five tincupfuls of flour put two teaspoonfuls of soda, four teaspoonfuls cream tartar, five eggs, one and one-half tincupfuls of sugar, one-fourth pound of butter, and pint of milk; add cinnamon and nutmeg.

CRULLERS.

MRS. DR. SMITH.

Two cupfuls of sugar; one-half cupful of butter; one-half teaspoonful of soda dissolved in a cupful of sour milk; cinnamon or nutmeg to taste; four eggs; flour enough to make a soft dough.

DROP GINGERCAKES.

MRS. WILLIAM CRAIGHEAD.

One pint of molasses; one teacupful of sugar; one cupful of butter; four eggs; two tablespoonfuls of ginger; same of ground cinnamon; one teaspoonful of salt; one tablespoonful of soda in a half-teacupful of hot water; flour enough to make a stiff batter. Drop on tins, and bake.

SAVORY CAKES.

MRS. ASHLEY BROWN.

Beat four eggs, whites and yolks separately; put them together and add one-half pound of white sugar. Beat very hard; stir in slowly one-quarter pound of sifted flour; flavor with vanilla; drop with a spoon in thin cakes on white paper; grate loaf sugar over the top, and bake in a quick oven.

SHREWSBURY CAKES.

MISS ARMSTRONG.

One pound of flour; one pound of sugar; one-half pound of butter; three eggs; flavor with cinnamon or caraway seed. Drop on tins.

CHOCOLATE JUMBLES.

MISS JENNIE A. EDGAR.

One pound of sugar; one-half pound of chocolate, grated; whites of eight eggs, or four whole ones, beaten very light; six ounces of flour; one teaspoonful of cinnamon, one of cloves. Drop with a teaspoon on well-buttered tins.

CHOCOLATE PUFFS.

MISS JOAN RENCH.

Beat stiff the whites of two eggs, and beat in gradually one-half pound of powdered sugar; scrape down very fine one and one-half ounces of best chocolate (prepared cocoa is better), and dredge it with flour to prevent it oiling; mix the flour well with it; then add the mixture of egg and sugar, and stir all very hard. Cover the bottom of a square tin pan with a sheet of white paper; place upon it spots of powdered sugar about the size of a half-dollar; put a portion of the mixture on each spot, smoothing it with a broad knife dipped in cold water; sift white sugar over the top of each; bake a few minutes in a brisk oven. When cool, loosen them with a broad knife.

DROP JUMBLES.

One pound of sugar; three-fourths of a pound of butter; yolks of eight eggs, or four whole ones; one cup of sour cream; one teaspoonful of soda; one pound of currants; flour sufficient to make the batter thick enough to drop from a spoon. Bake in buttered pans.

COCOANUT JUMBLES.

One pound of cocoanut, grated; three-fourths of a pound of sugar; three eggs; large ironspoonful of flour. Drop on buttered pans.

ALMOND MACAROONS.

MRS. M. EELLS.

One-half pound of almonds, blanched and pounded with a little rose-water or essence of lemon; one-half pound of white sugar; two eggs, whites well beaten. Dip your hands in water, and work the mixture into balls the size of a hickory-nut. Put them in a cool oven, and bake a light brown. Cocoanut can be grated and made into macaroons in the same way.

EGG KISSES.

MISS IRENE STOUT.

Take one-half pound of granulated sugar, and the whites of four eggs, beaten very stiff. Put writing-paper in a pan, and drop in spots with a teaspoon. Bake in a slow oven three-quarters of an hour.

MERINGUES.

MRS. D. W. STEWART.

The whites of nine eggs, beaten to a froth; mix with them one pound of powdered sugar. Drop on paper with a teaspoon, and bake a light brown, putting the paper on a board (not pine) on the bottom of a pan in the oven. When done, fill with whipped cream flavored with lemon.

COCOANUT CAKES.

Grate the white part of one cocoanut; allow an equal weight of white sugar; add the grated rind and juice of one lemon. Mix the ingredients well; make into cakes the size of a nutmeg, with a little piece of citron in each. Bake on buttered tins about twenty minutes in a moderate oven.

MADELEINES.

Blanch and chop rather fine some sweet almonds. Mix well together in a bowl three ounces of flour, three of sugar, and two eggs; then add one ounce of melted butter, and a few drops of essence to flavor. Butter slightly small tin moulds, and dust with equal parts of sugar and flour. Fill the moulds about two-thirds full; spread the almonds over the top, and bake in a quick oven. To be eaten cold.

CREAM CAKES.

MISS BIRGE.

Boil in one-half pint of water three-fourths of a cupful of butter, and stir in one and three-fourths cupfuls of flour. Take from the fire; put into a large bowl, and stir in five eggs, one at a time, without beating, and one-half teaspoonful of soda (dry). Drop in pans half the size you wish them; bake in a quick oven fifteen or twenty minutes.

FILLING FOR THE ABOVE.

One quart of milk; five eggs; one and one-half cupfuls of sugar; two tablespoonfuls of corn-starch; flavor with lemon or vanilla.

BOSTON CREAM CAKES.

MRS. I. BALDWIN.

One pint of water; one-half pound of butter; three-fourths of a pound of flour; ten eggs. Boil the water with the butter in it; stir in the flour dry while it boils; when cool, add a teaspoonful of soda, and the eggs well beaten. Drop the mixture on buttered pans with a dessert-spoon. Bake twenty minutes.

CREAM.

One cupful of flour; two of sugar; one quart of milk, and four eggs. Beat the flour, sugar, and eggs together, and stir them into the boiling milk. When the mixture is sufficiently scalded, set it to cool; flavor with lemon. When the cakes are cool, cut them open and fill in the cream.

PICKLES AND RELISHES.

In preparing pickles, avoid the use of metal vessels. If pickles are kept in them any length of time they will become poisonous. When it is necessary to boil vinegar, do it in a porcelain kettle, or in a stone jar on top of the stove. Always use the best vinegar. A small quantity of alum is an improvement to pickles, but too much is injurious. Keep them in glass or in hard stoneware.

CUCUMBER PICKLES.

MRS. G. W. ROGERS.

Two hundred small-sized cucumbers; three tablespoonfuls of white and three of black mustard-seed, three of celery-seed; one handful of juniper berries; one handful of small green peppers; two pounds of sugar, and a few small onions. Let the cucumbers stand three days in salt water closely covered. Boil a little alum in a half-gallon of vinegar, and pour over the cucumbers scalding hot; repeat three or four times. When ready to bottle, add one-half pound of ground mustard, and one bottle of English chow-chow. Take the vinegar from the chow-chow, and mix with it sufficient cold vinegar to cover well the pickles. Seal up in glass jars.

CUCUMBER PICKLES.

MRS. T. A. PHILLIPS.

Wash your cucumbers well, and place them in stone jars. To every gallon of vinegar add one-half teacupful of salt, one ounce of ginger-root, one ounce of allspice, one ounce of cloves, one ounce of cinnamon, one ounce of black pepper. Boil the vinegar and spices together for three mornings, and pour over the pickles hot; cover them closely. Will be ready for use in three days.

CUCUMBER PICKLES.

MRS. JAMES R. WALLACE.

Let the cucumbers lie in salt water forty-eight hours; put together two quarts of vinegar, some cinnamon, red peppers, and horse-radish, and let them boil hard for fifteen minutes; then throw in the pickles, and put in enough vinegar to cover them. Let them scald, not boil; then set the kettle upon the stove, and let the pickles remain in it (kept hot) until they are green; then pack them in jars, and scald fresh vinegar (adding one pint of sugar to every gallon of vinegar), and pour over the pickles. Seal them tight.

GHERKINS.

MRS. J. R. YOUNG.

Put the gherkins in brine for a week; if they are salty, soak one day; then take a kettle and line it with grape-leaves; put the gherkins in, and cover them with vinegar; put in a piece of alum the size of a hickory-nut; let them stand on the coolest part of the stove all day and keep warm, but not boil. If the vinegar is salty, put on fresh. Put the spices—cloves, cinnamon, mace, allspice, and pepper—in a separate vessel with vinegar, and boil. Pour it over the gherkins, and they are done.

INDIA PICKLES.

ADMIRAL SCHENCK.

One gallon of best vinegar; three ounces of salt; one-half pound of flour of mustard; two ounces of turmeric; three ounces of white ginger; one ounce of cloves, one of mace, one of white and long peppers each; four ounces of chalots, peeled; two ounces of garlic, peeled; two ounces of cayenne pepper. The mustard and turmeric must be rubbed together with a little cold vinegar, and stand until smooth; stir in the other ingredients just before it boils. As soon as it boils, remove it; let it cool, and it is fit for use.

YELLOW PICKLES.

MRS. R. P. BROWN.

Six gallons of best vinegar; six ounces of turmeric, six of white ginger, six of long peppers, one of mace, one of cloves, two of white mustard, one of white pepper, two of celery-seed; two pounds of brown sugar; two handfuls of garlic; oranges and lemons to taste. Into this pickle put any vegetable preferred, prepared as follows: Soak in cold brine for one week; after which expose them to the sun through the day; at night return them to the brine; then soak four days in vinegar, and afterward put them into the pickle. Onions should have boiling brine thrown over them and stand four or five days; then bleach as the others. Vegetables may be prepared as they come in season. This pickle will keep for years.

STUFFED CUCUMBERS.

MRS. H. STRONG.

Let the cucumbers lie in brine four or five days; then cut open one side and scrape out the inner part. If the inside is very salty, let them lie in cold water until the next day; if not, two or three hours will answer.

STUFFING.

American mustard-seed, cloves, black pepper, red pepper-pods, small onions, celery-seed, and horse-radish, chopped fine.

FILLING FOR CUCUMBER MANGOES.

MISS LOUIE PHILLIPS.

One-half pound of white mustard-seed; one ounce of cloves, one of black pepper; two of celery-seed; one cup of horse-radish, grated; one pod of garlic in each cucumber; four tablespoonfuls of table mustard, eight of oil, and one of turmeric. Mix the mustard in cold water, and boil; when cold, stir in the oil and turmeric, and then mix with the other ingredients. Onions, cabbage, and tomatoes may be chopped with the filling, if desired. Sweeten the vinegar.

RIPE CUCUMBER PICKLES.

Take bright yellow cucumbers, firm but not soft; pare and cut them in strips, and, after removing the seeds, put them in a weak brine for twelve hours; pour off the brine, and scald them in alum-water until clear; wash in cold water, and drain. To one gallon of vinegar, take three and one-half pounds of sugar, one stick of cinnamon, nutmeg, and mace. Boil, and pour over the cucumbers; repeat two or three times.

SLICED CUCUMBER PICKLES.

Take one peck of medium-sized cucumbers, and one-half dozen onions; slice, and sprinkle with salt; let them lie three or four hours; then drain, and boil in vinegar for ten minutes, with the following spices: one-half pound of yellow mustard-seed, two tablespoonfuls of cloves, one of mace, one of turmeric, and two of brown sugar. Pack in jars, and tie paper closely over them.

GREEN TOMATO PICKLES.

MRS. JUDGE SHERMAN.

One peck of green tomatoes, sliced thin; sprinkle with salt, and let them stand one night; slice twelve onions; put with the tomatoes, and boil in vinegar for two hours, with the following spices: four ounces of white mustard-seed, four of ground mustard, one-half ounce of turmeric, one ounce of cloves, one of allspice, one of ginger, one of pepper, one of cinnamon, one-fourth of a teacupful of salt, and one-half pound of brown sugar.

FRENCH PICKLES.

One-half peck of green tomatoes; one dozen of white onions; slice thin, and sprinkle with salt; let stand over night; drain in a cullender; then put them into a porcelain kettle; cover with vinegar and water, equal parts; boil slowly one hour; then drain one-half hour. Take one and one-half gallons of vinegar, and three pounds of brown sugar; boil and skim; then add one-half teacupful of French mustard, one ounce each of ground cloves, allspice, cinnamon, black pepper, and turmeric. Mix to a smooth paste with water, and stir into the vinegar while boiling. Use stone jars; put in a layer of pickles, and then a cup of the mixture. They are ready for immediate use.

PICKLED TOMATOES.

Take red tomatoes, not very ripe; puncture slightly with a fork, and cover them with strong brine; let them remain six or eight days; then soak them twenty-four hours in vinegar and water; drain off; and, for every gallon your vessel holds, take six ounces of ground mustard, four of ginger, two of celery-seed, one of cloves, and one dozen white onions, sliced. Mix the spices all together; put a layer in the bottom of the jar, then onions and tomatoes, and so on, alternately, until the jar is full. Fill up with strong vinegar.

PICKLED TOMATOES.

MRS. A. C. C.

Take pear-shaped tomatoes, yellow and red mixed; wash them off, and put in narrow-mouthed vessels, so that they can be made air-tight; to a quart of tomatoes take a teaspoonful of salt, some ginger-root, cinnamon, mace, and small red peppers mixed in among them; make the jars full, and fill up with vinegar. Set in a cool, dark place. In three or four weeks they will be ready for use.

GREEN TOMATO PICKLES (SWEET).

Scald and peel full-grown green tomatoes; drop them into strong ginger-tea, and scald well. For every two pounds of tomatoes take a pound of sugar and a pint of vinegar; make a syrup of this, and drop in the fruit; let them cook until perfectly clear; add mace, cinnamon, and white ginger. Cover well with the syrup, and tie up closely.

WALNUT PICKLE.

MRS. E. F. STODDARD.

Take white walnuts, fresh and tender; put them in salt and water for three days; then put in the sun until they turn black. Take half a pound of mustard-seed, two ounces of pepper, one-half ounce of cloves, one-half ounce of mace, one-half ounce of nutmeg, and a good stock of horse-radish, boiled in one gallon of vinegar. Cover the walnuts close, and let them remain three or four weeks. Pour off the liquid for catsup, if desired, and bottle it, covering the walnuts again with cold vinegar.

SMALL WHITE ONION PICKLES.

Take small white onions, and peel them; lay them in salt water for two days; change the water once; then drain them in a cloth, and put them in bottles. Boil mace, pepper, and vinegar together; let it cool, and pour over the pickles.

ONION PICKLES.

MRS. L. G. EVANS.

Put white onions on the stove in warm milk; when they commence to boil, take them out and rub the outside skin off with a coarse towel; then put them in jars, and sprinkle them lightly with salt; add a very little mace, about six sticks of cinnamon as long as your finger, a little horse-radish, and plenty of red pepper-pods. Cover them well with vinegar.

PICCALILLI.

MRS. J. F. EDGAR.

Take green tomatoes, chopped very fine; sprinkle well with salt; let stand twenty-four hours; drain off, and put in a stone jar. Take about half the quantity of cucumbers, and the same of cabbage; after they are chopped, put into jars separately, and cover with cold vinegar. Take about one-quarter as much white onions, chopped; salt, and pour boiling water on them; let stand a few hours; drain off, and cover with vinegar as above. Let all remain several days in a cool place; then press very dry and mix together; add some yellow and black mustard-seed, celery-seed, and a bountiful supply of grated horse-radish, with a few green peppers, chopped fine. Then take the best vinegar and about four pounds of brown sugar to each gallon. Boil it in part of the vinegar; skim well, and pour over the whole. Add as much cold vinegar as is required.

CHOW-CHOW.

Two dozen large cucumbers, sliced; three-quarters of a peck of green tomatoes, sliced; twelve large peppers (red and green), sliced; one-fourth peck of small white onions, peeled; one pint of small red peppers. Sprinkle one and one-half pints of salt over them, and let stand all night. In the morning drain them well; then add one ounce of mace, one ounce of white mustard-seed, one-half ounce of cloves, one ounce of celery-seed, one ounce of turmeric, three tablespoonfuls of ground mustard, one large piece of horse-radish, cut up; cover all with vinegar, and boil half an hour, or until tender.

PICCALILLI WITHOUT TOMATOES.

MRS. ROGER STEMBLE.

Two heads of cabbage; four dozen cucumbers; one dozen green peppers, one of white onions. Chop all but the onions; sprinkle with salt; let them stand one hour; drain well; then cover with cold vinegar, and let stand twenty-four hours. Chop the onions; pour hot water over them; squeeze it out, and mix all together. To one gallon of the mixture add one-half pound of sugar, one pint of mustard-seed, a little mace, and cloves. Boil the spices in the vinegar, and pour over hot.

OIL PICKLE CABBAGE.

MRS. W. B.

Trim and quarter six heads of good cabbage; boil in vinegar and water until a broom-splint can be passed through them. Prepare a paste of one-half pint of best sweet-oil, one pound of white mustard, one-half pound of black mustard, one quart of chopped horse-radish, one ounce of celery-seed, one ounce of turmeric, one teacupful of brown sugar. Put down one layer of cabbage; then cover with the above mixture, and alternate in this way, covering each layer with good vinegar.

SPICED NUTMEGS.

MRS. JOHN RENCH.

Take small nutmegs, not quite ripe; pare and quarter them; cover with vinegar, and let stand twenty-four hours. Then measure out one quart of the vinegar, and to each remaining quart add two pints of brown sugar; then add the quart of vinegar that has been measured out; put the vinegar and sugar on to boil a few minutes. Tie the spices—cloves, cinnamon, and mace—in a bag, and put in a jar with the nutmegs, and pour the vinegar over them. Boil this vinegar once a day for three successive days. The third time drop in the nutmegs, and let them boil fifteen minutes; then put them in stone jars, and in three weeks they will be ready for use.

WATERMELON PICKLES.

MRS. T. A. PHILLIPS.

Pare off the green of the watermelon rinds; cut in squares, and cover with weak alum-water, poured on hot; let it stand twenty-four hours; then soak in rain-water until well cleansed of the alum; put in a kettle; cover with pure water, and boil until tender; then press the water out with a napkin. Make a syrup of equal quantities of vinegar and sugar; add one stick of cinnamon, and race ginger. Put the fruit in and cook till clear; then take it out and cook the syrup a little more.

PICKLED PLUMS.

MRS. THEODOSIA DUBOIS.

Seven pounds of plums, three of sugar; one ounce of cinnamon, one of cloves, and one quart of vinegar. Put in a jar a layer of plums and a layer of spice; boil the sugar and vinegar, and pour it over the plums three days in succession, and the fourth day boil spices and all together. They will keep for years.

SWEET GRAPE PICKLE.

MRS. ADMIRAL SCHENCK.

Seven pounds of fruit; four pounds of sugar; one quart of vinegar. Spices should be tied in a thin cloth, and boiled in the syrup, which should be poured boiling hot, for three successive days, on the grapes. After that, they may be put away for use.

CHERRY PICKLES.

MRS. G. W. R.

Two pounds of cherries; one pound of sugar; one-half pint of vinegar; pour on boiling seven mornings in succession; the last time, if amber cherries, put them in and boil a few minutes; add cinnamon.

SWEET PICKLE CHERRIES.

MRS. DR. CRAIGHEAD.

To seven pounds of fruit take one quart of vinegar and three of sugar, one-half teacupful of broken cinnamon, and a few cloves. Seed one-half the cherries, and stew them rich.

SPICED APPLES.

Eight pounds of apples, pared; four pounds of sugar; one quart of vinegar; one ounce of stick cinnamon, and one-half ounce of cloves. Boil the sugar, vinegar, and spices together; put in the apples when boiling, and let them remain until tender. Take them out and put into a jar; boil down the syrup until thick, and pour it over.

SPICED CURRANTS.
MRS. J. L. BRENNER.

Three pounds of ripe currants; two pounds of sugar; one tablespoonful of cinnamon; nearly one-half tablespoonful of allspice; one-half tablespoonful of cloves, and nearly one-half pint of vinegar. Boil all one-half hour. Put into close glass jars.

SPICED PEACHES.
MRS. W. A. B.

Pare and halve one peck peaches, and place in a stone jar; boil three pints of vinegar and three pounds of sugar; skim, and pour over the fruit; repeat three times every other day; the third time add, while boiling, one-half ounce of cloves, one ounce of cinnamon, and one-quarter ounce of mace unground.

SWEET PICKLE PEACHES.
MISS B. PEASE.

One quart of vinegar, and four pounds of sugar; boil, and skim; peel seven pounds of fruit; put in and boil until a little soft; take them out; heat the syrup three times, and pour over hot; the last time boil it down. If not as sweet as desired, a little more sugar may be added.

SWEET PICKLE PEACHES.
MRS. WM. CRAIGHEAD.

To twelve pounds of peaches take six pounds of sugar and one pint of vinegar; add spice to taste.

SWEET CRAB-APPLE PICKLES.

Put half a bushel of crab-apples in a kettle with vinegar enough to cover them, and cook until tender; then take them out of the vinegar and put them in jars. Measure the vinegar, and add a pint more than will cover the fruit; and to each pint add one and one-half pints of brown sugar, one handful of stick cinnamon, three tablespoonfuls of cloves, and two of mace. Tie the spices in a bag, and boil in the vinegar half an hour; then put the fruit in the jars, and cover with the vinegar.

TO PICKLE PEARS WHOLE.

E. A. E.

Take three pounds of pears; peel them and cut out the ends, leaving the stems in; put them into a preserving-kettle, with one quart of water, and boil until a fork will go through them easily; then lay them out on a dish; add to the juice one and one-half pounds of sugar, one pint of vinegar, some stick cinnamon, whole cloves, and race ginger. Boil all five minutes, and skim; put in the pears and boil them until the syrup thickens; then take them out in a jar, and, after the syrup has boiled a little longer, pour it over them. If, after standing a few days, the syrup should become thin, take it off and boil it again.

TO PICKLE NASTURTIONS.

Take green nasturtions fresh from the vine; put them in salt and water for one day; then drain in a napkin. Put them in glass jars, and cover with strong vinegar; keep the bottles closely corked. Are equal to capers, with roast lamb.

CANNED FRUITS AND VEGETABLES.

CANNED PEACHES AND PEARS.

MRS. P. P. LOWE.

OF peaches, the white heath clings are preferred; of pears, the Flemish beauty. Take white clings tolerably ripe; pare, and keep them covered in a deep jar until ready to use; then to three pints of seeded peaches put one pint of water and four tablespoonfuls of pure white sugar; cook them a few minutes, or until a silver fork will enter them easily, but not enough for the fruit to break; then put in cans and seal immediately. This quantity usually fills a one-quart can. Pare only enough for four cans, and put them up before preparing more, unless two or three persons are at work; then let one person can steadily, using two kettles, and putting in each enough to fill two quart cans. First put in your kettle the water; add the sugar, and when that is dissolved put in the peaches. Can as soon as possible after peeling, to prevent their discoloring by exposure to the air.

CANNED PEACHES.

MRS. J. R. REYNOLDS.

Take nice ripe peaches; after paring, put them in a boiling syrup of sugar and water (four tablespoonfuls to one quart); cook ten minutes. Can and seal boiling hot.

BRANDY PEACHES.

MRS. J. R. YOUNG.

Take nice peaches, pared smoothly; scald them in an ordinary syrup until soft enough to run a straw in; place them in a jar; make a fresh, rich syrup. To one pint of syrup add one pint and a half of best whisky; pour this over your peaches and let stand over night; if the syrup looks thin, boil over and add more sugar.

TO PRESERVE PEACHES FOR PIES.

Take five pounds of sugar to fifteen pounds of peaches; boil half an hour; then add one and one-half pints of vinegar, and let boil fifteen minutes. Bottle and seal up.

TO PRESERVE STRAWBERRIES.

MISS ARMSTRONG.

To two pounds of fine large strawberries add two pounds of powdered sugar; put them in a preserving-kettle over a slow fire until the sugar is melted; then boil them precisely twenty minutes, as fast as possible. Have ready a number of small jars, and put the fruit in boiling hot; cork and seal the jars immediately; keep in a dry place. The jars must be heated before the hot fruit is put in, otherwise they will break.

PRESERVED QUINCES.

MRS. THEODOSIA DUBOIS.

Take fine apple quinces; cut them in half; pare and remove the cores; weigh them, and to each pound of quinces allow one of sugar. Then put them into a kettle; cover with cold water, and boil until they are tender enough to pass a broom-splint through. Take out one at a time, and put them on dishes to cool and drain. Put sugar in a kettle with water enough to dissolve it; then put the quinces into the syrup and let them cook until of a light color, skimming them all the time. Do not let them remain long, or they will turn dark. Lay them on dishes, and when cool put in jars. Skim the syrup and strain through a hair sieve and pour over the quinces.

BLACKBERRIES.

Allow one pint of currant-juice and one pint of water to six pounds of blackberries. Give them their weight in sugar; boil until the syrup is rich.

TO PRESERVE CRAB-APPLES.

Put the crab-apples in a kettle with grape-leaves in and around them, and a small bit of alum. Keep them scalding hot about one hour; then take them out; skin, and take out the seeds with a small knife, leaving on the stems; lay them in cold water. Make a syrup of one pound of sugar to one pound of apples; wipe, and put them in; stew gently until they look clear; take them out and boil the syrup longer.

TO PRESERVE ORANGES.

Boil the oranges in soft water until you can run a straw through the skin. Put three-quarters of a pound of sugar to each pound of fruit; take the oranges from the water and pour the hot syrup over them; let them stand over night; next day boil them in the syrup until it is thick; then take them out and strain it over them.

GREEN GAGE PLUMS.

Take an equal quantity of fruit and sugar; pour boiling water on the plums, and wipe them dry; prick them. Then make a syrup of the sugar and one-half pint of water; when it boils, put in half the plums; let them do slowly until they look clear; then take them out and put in the balance. If the syrup is thin, boil it longer.

CITRON MELON.

Pare the melons; take out the seeds, and cut in squares half an inch thick; lay in salt and water one hour; then wash off, and boil in strong ginger-tea. Make a weak syrup of sugar and water, and boil ten minutes; then make a syrup of one pound of sugar to one pound of citron; boil in this until it looks clear; season with lemon-peel.

GOOD APPLE SAUCE.

Peel, quarter, and core as many apples as you desire; put them in a vessel with just enough water to stew them. While they are cooking have a vessel on the fire with one-half pint of water, one tablespoonful of butter, one of sugar, and one-quarter of a nutmeg, grated. When this boils, stir in enough paste-thickening to make it of the consistency of cream; put your apples in a dish, and pour this over them.

RASPBERRY JAM.

MRS. S. CRAIGHEAD.

Take the best of red Antwerp raspberries; to every pound of fruit allow three-quarters of a pound of white sugar; mash them up well and mix with the sugar. Put them into a preserving-kettle (porcelain is best), and let them boil one-half hour, skimming them frequently; put into close glass jars; keep in a cool, dark place.

JAM.

MRS. THEODOSIA DUBOIS.

Seven pints of white currants, ten of red raspberries; twelve pints of sugar. Boil slowly one-half hour; then put in the sugar, and boil well three-quarters of an hour, stirring most of the time to prevent its burning.

PEACH JAM.

Take ripe freestone peaches; pare, and cut in small pieces; to every pound of peaches allow one-half pound of white sugar; put the sugar over the peaches, and let them stand two hours; then put them into a porcelain kettle on the fire, and boil slowly; stir all the time until the fruit is mashed smooth, and it almost jellies; put into glass jars.

CHERRY JAM.

To each pound of cherries allow three-quarters of a pound of white sugar; seed them; and as you do so, throw the sugar gradually into the pan with them; cover, and let them stand over night; next day boil them until they form a thick paste.

ORANGE MARMALADE.

Separate the pulp from the skin and seeds of the oranges; soak the skins over night in cold water (if the oranges are bitter, put a little salt in the water). Scrape the skins well, carefully removing all the white; then cut the yellow part into shreds as fine as possible, and add to the pulp. Add one pound of sugar to every pound of fruit. Boil twenty minutes.

PINE-APPLE JAM.

Peel pine-apples, carefully cutting out black specks with a pen-knife; grate on a coarse grater. Use one pound of sugar to one pound of pine-apple; boil until clear (about three-quarters of an hour). Put in small glass jars, and seal up.

TOMATO JAM.

Take one-half pound of sugar to one pound of tomatoes; put together in a stone jar, and let stand twenty-four hours; then take off the juice and strain it. Put it in a porcelain kettle; bring to a boil, and skim; then put in the tomatoes with a handful of stick cinnamon tied in a cloth; stir all the time. About ten minutes before removing from the fire, take out the cinnamon, and add one teacupful of good vinegar to one gallon of jam. Boil until the jelly will not separate.

FOR CANNING CORN.

MRS. J. R. YOUNG.

Get the best sweet corn; scald it on the ear, and cut it off while hot; put it in a pan over a kettle of boiling water, to keep it hot until you get enough cut to fill a can.   Have a kettle of weak brine boiling in a porcelain kettle.   Fill your can within an inch of the top with corn ; cover the corn with the brine, leaving room for it to swell, seal the can while boiling hot.

FOR CANNING CORN.

Dissolve one and one-fourth ounces of tartaric acid in one-half pint of water ; cut the corn from the cob ; put it in a vessel over the fire, and bring to the boiling-point ; to each pint of corn allow one tablespoonful of this solution.   Boil one-half hour, stirring occasionally ; then put the corn in quart cans, and seal tightly.   When wanted for use, pour the corn into a bowl, and stir in two-thirds of a teaspoonful of soda to each quart of corn.   Let it stand one hour before cooking.

TO CAN GREEN CORN.

Cut the corn off the cob ; pack very closely into quart cans ; then solder so that every particle of air is excluded.   Set the cans in a kettle of cold water and bring it to a boil ; let the corn boil two and a half hours in this sized cans (larger cans will re-quire more time).   When done, pour cold water into the kettle to cool the cans and enable you to remove them carefully.

DRINKS FOR FAMILY USE.

TO MAKE CHOCOLATE.

TAKE three tablespoonfuls of chocolate (scraped) and dissolve it in one teacupful of boiling water; add to it one pint more water, and when it comes to a boil, stir in as much milk as is desired. Boil five minutes.

TO MAKE COFFEE.

First have the coffee roasted an even, rich brown; do not grind it too fine; allow one tablespoonful of ground coffee for each cup of coffee; put it into the coffee-boiler; stir into it the white of one egg, and just enough cold water to mix it; then pour on boiling water. For six tablespoonfuls of coffee put in three pints of water; boil twenty minutes; set it aside, and pour in one teacupful of cold water to settle it; then transfer it to the urn.

Coffee for forty persons.—Three pints of ground coffee and two gallons of water.

TO MAKE TEA.

First scald the teapot; pour out that water, and put in two teaspoonfuls of green tea; add a cupful of water; let it stand ten minutes; fill up with boiling water.

GRAPE WINE.

To every quart of grape-juice take one pound of sugar and one quart of water. Put it in jugs, filling them, and keeping out enough to supply the jugs as it works over; when it is done fermenting, put the corks in loosely, and let stand six weeks; then bottle, and cork tight.

ELDERBERRY WINE.

To two quarts of berries put two quarts of water; boil half an hour; strain the liquor through a hair sieve; then to every quart put three-quarters of a pound of brown sugar, four ounces of ginger, and two of cloves. Boil the whole fifteen minutes. Pour it into a tub, and, when cool, put into a jug or keg, with a piece of toast dipped in yeast. Keep it in a warm place; in four or five days put in one pint of brandy. It will be ready to bottle about Christmas.

BLACKBERRY WINE.

Measure the berries and bruise them; to every gallon add one quart of boiling water; let them stand twenty-four hours, stirring occasionally; strain the juice through a flannel bag; to every gallon add two pounds of brown sugar; pour it into a cask, and let it stand till through fermenting; then bung up tight.

CURRANT WINE.

MRS. J. F. E.

Take one quart of juice, two of water, and three pounds of sugar; dissolve the sugar in the water; then mix all together, and fill the vessel to the brim, leaving the bung out until fermentation ceases; fill up every morning with fresh juice and water, so that the scum may throw itself off; when it has stopped fermenting, add two quarts of whisky to one barrel. Bung up tightly until February or March, when it may be racked off and bottled.

CURRANT SHRUB.

To a pint of strained currant-juice put a pound of sugar; boil gently together eight or ten minutes; then set it to cool; when lukewarm, add a wine-glass of brandy to every pint of syrup; bottle, and cork tight. Keep in a cool place.

RASPBERRY SHRUB.

MRS. GRAHAM.

One gallon of red berries, and one-half gallon cider-vinegar; let it stand over night; then strain; put in six pounds of white sugar; let it boil; skim, and let it stand until cool; then bottle it, and, when used, put in two-thirds ice-water.

RASPBERRY VINEGAR.

Put two quarts of raspberries in a stone jar; pour over them one quart of the very best vinegar; let it stand twenty-four hours; then strain, and pour the liquor over fresh fruit, and let it stand in the same way; allow one pound of sugar to a pint of juice; put it into a stone jar, and set it in a pot of boiling water for one hour; skim well; put into bottles, cork, and seal tight. Diluted with water, it is a very nice drink for the sick. Toasted bread may be eaten with it.

STRAWBERRY ACID.

Twelve pounds of fruit; two quarts of water; five ounces of tartaric acid. Put the acid in the water, and, after it is dissolved, pour it over the fruit; let it remain forty-eight hours; and then strain it. To one pint of clear juice add one and one-half pounds of white sugar; let it stand two or three days, stirring once or twice a day to dissolve the sugar, then bottle it. Place a cork loosely in each bottle until a slight fermentation takes place, then cork tight, and keep the bottles erect. The whole process to be cold, and no tin vessel must be used.

ELDERBERRY SYRUP.

Wash and strain the berries, which should be ripe; to a pint of juice add a pint of molasses; boil twenty minutes, stirring constantly. When cold, add to each quart four tablespoonfuls of brandy; bottle, and cork tight. Is good for a cough.

ORANGE SYRUP.

Select ripe and thin-skinned fruit ; squeeze the juice through a sieve, and to every pint add one pound of white sugar. Boil slowly ten minutes, and skim as long as any scum rises ; when cold, bottle. Two tablespoonfuls of this syrup, mixed with melted butter, makes a good sauce for puddings. Three table-spoonfuls of it in a glass of ice-water makes a nice drink.

LEMON SYRUP.

To every pint of strained juice add one and one-quarter pounds of sugar. Let it simmer until it becomes clear ; when cold, bottle, and cork tightly.

PINE-APPLE SYRUP.

Pare and cut the pine-apples in pieces, and to every three pounds add a quart of water ; cover them, and boil until very soft ; then mash and strain. To one pint of this juice add one pound of sugar ; boil to a rich syrup, put in bottles, and cork tightly.

BLACKBERRY CORDIAL.

MRS. G. W. ROGERS.

To a peck of berries take one pint of water ; boil and strain them ; to three quarts of juice add three pounds of crushed sugar ; boil and skim ; stir in one ounce each of cloves and cin-namon ; when cold, add one quart of best brandy, and two nut-megs, grated ; bottle, and seal up.

QUINCE CORDIAL.

Grate the quinces, and strain them through a flannel bag. To every three quarts of juice add one quart of brandy, two pounds of sugar, spice if you wish. Bottle tight ; keep in a cool place.

CHERRY CORDIAL.

Mash and strain the cherries, and to one gallon of juice put two pounds of sugar. Boil together, and add one-half pint of spirits to a gallon. When cold, bottle.

SUMMER DRINK.

One large lemon; one ounce of ginger-root; one and one-half pounds of sugar; one gill of yeast; one ounce of tartaric acid; two and one-half gallons of water. Slice the lemon; bruise the ginger, and mix all together except the yeast; pour the water boiling hot upon the mixture, and let stand until it is milk-warm; then add the yeast, and set in a warm place for twelve hours; then bottle; tie the corks down tightly. It will be ready for use in forty-eight hours.

CREAM NECTAR.

Three pounds of white sugar; two ounces of tartaric acid dissolved in one quart of soft water over night; stir in the whites of three eggs, well beaten; flavor to taste; bottle, and keep in a cool place. Allow three tablespoonfuls of the syrup to one glass of water; add soda enough to make it effervesce; put the soda in the water first.

EGG–NOG.

Twelve eggs; one and one-half pounds of sugar; three pints of cream, one of new milk; two tumblerfuls of Jamaica spirits, one of brandy. Beat together for one hour; then heat over hot water until milk-warm; then beat until cold.

EGG–NOG.

MRS. WILLIAM CRAIGHEAD.

Twelve eggs; one pound of granulated sugar. Beat the yolks of eggs and the sugar together until very light; set them over a pot of boiling water, beating constantly until they are warmed through. Add from four to six wine-glasses of brandy, five pints of milk, and the whites, beaten to a stiff froth, last.

BEER.

One pint of molasses; one pint of yeast; one tablespoonful of cream tartar; one ounce of ginger, and six quarts of cold water. Mix, and let stand twelve hours before bottling.

SPRUCE BEER.

Take four ounces of hops; boil half an hour in one gallon of water; strain it; add sixteen gallons of warm water, two gallons of molasses, eight ounces of essence of spruce dissolved in one quart of water. Put it in a clean cask; shake it well together; add one-half pint of yeast; let it stand and work one week; if warm weather, less time will do. When drawn off, add one tablespoonful of molasses to each bottle.

HARVEST BEER.

To make fifteen gallons of beer, put into a keg three pints of yeast, three pints of molasses, and two gallons of cold water. Let it stand a few minutes; then mix well together three quarts of molasses, three gallons of boiling water, with one ounce of ginger, and pour all into the keg; fill it up with cold water. A decoction of sassafras is an addition to the flavor of the beer.

FOOD FOR THE SICK.

In preparing articles of diet for the sick, be careful to use cooking-utensils that are perfectly sweet and clean.

Food should be prepared in small quantities, and served in the most inviting manner.

BEEF TEA.

Cut one pound of lean, fresh, juicy beef into thin slices; sprinkle with a little salt; put it into a wide-mouthed glass or stone jar; cover closely; set it in a kettle of water which must boil hard for one hour; take out the jar, and strain the essence of the beef into a bowl. Chicken tea may be made in the same manner.

MUTTON BROTH.

Boil a piece of mutton until it will fall from the bone; then strain the broth and let it get cold, so that the fat will rise, which must be taken off; then warm the liquid and put in a little salt. Swelled rice or barley may be added to it. Veal or chicken broth is made in the same way.

GRUEL FOR THE SICK.

Gruel can be made from oat-meal, arrow-root, wheat flour or corn-meal. In all cases these things should be first mixed smoothly with a little cold water, and afterwards more water added; boil, and season to taste. Two tablespoonfuls of any of them is enough to make one pint, when boiled. A few raisins boiled in gruel is an improvement.

EGG GRUEL.

Beat the yolk of one egg with one tablespoonful of white sugar; pour one teacupful of boiling water on it; add the white of the egg beaten to a froth, with any seasoning or spice you may desire. To be taken warm.

PANADA.

Toast a slice of bread very dry, until a nice brown color, but do not scorch it; break in small pieces into a bowl; put in sugar and a little grated nutmeg, and pour boiling water over it. If the patient has no fever, one-half glass of wine may be added.

BARLEY PANADA.

Boil a small teacupful of barley in water (with a few raisins) until it is soft. Put in sugar and a little grated nutmeg; break in bits of toast or dry rusk after it is taken from the fire.

EGG PANADA.

Boil one handful of good raisins in one pint of water; toast a piece of bread nicely, and cut it up into a bowl; beat one egg with a teaspoonful of sugar and put with the bread. When the raisins are soft, pour them, with the water in which they were boiled, over the toast and egg, stirring all the time; season to taste with wine, nutmeg, and butter, if the patient can bear it.

TOAST WATER.

Cut slices of bread very thin; toast it dry and brown, but do not let it burn; put it in a pitcher and pour boiling water on it. Toast water will allay thirst better than almost anything else.

APPLE WATER, ETC.

Roast two nice, tart apples; mash, and pour over them one pint of water, or slice raw apples and pour boiling water over them. Tamarinds, currant or grape jellies, cranberries, or dried fruits of any kind, mixed with water, make a good drink.

WINE WHEY.

Boil one pint of milk; when it rises to the top of the sauce-pan, pour in a large glassful of sherry or Madeira wine; let it boil up; if it separates, take it off the fire; let it stand a few minutes, but do not stir it. Strain it through Swiss muslin.

BUTTERMILK WHEY.

Put one quart of buttermilk in a sauce-pan over the fire; when it boils, put in the beaten yolk of one egg, and, if it can be allowed, a little cream or butter; beat the white of the egg very light and stir in; add sugar and spice to taste.

TAMARIND WHEY.

Mix one ounce of tamarind pulp with one pint of warm milk; strain it, and add a little sugar to the whey.

MULLED WINE.

Beat together one egg, one glass of wine, and one table-spoonful of sugar; add to it one-half pint of boiling water; stir all the time to prevent curdling; pour it into a tumbler, and grate a little nutmeg over it.

MULLED JELLY.

Take one tablespoonful of currant or grape jelly; beat with it the white of one egg and a little loaf-sugar; pour on it one-half pint of boiling water, and break in a slice of dry toast or two crackers.

EGG-NOG.

MRS. WILLIAM CRAIGHEAD.

Beat up one egg, one and one-half tablespoonfuls of sugar, three tablespoonfuls of cream, and one of liquor.

BLACK TEA.

Put one teaspoonful of tea in a vessel that will hold one pint; pour over it two small teacupfuls of boiling water; cover closely, and set by the fire to draw.

COFFEE.

Put two teaspoonfuls of ground coffee in a small tin cup. Pour boiling water on it; cover, and set over the fire five minutes; then let it settle, and pour off in a cup; add sugar and cream if desired.

CHOCOLATE.

To make a single cup of chocolate, grate one dessert-spoonful in a tin cup and pour on it a teacupful of boiling water; cover, and let stand over the fire five minutes; just before taking it off, stir in a teaspoonful of cream.

IRISH MOSS BLANC MANGE.

Pick over carefully one teacupful of Irish moss; wash it first in saleratus water; then rinse it several times in fresh; put it in a tin bucket, with one quart of milk; cover closely, and set in a pot of boiling water. Let it stand until the milk begins to thicken, then strain through a fine sieve, and sweeten with powdered sugar; flavor with lemon or vanilla; wet the mould in cold water; pour in the blanc mange, and set in a cool place. When quite firm, loosen the edges from the mould and turn out on a dish. To be eaten with sugar and cream.

RYE MUSH.

Take four tablespoonfuls of rye flour; mix smooth with a little water, and stir it into one pint of boiling water; boil twenty minutes, stirring frequently. To be eaten with cream or milk.

OYSTER TOAST.

R. L. E.

Make a thick slice of well-browned and buttered toast; lay it in a hot dish. Put six oysters, half a teacupful of their own liquor, and not quite one-half teacupful of milk, into a tin cup. Boil one minute. Season with butter, pepper, and salt, and pour over the toast.

BOILED CUSTARD.

Beat up one egg, with a heaped teaspoonful of sugar; put it into a teacupful of boiling milk; stir until it thickens. Pour it into a bowl over a slice of toasted bread. Spice to suit.

MEIG'S DIET FOR INFANTS.

A piece of sheet gelatine two inches square, soaked for a short time in cold water, then boil in one-half pint of water about ten minutes; add, with constant stirring, one teaspoonful of arrow-root, dissolved, and one-half pint of milk; add a little cream just before removing from the fire, and a moderate quantity of sugar.

DRIED FLOUR FOR INFANTS.

Take one teacupful of flour; tie it up tightly in a close muslin bag; put it in a pot with cold water; boil three hours; then take it out and dry the outside. When used, grate it; one tablespoonful is enough for one teacupful of milk (which would be better with one-third water); wet the flour with a little cold water; before stirring it into the milk add a very little salt. Boil five minutes.

BEEF TEA FOR INFANTS.

Take one and one-half pounds of the best steak; cut it into very small pieces, and put them into a glass jar with enough cold water to cover the meat; tie the top of the jar on, and put it into a sauce-pan full of cold water; place it on the fire, and boil three hours.

MISCELLANEOUS.

FOR DIPHTHERIA.

MAKE two small bags out of close drilling, long enough to reach from ear to ear; fill them with equal parts of wood-ashes and salt; wring one at a time very dry, out of hot water, and apply to the throat; cover it up with dry flannel; when it becomes cold, change for a warm one, and continue to do so until the skin is slightly irritated. For children, put flannel between the bag and the throat; or, the salt and ashes may be heated before putting them into the bags, and applied dry to the throat. Make a gargle of one teaspoonful of molasses, one of salt, and one-half teaspoonful of cayenne pepper; mix these with one teacupful of hot water; when cool, add one-quarter of a cup of cider-vinegar. Gargle every fifteen minutes.

COUGH SYRUP.

Take one ounce of thorough-wort, one of slippery elm, one of stick licorice, and one of flax-seed. Simmer together in one quart of water until the strength is extracted; then strain, and add one pint of molasses, and one-half of a pound of loaf-sugar; simmer well together. When cold, bottle tight. Dose.—One tablespoonful at a time, as often as the cough demands.

EXCELLENT COUGH MIXTURE.

Take a handful of hoarhound; boil it in a quart of water; add one pint of Orleans molasses, and one pound of brown sugar. Boil to a thin syrup. Put all in a bottle, and add one tablespoonful of tar. Shake while warm, until the tar is cut into small beads.　Dose.—Take one tablespoonful whenever the cough is troublesome.

FOR A COUGH.

Roast a lemon very carefully, without burning it.　When it is thoroughly hot, cut, and squeeze the juice into a cup over two tablespoonfuls of powdered sugar.　Dose.—A tablespoonful.

REMEDY FOR BURNS.

One pint of lard, warm ; one tablespoonful of brimsone (pulverized), one of tar, and one teaspoonful of verdigris.

SIMPLE REMEDY FOR RHEUMATISM.

Bathe the parts affected with water (in which potatoes have been boiled) as hot as can be borne.　This has been tested, and found to be very efficacious.

DYSPEPSIA REMEDY.

One cup of sugar ; one pint of bran.　Mix well together, and brown it in the oven same as coffee, stirring often.　Eat of it two or three times a day.

CURE FOR FEVER AND AGUE.

MRS. A. C. CLARK.

One ounce of Peruvian bark, one ounce of cream tartar, and sixty cloves, all pulverized, and put into one quart of whisky. Dose.—One-half a wineglassful three times a day.

AGUE BITTERS.

MRS. P. P. LOWE.

Ten cents' worth of prickly-ash berries ; five cents' worth of dogwood-bark, same of sarsaparilla, and the same of wild cherry. Put the above into a bottle large enough to hold them, with one quart of the best whisky. Let stand a day or two before using. Dose.—For an adult, a little more than one-half a wineglassful three times a day ; use it until there is only enough left for three doses for the ninth day, or whatever day precedes the one on which the chill is likely to return.

ANTIDOTES FOR POISON.

Swallow instantly a glass of warm water, with a heaping tea-spoonful of common salt, and one of ground mustard, stirred together. This will serve as an emetic; afterward, take the whites of two raw eggs. If you have taken corrosive sublimate, take one-half dozen of raw eggs, besides the emetic ; if laudanum, a cup of very strong coffee ; if arsenic, first the emetic, then one-half cup of sweet oil, or melted lard.

TO PREVENT LOCKJAW.

In case of any wound or scratch from which lockjaw may be apprehended, bathe the parts freely with lye or saleratus-water. A rind of salt pork bound upon a wound occasioned by a needle, pin, or nail, prevents lockjaw. It should always be applied until medical aid can be procured.

FOR FROSTED LIMBS

Two drachms of beeswax, two of Venice turpentine ; one and one-half drachms of chloroform ; one-half drachm of camphor, and one-half ounce of lard. Melt the beeswax, turpentine, and lard over a slow fire ; then add the camphor and chloroform. Bathe the frosted parts in warm water, and rub the ointment on by the fire.

TO STOP THE FLOW OF BLOOD.

Bind the cut with cobwebs and brown sugar, pressed on like lint, or with the fine dust of tea. When the blood ceases to flow, apply laudanum.

CURE FOR WASP-STING.

Make a poultice of saleratus-water and flour, and bind on the sting. For a bee-sting, apply sliced raw onion.

CURE FOR SPRAINS.

Beat up an egg to a thick paste with fine salt; spread it on a cloth, and bind on the part affected. Renew occasionally.

TO REMOVE TAR FROM THE HANDS OR CLOTHING.

Rub well with clean lard, and afterward wash with soap and warm water.

TO REMOVE DISCOLORATION BY BRUISING.

Apply a cloth, wrung out of very hot water, and renew frequently, until the pain ceases.

TO CLEANSE THE HAIR.

Beat up the yolk of an egg, with a pint of soft water; apply it warm; rub well, and afterward rinse with clean soft water.

CAMPHOR ICE.

MRS. WM. CRAIGHEAD.

One ounce of white wax, two of spermaceti, and one of gum camphor, well pulverized. Put all in a tin cup, and nearly cover with olive oil; put it on the stove and let simmer for fifteen minutes, but not boil.

COLOGNE.

MRS. J. R. YOUNG.

Three ounces of oil of bergamot, two of lemon, two of lavender; rose, one hundred and twenty-eight drops; alcohol, two gallons; twenty-eight drops neroli.

COLD CREAM.

One ounce of rose-water; one-half ounce of spermaceti; one drachm of white wax, and fourteen drachms of almond oil. Melt the last three in a china cup, in hot water; then add the rose-water gradually.

SALVE.

MRS. W. C.

Four ounces of mutton-tallow, two of beeswax, one of rosin, and one-half ounce of gum camphor. Simmer well together; take off the fire, and then add one gill of alcohol. Good for all kinds of sores and wounds.

BROWN SALVE.

Two pounds of mutton-tallow; put in as many Gympson (Jamestown-weed) and plantain-leaves as possible; fry until they crimp up, and then strain; to this add about two tablespoonfuls of tar; let it boil up; then pour it into the vessel in which it is to be kept, and let cool.

EXCELLENT LINIMENT.

One ounce of spirits turpentine, two of olive oil, one of spirits camphor, and two of spirits ammonia.

EXCELLENT LINIMENT FOR CUTS.

Take four ounces of balm of Gilead buds, and steep them two or three days in one quart of alcohol; then strain off the liquor, and add to it three ounces of turpentine, four of gum camphor, three of oil of origanum, and two of sweet oil. Is good for either man or beast.

CURE FOR A FELON.

Take rock salt, and heat it in the oven; then pound it fine, and mix it with turpentine, equal parts; put it on a cloth, and wrap around the part affected; as it dries out, make a fresh application, and so on until cured.

LYE POULTICE.

Tie a tablespoonful of wood-ashes in a rag, and boil it in one pint of water fifteen minutes; take out the ashes, and thicken with corn-meal. Stir in a teaspoonful of fresh lard; spread on a cloth, and apply warm.

CREAM POULTICE.

Put to boil one teacupful of cream; mix two tablespoonfuls of flour in milk, and stir into the boiling cream.

LILY ROOT POULTICE.

Pound the roots of the sweet white lily, and put them on to boil in rich milk; when soft, thicken with bread-crumbs. This is a most valuable poultice for a gathering.

HOP POULTICE.

Boil a handful of hops in a pint of water until very soft; then thicken with corn-meal. It is good for a sore throat or swelled face.

POTATO POULTICE

Is said to be better than one made of bread. It is more efficacious; keeps heat longer, and can be reheated if necessary. The potatoes are pared, boiled, and mashed fine; put into a thin muslin cloth, and applied quite moist, and as warm as the patient can bear it.

FOR KEEPING CIDER.

MRS. L. A. TENNY.

Two quarts of milk; one pound of best mustard (in box); one full barrel of cider, and four extra gallons. As it ferments, fill it up until it becomes quiet; then rack it off; put in a clean barrel, and place it in the cellar.

TO PRESERVE MILK.

Put a small piece of horse-radish into a pan of milk, and it will keep it sweet.

FOR PRESERVING BUTTER.

Take two parts of the best table salt, one part of sugar, and one part of saltpetre; blend the whole completely. Take one ounce of the composition for one pound of butter; work it well into a mass; then pack it solid into a stone jar.

TO KEEP BUTTER.

MRS. A. C. COBURN.

Make a brine of rock-salt that will bear up an egg; boil and skim it well; pour into a clean vessel to cool. Then pour off into a stone or wooden vessel that has not been used for anything else; tie up rolls of butter in cloths and drop in the brine. Be careful to keep the vessel covered, and the butter under the brine.

FOR KEEPING PICKLES IN BRINE.

MRS. G. ARNOLD.

Wash them clean. Put into the bottom of a cask one-half inch of dry salt; then a layer of pickles; then a layer of salt (no water). Put a board on, and a light weight to keep them down; they will draw their own brine.

When wanted for use, put the pickles into a porcelain kettle; not more than half full; fill up with cold water; cover, and set it on the top of the stove; stir the pickles frequently; when almost boiling, pour off the water and fill up as before. Repeat this process several times, or until the salt is extracted; put a small lump of alum in the last water with part vinegar; throw that away, and boil vinegar with any spice you desire, and when cold, put in the pickles. They will be ready for use in a few days.

CURING HAMS.

MR. PRUGH.

As soon as the hams are cut and ready, rub them thoroughly, with a mixture of salt and saltpetre, dry, in the proportion of three tablespoonfuls of salt and one tablespoonful of saltpetre (pulverized) to four hams. Let them lie for twenty-four hours; then put them down into a tub and cover them well with brine strong enough to bear an egg. Leave the hams in this liquor for five weeks; then take them out and wash off with warm water. Have ready plenty of ground black pepper, and rub the whole ham well with it, especially on the cut sides; rub it very thick, and in any little cracks and about the bone. Then hang up and smoke with green sugar-tree wood.

TO SUGAR-CURE HAMS.

For one hundred pounds of meat take five pounds of sugar, two ounces of pulverized saltpetre, and seven pints of salt. Rub the hams first with the saltpetre and then with the sugar; then pack them in a meat-tub and let them remain one week; rub salt into them and pack them again in the same tub. They will be ready for the smoke-house in from four to six weeks, depending upon the size of the hams. The position of the hams ought to be changed several times, so that all will be equally salted.

TO CURE TONGUES.

Wet each tongue with molasses; rub on it a teaspoonful of pulverized saltpetre, and as much salt as will stick to it, besides putting a little loosely in the cask. Let them lie three weeks in the brine, turning frequently, then rinse off and hang up to dry.

TO PRESERVE EGGS.

One heaping pint of salt, one scant pint of lime, and six quarts of water. Let the pickle stand a few days, stirring it occasionally; drop the eggs in carefully without cracking them. They must be fresh.

FOR KEEPING EGGS.

One and one-half pints of lime, and five cents' worth of beef suet. Slack the lime; then add one and one-half gallons of water. Render out the suet and put with it; let all come to a boil. Have a wire ladle ; dip a few eggs at a time in the boiling solution for a minute; then lay them on something to dry; then pack away in a box, in either saw-dust or bran.

TO PRESERVE SAUSAGE.

Heat ground sausage-meat slowly in a tin pan or kettle, while mixing in the salt, sage, and pepper; not permitting it to cook or burn. When thoroughly mixed and while hot, put in a tight jar and pour melted lard over the top one-half inch thick. Keep it in a cool place. For use during the summer.

WASHING-FLUID.
MRS. W. R. S. A.

Take two pounds of potash ; put it in an earthen vessel and add two gallons of boiling rain-water, one ounce of sal ammoniac, and one ounce of salts of tartar. Put them in an earthen vessel; add one quart of boiling rain-water, and let stand twenty-four hours. Then strain all through a flannel bag; put together in a stone jug, and cork tight. Have the water in the boiler near boiling; then put in one teacupful of the fluid and use less soap. After the clothes have been well washed through one water, put them in and boil for half an hour. Then rub the clothes out of the boil, and rinse; for each boiler of clothes after the first, use only half the quantity of the fluid.

CLEANSING-FLUID.

Two drachms of chloroform; one-half ounce of sal soda; one-half ounce of alcohol; two ounces of white castile soap; two and one-half ounces of aqua ammonia; cut the soap fine, and dissolve it in one gallon of soft water; strain it, and then add the other ingredients. This fluid will remove grease and spots from any fabric.

CLEANSING-CREAM.

Three ounces of castile soap, and one of borax ; dissolve together, in one quart of rain-water, over the fire. When dissolved, add four quarts more of cold water; then add the spirits,—four ounces of alcohol, three of ammonia, two of ether,—and one ounce of glycerin. This is nice to take out grease, paint, etc., from all materials.

HARD SOAP.

Pour four gallons of boiling water on six pounds of sal soda and three pounds of unslaked lime. Stir, and let stand over night; pour off carefully, and add six pounds of perfectly clean grease; boil two hours, stirring most of the time. If it does not seem thick enough, put another pailful of water on the settlings; stir well, and when settled, drain off carefully, and add to the mixture as is required; try it by taking a little out to cool. When ready to take off the fire, stir in one handful of salt; rinse out a tub with cold water; put the soap into it, and let stand until solid; then cut into strips and lay on a board to dry.

SODA-ASH SOAP.

MRS. W. R. S. AYRES.

To five pounds of soda-ash take four pounds of unslaked lime, eight gallons of rain-water, and fifteen pounds of grease. Put lime, soda, and water into a kettle, and boil twenty minutes; then pour out into a tub, and let it stand all night; in the morning, dip the clear water off carefully; put into a kettle; add the grease (cleaned), and boil one hour; then dip it out into tubs to cool. Be careful not to get any of the lime from the bottom of the kettle.

SOFT SOAP.

MRS. ELIZA PIERCE.

Fifteen pounds of clean grease; fifteen pounds of crude potash. Put the potash in a bucket of boiling water to dissolve; put the grease into a barrel and pour the potash-water over it; every day add a bucket of hot water until the barrel is full. Stir well each time.

A HINT TO THE LAUNDRESS.

Take some beeswax and tie it in a piece of white cotton cloth. When ironing starched linen, rub the wax over the iron once or twice; then over the cleansing cloth to make sure there is nothing on the iron to soil the clothes; this will prevent the starch from rolling, and imparts a gloss to the linen.

A little salt sprinkled in starch while boiling, and a sperm candle stirred around in it a few times, will keep it from sticking.

A large spoonful of alum stirred into a hogshead of muddy water will so purify it that in a few hours the dirt will sink to the bottom.

TO WASH BLANKETS.

Put two large tablespoonfuls of borax and one pint-bowl of soft soap into a tub of cold water; when dissolved, put in a pair of blankets, and let them remain over night. Next day rub and drain them out; rinse thoroughly in two waters, and hang them out to dry. Do not wring them.

TO WASH BROWN HOLLAND CHAIR-COVERS.

After being washed in the usual manner, they must be rinsed at the last in water in which some hay has been boiled. This will restore the color that has been washed out. It is also good for crumb-cloths and covering for stair-carpets.

Straw matting should always be washed in salt and water, and wiped dry with a coarse towel. It will prevent its turning yellow.

TO CLEAN LIGHT KID GLOVES.

Take a flannel rag; rub on soap and dip in milk, wetting lightly; rub the glove while on your hand.

FOR WASHING SILK.

MISS MAGGIE CONNELLY.

Mix together one tablespoonful of molasses, two tablespoonfuls of soft soap, and three of alcohol; add to this one pint of hot rain-water; lay your silk on a bare table, and rub on the mixture with a small clothes-brush. Have ready a tub of lukewarm rain-water; dissolve five cents' worth of white glue and put in the tub of water. As you clean each piece of silk, throw it in the water and let it lie until you have finished; then dip each piece up and down in the water, but do not wring it. Hang it up to dry by the edges, and iron it before it is quite dry.

FOR CLEANING SILK.

Pare and slice three potatoes (very thin); pour on one-half pint of water, and add an equal quantity of alcohol. Sponge the silk on the right side, and, when half dry, iron on the wrong side.

FOR RENOVATING SILK.

MRS. MCVEY.

Take an old kid glove; dark-colored, if the silk is dark; light, if the silk is light. Tear it in pieces; put it in a tin cup, and cover with water. Set it on the stove, and let it simmer until the kid can be pulled into shreds. Take a cloth or sponge; dip it in this water; rub it over the silk, and iron immediately. This process will cleanse and stiffen old silk, and give it the appearance of new.

TO CLEAN BLACK DRESSES.

Two tablespoonfuls of ammonia to one-half gallon of water. Take a piece of black cloth and sponge off with the preparation, and afterwards with clean water.

FOR CLEANING ALPACA.

MISS SIDNEY SIMS.

Put the goods into a boiler half full of cold rain-water; let it boil for three minutes. Have ready a pail of indigo-water (very dark with indigo), and wring the goods out of the boiling water, and place in the indigo-water. Let remain for one-half hour; then wring out and iron while damp.

TO REMOVE INK-STAINS.

While an ink-spot is fresh, take warm milk and saturate the stain; let stand a few hours; then apply more fresh milk; rub the spot well and it will soon disappear. If the ink has become dry, use salt and vinegar, or salts of lemon.

TO REMOVE FRUIT-STAINS FROM TABLE LINENS.

Spread the stained parts over a large bowl, and pour on boiling water. Repeat several times before putting into soap-suds.

TO CLEAN STRAW HATS.

Make a paste of pounded sulphur and cold water; wet the hat, and cover it with the paste until the straw cannot be seen; rub hard, and hang the hat where it will dry; then rub the sulphur off with a brush, until the straw looks white.

TO CLEAN BOTTLES.

Put them into a kettle of cold water, with some wood-ashes, and boil; then rinse in clean soft water.

TO KILL MOTHS IN CARPETS.

Wring a coarse cloth out of clean water; spread it smoothly on the part of the carpet where moths are suspected to be, and iron it with a hot iron. The steam will destroy the moth and eggs.

TO PRESERVE FURS FROM MOTHS.

Moths deposit their eggs in the early spring, and that is the time to attend to furs. Beat them with a light rattan, and air for several hours; then comb with a clean comb carefully; wrap them up in newspapers perfectly tight, and put in a close linen bag, or cedar chest. Examine them several times during the summer, and each time repeat the combing.

TO DESTROY COCKROACHES.

Pulverized borax, scattered about where they are, will banish them effectually.

TO DESTROY BEDBUGS.

Mix together one ounce of corrosive sublimate, one of gum camphor, one pint of spirits turpentine, and one of alcohol. Put in a bottle; apply with a feather. Rank poison,—be very careful.

TO CLEAN PAINT.

Smear a piece of flannel in common whiting, mixed in warm water to the consistency of common paste. Rub the surface to be cleaned quite briskly, and wash off with warm soft water. Grease-spots will in this way be easily removed, and the paint retain its brilliancy unimpaired.

Wood-ashes and common salt, wet with water, will stop the cracks of a stove and prevent the smoke from escaping.

TO PREVENT METALS FROM RUSTING.

Melt together three parts of lard and one of rosin, and apply a very thin coating with a brush. It will preserve stoves and grates from rusting through the summer.

TO CLEAN STEEL OR IRON.

One ounce of soft soap and two ounces of emery made into a paste. Rub the articles for cleaning with wash-leather. It will give a good polish.

TO REMOVE RUST FROM STEEL.

Rub well with sweet oil; let it remain two days; then rub with pulverized lime.

TO TAKE OUT IRON-RUST.

To one gallon of buttermilk add a large handful of grated horse-radish; let the goods remain in the milk from twelve to twenty-four hours, rubbing occasionally; then wash out in clean water.

Another way is to rub the spots of rust with oxalic acid mixed in a little water, and expose to a hot sun.

RUBBER CEMENT.

Shreds of india-rubber, or gutta-percha, dissolved in refined turpentine, will make a good cement for rubber-shoes, shoe-soles, etc.

Plaster of Paris, stirred into the white of an egg tolerably thick, makes a strong cement for glass and china.

TIN POLISH.

Six cups of water; five tablespoonfuls of nitric acid; one tablespoonful of emery, and two of pumice-stone.

SILVER POLISH.

Four ounces of Paris white, with one pint of hot water; put it over the fire, and let come to a boil; when cool, add one ounce of ammonia.

FOR VARNISHING GILDED FRAMES.

Take pure white alcoholic varnish, such as is used for transferring engravings. Apply with a soft brush. The frames can afterwards be cleansed with a damp cloth without injury.

VARNISH FOR GRATES.

Take one tablespoonful of sugar, and one-half teacupful of vinegar. Mix, and apply with a cloth.

FOR SWEETENING KITCHEN SINKS.

One-half pound of copperas, and one quart of pulverized charcoal, dissolved in two gallons of water. Heat the mixture to nearly a boiling point, and pour a quart of it or more at one time down the sink-pipe. This mixture will remove strong, disagreeable odors from either glass or earthen vessels, by simply rinsing them thoroughly with it.

TO MAKE COLORS PERMANENT.

Three gills of salt, in four quarts of boiling water. Put the calicoes in while hot, and let them remain until cold.

Alum, or vinegar, is good to set colors of red and green.

TO COLOR BLACK.

To every pound of goods take one ounce of extract of logwood, one ounce of blue vitriol. Put the blue vitriol in sufficient water to cover the goods without corroding, or it will spot; let it boil; have the goods clean and free from grease; wet thoroughly before you put them in; let them simmer twenty minutes; then take them out and hang up to air. Dissolve the extract of logwood and put it in the kettle with the vitriol; put back the goods and let them simmer as before, twenty minutes. Take out the goods; let them dry, and soak in sweet milk over night; wash thoroughly next day in soap-suds.

LYE COLOR.

To eight pounds of yarn take one pound of copperas and as much water as will cover the yarn; bring the water to a boil; put the copperas in, and let it be well dissolved; then pour it out in a tub; put the yarn in, and let it remain one-half hour; take weak lye, as much as will cover the yarn, and bring it to a boil; take the yarn out of the copperas-water, and let it air one-half hour; then put into the lye one-half hour; repeat the process, until the color is sufficient. Wash well in hard water; then in hard soap-suds soak one-half hour; afterward wash in hard water.

CAPITAL CITY

COOK BOOK

REVISED 1906.

STATE JOURNAL PRINTING COMPANY.

DAVID ATWOOD,
PRINTER AND STEREOTYPER,
MADISON, WIS.

CAPITAL CITY

COOK BOOK.

We may live without poetry, music and art;
We may live without conscience, and live without heart;
We may live without friends; we may live without books;
But civilized man cannot live without cooks.

THIRD EDITION.

MADISON, WIS.:
PUBLISHED BY GRACE CHURCH GUILD.
1906.

FOREWORD.

Just twenty-three years ago the Woman's Guild of Grace Church published its Cook Book. It contained the favorite recipes of many of the good housekeepers of Madison and met with immediate and lasting success. For a long time the book has been out of print and impossible to obtain. Owing to the frequent demand for it the Guild has decided to publish it again. It is here presented containing all of the old recipes and a great many new ones; nearly one-third of the recipes being added at this time. That it may meet with the success which greeted the first edition is all that can be wished.

The Guild wishes to take this opportunity of thanking the advertisers whose generous patronage has made the bringing out of the book possible. It asks that a careful reading and regard be given to the advertisements which are contained in the book. Our merchants are always generous and the Guild is appreciative of their good works.

WOMAN'S GUILD OF GRACE CHURCH.
Madison, *Wisconsin*, May, 1906.

INDEX TO ADVERTISERS.

INDEX.

CAPITAL CITY COOK BOOK.

SOUPS.

SOUP STOCK.

Use a porcelain-lined kettle. Four pounds of lean meat, five quarts of water; add to this, if you wish it very rich, a knuckle of beef or veal; add bones of fowls whose marrow is very rich; a bunch of sweet herbs in a muslin bag, three onions, three carrots, a few blades of celery, one-half of a good sized turnip; let this come to a boil slowly and skim, then shove back on stove where it will simmer (not boil) slowly for two hours, then throw in salt; let cook six or eight hours.— *Miss Mary L. Atwood.*

AMBER SOUP.

A large soup bone (two pounds), a chicken, a small slice of ham, an onion, two sprigs of parsley, half a small carrot, half a parsnip, half a stick of celery, three cloves, pepper, salt, a gallon of cold water, whites and shells of two eggs and caromel for coloring. Boil the beef, chicken and ham for five hours, add vegetables, and cloves to cook the last hour (having first fried the onion in hot fat, and in it stick the cloves). Strain into an earthen bowl and add the beaten whites of the eggs and their shells. Boil quickly half a minute, then skim off all scum and whites from the top, not stirring the soup. Pass through a jelly bag. It should be perfectly clear. Add a table-spoonful of caromel to give a richer color and flavor. Use the cleanest of kettles.— *Mrs. C. Hawley.*

BUILLON.

Take about six pounds of beef and bone (soup bones) for ten persons. Cut up the meat and break the bones, add two quarts of cold water, and simmer slowly until all the strength is extracted. It will take about five hours. Strain it through a fine sieve, removing every particle of fat; and if there is more than ten cupfuls, reduce it by boiling to that quantity. Season with pepper and salt.— *Miss Emma Hawley.*

BLACK BEAN SOUP.

One quart of black beans soaked over night and drained, cover these with fresh water and put on the fire to boil a few moments and drain again. Add the beans to two quarts of beef stock, two quarts of cold water, one onion chopped fine, and one-half pound of salt pork which has been put in cold water and boiled ten minutes. Boil the soup slowly four hours, season with pepper, strain into the tureen, and serve with thin slices of lemon.— *Mrs. Breese J. Stevens.*

TOMATO SOUP.

Make one gallon of beef stock; take one quart ripe tomatoes, two carrots, two onions, one turnip cut fine; boil all together one hour and a half, then strain all through a sieve. Put in a saucepan a quarter of a pound of butter, which must be heated until of a light brown color; then add two table-spoonfuls of flour, one table-spoonful of sugar; add this to the soup; season with salt and pepper; stir well, until it boils; then skim, and strain into the tureen.— *Mrs. Breese J. Stevens.*

Soup a l'Italienne.

Take the fat from the top of soup stock, strain and heat to scalding; heat in another vessel a pint of milk, pour it upon three beaten eggs; return to the same pan, with a little salt and a pinch of soda, and cook two minutes, stirring all the while. Have ready four table-spoonfuls of grated cheese in the bottom of a tureen; pour in first the milk and eggs, then the soup; stir all well and serve.— *Mrs. G. W. Oakley.*

Tomato Soup.

To one pint of tomatoes, or four large raw tomatoes cut up, add one pint boiling water, and let them boil; then add one tea-spoonful soda; when it will foam, immediately add one pint sweet milk, salt, pepper and plenty of butter, and when it boils add a few cracker crumbs.— *Miss Bertha Schaal.*

Tomato Soup.

One soup bone, three quarts of water; put in three whole cloves, three pepper-corns, and one small red pepper. Boil two and one-half hours, then add half a can of tomatoes and one onion chopped fine; season with salt to taste, and boil from half to three quarters of an hour longer; thicken it with one table-spoonful of flour, and strain through a colander. One half cup

tomato catsup can be used in place of the plain tomatoes, and is an improvement.— *Mrs. C. Hawley.*

VERMICELLI SOUP.

The day before it is required, make four quarts good
stock, and boil in it one carrot, one turnip, four onions,
one or two parsley roots. three blades mace, salt and
white pepper; strain it, and before using take off all
the fat. Boil in some of the liquor, crumbs of three
French rolls, till soft enough to mash smooth; boil
the soup, and stir in the mashed crumbs; boil it
fifteen minutes, and before using add yolks of two eggs
beaten with three table-spoonfuls of cream; boil in a
little water two or three ounces vermicelli, for twenty
minutes; strain and put in tureen, and pour the soup
upon it.— *Mrs. R. W. Hurd.*

VEAL SOUP.

A knuckle of veal, three quarts of cold water, one
table-spoonful of rice; boil slowly for four hours. Put
the yolk of one egg well beaten in the tureen and stir
well into it a tea-cupful of sweet cream or new milk.
Add a piece of butter size of a walnut. On this pour the
soup, boiling hot, stirring all the time.— *Mrs. Charles
S. Mears.*

WHITE SOUP.

To six pounds of veal — from fore shoulder — put a
gallon of water and simmer four or five hours. Clarify
with egg shells, flavor with celery or celery salt, salt
and pepper; strain. When cold remove all fat hardened
on top. Heat the stock for use and thicken with mashed
potato, beaten very smooth, with a pint of cream. Strain
again.— *Mrs. A. J. Ward.*

ALMOND PUREE.

Eight pounds chicken, three pounds veal to make stock; one pint cream; one table-spoon corn starch to thicken; one tea-spoon almond extract; salt and white pepper to taste; four blanched almonds chopped fine to each cup; last add dessert-spoon of whipped cream to each cup. Serve hot. This will serve twenty-four people. — *Mrs. M. G. Ford.*

ASPARAGUS SOUP.

Cook for one hour the tough part of asparagus in the water in which it was boiled; press through colander, and to each pint add a table-spoon of butter, a pint of milk, two table-spoons of flour rubbed into butter, a level tea-spoon of salt, a dash of pepper and a little onion. — *Mrs. A. B. Morris.*

CORN SOUP.

One pint milk, one-half can corn, put through sieve into milk; four large table-spoons butter, one and one-half table-spoons flour mixed with butter. Cook about one-half hour, and just before taking from fire stir in a cup of whipped cream.— *Mrs. David Atwood.*

MUSHROOM SOUP.

Dissolve one tea-spoon of beef extract in one quart of hot water, add two table-spoons of flour dissolved in two table-spoons of melted butter; add a can of mushrooms sliced and let it boil or simmer; heat one quart of cream in double boiler, which add to the mixture just before serving.— *Mrs. E. P. Vilas, Milwaukee.*

Normandy Veal Soup

Knuckle of veal with a good deal of meat on it, six quarts water, one table-spoon of salt, eight small white onions, one table-spoon whole mace. Boil down to one-half the quantity, strain and cook; skim off *all* grease. Heat one pint cream; add to hot soup. Chop fine three hard boiled eggs and add to soup.— *Miss Kate A. Chittenden.*

Puree of Peas.

One can marrowfat peas, one and one-half tea-spoon sugar, one pint water or white stock, one pint milk, one sliced onion, two table-spoons butter, two table-spoons flour, one tea-spoon salt, *even*, one-eighth tea-spoon white pepper. Drain peas from liquor, rinse them in cold water, add sugar, water or stock and simmer twenty minutes; rub through a puree sieve, return to range, bring to boiling point, thicken with flour and butter cooked together; scald milk with onion in double boiler; add milk to first mixture; season with salt and pepper. — *Mrs. A. B. Morris.*

FISH.

ESCALOPED FISH.

Three pounds of fresh fish, white fish the best, but *any* can be used. Boil or steam until done; when cold remove all bones, skin and rub up fine with the fingers. Then make a dressing as follows:

" FISH DRESSING."—To one pint of milk, add one half of a small chopped onion, one large cup butter rubbed into two heaping table-spoonfuls of flour; stir this into the boiling milk, then add a pinch of parsley and summer savory, together with plenty of salt and pepper; make it quite salt. Grease an oyster dish, pour in a layer of fish, then a layer of dressing, and so on until the dish is filled; allowing the dressing for the top layer, over which grate a little cheese, and bake about twenty minutes.— *Mrs. F. W. Oakley.*

TURBOT.

Boil a white fish, take out the bones, and cut in small pieces. Make a dressing of one quart of milk, one small onion, parsley and thyme, two ounces of flour; stir until it thickens, then add one-fourth pound of butter; strain it through a gravy strain on the beaten yolks of two eggs; season with salt and pepper. Alternate layers of fish and dressing; lastly a layer of rolled crackers and grated cheese, and bits of butter; bake until lightly browned. Two medium sized white fish are sufficient for this quantity of dressing. The cheese can be used or not, as one chooses; only a little, if used; is nice without it.— *R. L. Garlick.*

FISH CHOWDER.

Six pounds of fresh fish cut in rather small pieces, six potatoes pared and sliced, three onions sliced very thin, half a pound of salt pork cut in small squares, half a pound of butter, one quart of milk, two pounds of butter crackers, pepper and salt. Put the pork in a kettle and fry until brown, taking care not to scorch; then a layer of fish, potato, and onion, seasoned with pepper, salt and butter, then a layer of crackers; repeat this order until your materials are exhausted; let the top layer be crackers; pour over all boiling water enough to just cover, cover kettle tight and stew gently for half an hour (should sink too low, replenish with boiling water); lastly add the milk, and simmer five minutes more.— *Mrs. John M. Sumner.*

BROILED WHITE FISH.

Wash the fish thoroughly in salt and water. Spread it out flat on a wire broiler. Sprinkle with salt, and set in the oven. Bake twenty minutes and then brown over hot coals. Pour melted butter over and serve. A medium-sized fish is preferable.— *Mrs. Charles E. Bross.*

DROPPED FISH BALLS.

One pint-bowl-full of cod-fish, picked up fine, two heaping bowlfuls of pared potatoes, two eggs, butter the size of an egg, and a little pepper. Put potatoes into boiler with the fish on top of them, cover with boiling water and boil half an hour, drain off water and mash fish and potato together, then add butter, pepper, and eggs well beaten. Have a kettle of boiling fat, dip a table-spoon in it, then take up a spoonful of the mixture, drop into boiling fat, and cook until brown. The spoon should be dipped into the fat every time.— *Mrs. G. W. Oakley.*

Cod-Fish Balls.

Take cod-fish that has been boiled before. Carefully remove the bones, and mince the flesh. Mix with it a quantity of warm mashed potatoes (mashed with butter and milk) in the proportion of one-third cod-fish, and two-thirds mashed potatoes. Add sufficient beaten egg to make the whole into a smooth paste. Season it with cayenne; and if the mixture seems dry, moisten and enrich it with a little butter. Make it into cakes about an inch thick. Sprinkle them well with flour. Fry them in lard. Drain them and send them to the table.— *Mrs. C. Hawley.*

Clam or Oyster Cocktails.

Allow one-half dozen small oysters or clams for each guest. For six glasses use one tea-spoon grated horse-radish, one-half tea-spoon catsup, one-eighth tea-spoon salt, a dash of cayenne, two table-spoons lemon juice and five drops tabasco sauce. Pour over the clams or oysters in small glasses about ten minutes before serving.— *Miss M. L. Atwood.*

Codfish Balls.

One cup codfish (light kind, picked and shredded), one pint potatoes, one salt-spoon butter, one egg well

2

beaten, one-quarter salt-spoon pepper. Cook potatoes until half done; drain and mash potatoes and codfish together, keeping as dry as possible. If the balls don't stick together well add a little flour. Fry in deep fat one at a time; cook about one minute; drain on brown paper and serve hot.— *Mrs. Florence Bashford Spensley.*

FISH CHOWDER.

Two slices of fat salt pork, diced and fried crisp; six large potatoes (raw) sliced; two or three pounds fish, boned and cut in small pieces; half minced onion. To the fried pork add layers of potatoes and fish, cover with boiling water and cook slowly for one hour or longer. Add one can of tomatoes and cook half an hour longer. Season with pepper, salt and a few drops of tabasco. Add three table-spoons of rolled cracker crumbs.— *Mrs. Charles F. Lamb.*

FISH FOR RAMAKINS

One can shrimp, one can mushrooms, one cup cream, one-half cup milk; put three-fourths table-spoon butter and one table-spoon flour in pan to cook, add cream and milk and salt and white pepper to taste; add fish and mushrooms, and cook thoroughly; put in ramakins, grate old cheese on top of each dish, a tea-spoon sherry, and grate hard boiled egg just before serving, with a dash of paprika and a sprig of parsley.— *Mrs. A. B. Morris.*

LOBSTER A LA NEWBURG.

Split and remove the meat of a whole live lobster; cut into pieces one-half inch long; braise with fresh butter; add one glass Madeira or Sherry, and when thoroughly heated, add the yolk of one raw egg and a cup of cream; season with salt and pepper; serve *hot* on dry toast.— *Mrs. Frank Van Pierce.*

TURBOT.

Take a white fish (or pickerel), boil or steam until tender; remove skin and bones; season with salt and pepper. For dressing, heat one pint milk and thicken with one-quarter pound of flour; when cool, add one or two eggs and a large piece of butter, season with a very little onion and parsley; put in buttered baking dish a layer of fish, then a layer of sauce until full, cover top with cracker crumbs and bake one-half hour.—*Mrs. Charles F. Lamb.*

OYSTERS

OYSTER SOUP.

For one can of oysters carefully picked over, use the liquor of the oysters strained through a sieve into a porcelain kettle, one quart of boiling water, a pint of new milk; skim this before putting in a piece of sweet butter as large as an egg, salt and pepper to taste; let this come to a boil, and drop the oysters in and take out immediately, putting them into a hot tureen, and after the soup has boiled again, pour it over the oysters, and serve.— *Mrs. David Atwood.*

FRIED OYSTERS.

Carefully pick over select oysters and drain in a colander. Season with pepper and salt to taste, then dip singly into crackers rolled very fine, and fry in equal quantities of butter and lard made very hot before putting in oysters.— *Mrs. David Atwood.*

ESCALOPED OYSTERS.

Butter the dish (common earthen pie-plates are the best), put in a layer of oysters, seasoned well with butter, salt and pepper; alternate with bread crumbs and oysters until you have three layers, finish with crumbs; add a tea-cup of cream or milk; bake half an hour.— *Mrs. A. C. Mills.*

ESCALOPED OYSTERS.

Pick over oysters carefully to remove pieces of shell, and season with pepper and salt to taste; roll crackers, not too fine, and cover with them the bottom of a baking dish that has been buttered; then spread a layer of oysters over the crumbs, and drop on bits of butter; pour on part of the liquor, then a layer of crumbs, alternating them with the oysters until dish is full, adding liquor each time; if there is not sufficient oyster liquor to moisten thoroughly, add water; have the crumbs for the top layer with bits of butter on top. Bake three-fourths of an hour in a very hot oven.— *Mrs. David Atwood.*

OYSTER CROQUETTES.

Drain the oysters as dry as possible, using first a colander and then a napkin; chop fine and measure them; then measure an equal quantity of potatoes that have been boiled and mashed very fine; season to your taste, and, if possible without making too moist, add a little cream and butter. Make into rolls, dip in egg, and roll in fine cracker crumbs; cut a piece of paper to fit the bottom of your egg boiler, lay your croquettes very carefully in this to fry, as they are so delicate they will fall to pieces if dropped at once into the kettle of hot lard.— *Mrs. W. W. Daniells.*

OYSTER SHORTCAKE.

Put liquor of oysters with one-half of a cup of water on the stove, and let it come to a boil; skim, add one cup of milk, butter, pepper, salt, and a little flour to thicken; add oysters, and let all come to a boil. Make shortcake same as for strawberries; open it, and pour oysters and part of liquor between; the remainder pour over the top.— *Miss Frank L. Clark.*

OYSTER SALAD.

One quart of oysters cut into small pieces, one bunch of celery cut in small pieces, two hard-boiled eggs, two raw eggs, well whipped; one table-spoonful of salad oil, one tea-spoonful sugar, one tea-spoonful of salt, one tea-spoonful of pepper and made mustard, one-half cupful best vinegar. Drain the liquor from the oysters, cut in dice, cut the celery into pieces of corresponding size; set aside in a cool place while the dressing is prepared. Beat eggs stiff, mix in the sugar, whip gradually in the oil until it is a light cream; have ready the boiled yolks rubbed to a powder; add to them salt, pepper and mustard. Beat these into the oil-yolk, and then add, two or three drops at a time, the vinegar, whipping the dressing briskly for two minutes; serve as soon as possible; keep on ice until wanted.— *Mrs. C. A. Belden.*

DEVILED CLAMS (OR OYSTERS)

One pint of clams and liquor, to which add one gill of water, after which throw away one gill of the mixed liquor and water; let this come to a boil, then pour all into a colander; add to the strained liquor two table-spoonfuls of butter, two and one-half table-spoonfuls of flour; boil until it thickens, then stir in two eggs, one table-spoonful chopped parsley, pepper and salt to taste; chop the clams fine and add them to the mixture; let it boil one minute, and then put away to cool; put the mixture into the shells, and cover them with cracker crumbs; put into the stove and brown nicely. For oysters, no water is needed with the liquor.— *Mrs. C. M. Macomber.*

PICKLED OYSTERS.

Put your oysters into a kettle with just enough liquor to prevent them from burning. Let them cook until they curl. Have ready enough vinegar to cover them, lightly spread with mace and pepper-corns. Skim the oysters out of the liquor, and pour over the vinegar boiling hot; take care that it is not too strong or it will soften the oysters. Add a little salt while stewing, to taste. They require to stand five or six hours before eating.— *Mrs. L. B. Vilas.*

STEWS

GUMBO — A STEW.

To the stock and meat of a fifteen cent soup bone (or a chicken) add one can tomatoes, or its equivalent of fresh tomatoes sliced, six or eight large onions sliced fine, one can or six ears of corn, twelve medium sized pods of okra sliced, one can lima beans. Cook slowly for four or five hours; add vegetables to the stock and meat in the following order: The tomatoes and onions at the first; the beans three-quarters of an hour before serving; and the okra and corn half an hour before serving; season with salt, tabasco sauce or cayenne pepper.— *Mrs. Charles F. Lamb.*

SCOTCH STEW.

Two pounds mutton, one-half cup pearl barley, two or three quarts cold water, two table-spoons butter, one-half cup each chopped carrot and onion, one table-spoon flour, one tablespoon chopped parsley, two tea-spoons salt, one salt-spoon pepper, a few drops of tabasco. Soak barley over night in cold water; remove fat and skin from meat and cut in small pieces, put on to cook in cold water, skim; add barley and skim again. Add vegetables and let simmer for three or four hours. Thicken with the butter and flour; add parsley, salt, pepper and tabasco. Simmer a few minutes longer and serve without straining.— *Mrs. Charles F. Lamb.*

MEATS.

BEEF À LA MODE.

Take a piece of beef four or five inches thick, and with a knife make small holes entirely through, at a small distance apart; take strips of fat salt pork, roll them in pepper and cloves, lay all on a pan and cover closely, and put in a steamer and steam three hours. When done thicken the gravy in the pan with a little flour. This is excellent, eaten as cold meat.— *Mrs. Wm. F. Vilas.*

BEEF LOAF.

Two pounds round beefsteak chopped, two-thirds cup rolled crackers, three eggs, one cup butter, one table-spoon salt, a little pepper. Bake three-quarters of an hour.— *Mrs. Herbert W. Chynoweth.*

VEAL LOAF.

Three and one-half pounds of veal, three table-spoons of butter, one nutmeg, salt and pepper to taste, one slice of salt pork, two eggs, Boston or soda crackers; put it through a sausage grinder, make in loaf, and bake two hours or more, basting often.— *Mrs. Wm. F. Vilas.*

VEAL LOAF.

Three pounds of veal chopped fine, one slice of salt pork, a few crackers rolled fine, butter size of an egg, two eggs, one table-spoon each of salt, pepper, and sage, three table-spoons of extract of celery; mix thoroughly. Pack tightly in a deep square tin, cover with fine cracker crumbs, and bits of butter; bake two hours.— *Miss Frank L. Clark.*

VEAL LOAF.

Three pounds of veal, one-half cup of rolled crackers, one-half cup of butter, two eggs, one table-spoonful of salt, one table-spoonful of pepper, spread butter over the top, and bake three-quarters of an hour.— *Mrs. C. M. Macomber.*

VEAL CROQUETTES.

Chop the veal fine; mix half a cup of sweet milk with a tea-spoonful of flour; melt a piece of butter the size of an egg and stir the milk and flour into it, then let it come to a boil. Mix this thoroughly with the meat, form it into balls, lay on a platter, scatter a little pepper and salt over them, and let stand until morning. Then beat one egg very light, add a little milk, dip the meat balls in the egg and then in cracker crumbs. Fry in hot lard until brown.— *Mrs. J. H. Palmer.*

TO ROAST DUCKS

After the ducks are dressed fill them with a stuffing prepared with bread crumbs, sage, a little onion, butter, salt, and pepper. Put them in a steamer and steam them for one hour; then take them up, lay them in a dripping pan with a little of the water from the kettle they were steamed over, sprinkle with salt and pepper, add a little butter, and bake a nice brown in a quick oven.— *Mrs. F. Durlin.*

SWEET BREAD.

Dip into boiling water to remove tough parts, cut into strips, dip into egg and then into rolled cracker crumbs prepared with salt and pepper as for fried oysters, and fry in butter and lard.— *Mrs. J. W. Curtis.*

ESCALOPED CHICKEN.

Boil one chicken very tender, take out bones, skin, et cetera, cut in small pieces, have a little gravy well seasoned, and thickened, boil the chicken in it, put a layer of bread crumbs in the bottom of a dish, pour in the chicken, and put a thick layer of crumbs on top. Moisten the crumbs with the gravy; if it gives out, use milk; put some pieces of butter on top, and bake twenty minutes or until nicely browned.— *Mrs. J. W. Curtis.*

TO BROIL PARTRIDGES, ETC.

Place them in salt and water an hour or two before broiling; when taken out wipe them dry, and rub them all over with butter, pepper and salt. First broil the under or split side on the gridiron, over bright, clear coals, turning until the upper side is of a fine, light brown; it must be cooked principally from the under side. When done rub well again with fresh butter, and if not ready to serve them immediately, put them in a large shallow tin bucket, cover it, and set it over a pot or kettle of boiling water, which will keep them hot without making them hard or dry, and will give time for the many "last things" to be done before serving a meal. When served, sift over them powdered cracker, first browned.

ROAST TURKEY.

Wash the turkey thoroughly inside and out, having removed the insides. Make a dressing of bread soaked in cold water, drained and mashed fine, a small piece of melted butter, pepper, salt, sweet herbs, a hard boiled egg chopped fine; the body and crop must be filled with the dressing and sewed up. The giblets ought to be boiled tender for gravy, adding a little of the turkey drippings, seasoning with pepper and salt, and thickening with a little flour and water mixed smoothly; place where it will boil. When the fowl is put on to roast put a little water in the dripping pan; at first roast slowly and baste frequently; tie up the wings and legs before roasting and rub on a little butter and salt.— *Mrs. David Atwood.*

CHICKEN CURRY.

Boil the chicken until it is tender, in a little water seasoned with salt and some mace; take the meat off the bones and cut it in squares, or leave it on the joints, as you please. Take about a pint of the water in which the chicken was boiled, put in a sauce-pan with one and one-half table-spoonfuls of flour rubbed into a little butter, and one tea-spoonful of curry powder; when it boils lay in the chicken for a few minutes so as to be thoroughly flavored with the curry. Have a tea-cupful of rice boiled in water with a little salt; it takes about fifteen minutes to boil it; line your dish with the rice, and place your curry in the center; garnish with pickled gherkins or sliced lemon. Fish broiled and cut into small pieces can be curried in this way; also frog's legs; garnish with parsley or limes.— *Mrs. W. H. Fox.*

BRAISED TONGUE.

Boil fresh tongue until tender; take out roots and grissle; also remove skin; curl it up in dish to fit, allowing room for sauce. Sauce: Chop fine one table-spoon celery, one table-spoon parsley, one table-spoon carrots, one table-spoon parsnips, one table-spoon turnips; brown in frying pan with two table-spoons each of flour and butter; when brown, add one and one-half pint of liquor which tongue was boiled in; season well with salt and pepper and Worcestershire sauce; allow mixture to thicken; pour over tongue; cover tightly; bake two hours; serve on hot platter garnished with parsley and red pepper; cut in strips with sauce poured over.— *Mrs. Florence Bashford Spensley.*

CASSEROLE OF RICE AND BEEF.

Line bottom and sides of a good sized mold with boiled rice. Fill the center with minced cold beef, highly seasoned and moistened with gravy; cover the top with rice and steam one hour. Turn out on a platter and pour around it tomato sauce.— *Miss M. L. Atwood.*

CHOPS A LA MAINTENON.

Put one table-spoon of butter in a frying pan; when hot, add one table-spoonful of flour; cook a few minutes; then add four table-spoonfuls of chopped mush rooms, one tea-spoonful of parsley, one-half tea-spoon of salt, and a dash of pepper; moisten with three table-spoonfuls of stock; mix well together and set aside to cool. Have six French chops cut one inch thick. With a sharp knife split the chops in two without separating them at the bone; spread the mushroom mixture between the opened chops; press the edges well together, and broil for eight minutes; serve with an olive sauce.— *Miss M. George.*

CORNED BEEF.

Take six pounds of salt, two pounds brown sugar, two ounces of saltpeter, six gallons of water; boil till transparent; when cold, put on beef. Sprinkle your beef with salt a day or two before.— *Mrs. R. M. Bashford.*

MEAT SOUFFLE.

Three cups ground meat, one or several kinds of cooked meat, one pint milk, one-half cup ground bread crumbs (stale), one small onion, through chopper, pinch of cayenne pepper, white pepper and salt to taste, one egg beaten; mix altogether well; put in baking dish with a table-spoon melted butter. Take one tea-spoon butter, one-half cup grated bread crumbs; heat on the stove and mix; then sprinkle over top; always butter your dish to cook meat with milk.— *Mrs. A. B. Morris.*

VEAL LOAF.

Three pounds veal and one-half pound salt pork chopped fine; three beaten eggs. Mix together one small tea-spoon black pepper, one tea-spoon salt and one table-spoon powdered sage. Season meat and egg with this, and add eight large table-spoons rolled crackers; then add a piece of butter the size of an egg, dissolved in a cup of hot water. Mix thoroughly; make into a loaf, and press down thoroughly into a tin. Bake in a moderate oven about three hours.— *Mrs. John Corscot.*

MELTON LOAF VEAL.

Boil two pounds veal until tender. When cool, chop fine; season with pepper, salt and a little lemon juice; add two or three table-spoons cracker crumbs; moisten with stock meat was cooked in. Take one-third as much boiled ham, chopped fine. Season this with mustard and cayenne, and add two table-spoons cracker crumbs; moisten with stock. Butter a mold and line it with slices of hard boiled eggs. Put in the mixture irregularly or in layers; press in closely and steam forty-five minutes. Cool, remove from mould and serve whole or sliced. Garnish with very thin slices of peeled lemon.— *Mrs. Charles F. Lamb.*

HOT MUSTARD SAUCE FOR HOT BOILED OR BAKED HAM.

One tea-spoon flour, yolks of two eggs, one desert-spoon sugar, two table-spoons dry mustard, one and one-half cup water, vinegar to taste, one table-spoon butter. To be thoroughly mixed and cooked in a double boiler until thick.— *Mrs. Lucius Fairchild.*

OLIVE SAUCE FOR CHOPS.

One dozen olives, one cup of brown stock, one table-spoon of butter, one table-spoon of flour, one table-spoon each of chopped onion and carrot, one clove, one tea-spoon salt. Dash of pepper. Put the butter in a sauce-pan, when it bubbles add the chopped onion and carrot and let them brown; then the flour and let that brown. Then add slowly the stock; season; let simmer for twenty minutes and strain. Stone the olives, leaving the meat in one piece; boil them in a little water for

3

half an hour.   Add the cooked olives to the strained
sauce, and cook for five minutes.— *Miss M. George.*

SAUCE FOR COLD BOILED HAM.

Two table-spoons butter, two table-spoons tomato
catsup, two table-spoons sherry, one table-spoon Worce-
tershire sauce, one-half tea-spoon dry mustard, mixed
with one table-spoon tarragon vinegar.   Melt all together
in the blazer of a chafing dish, put in the slices of ham and
serve very hot.   This sauce may also be used for other
meats.— *Mrs. Geo. C. Comstock.*

TOMATO SAUCE.

Stew a half can of tomatoes, with four cloves, pepper
and salt, a slice of onion, a sprig of parsley, for fifteen
minutes.   Strain, put on stove and thicken with lump
of butter and a table-spoon of flour.— *Mrs. Frank Van
Pierce.*

VEGETABLES.

ESCALOPED POTATOES.

Take six ordinary sized potatoes, slice thin the raw potatoes. Butter an escaloping dish and put them in layers, with salt, pepper and butter. Cover with a quart of cream or rich milk, add more butter, and bake half an hour.— *Mrs. A. J. Ward.*

POTATO CROQUETTES.

Season cold mashed potatoes with pepper, salt and nutmeg. Beat to a cream with a table-spoonful of melted butter and one of cream to every cupful of potato, roll into oval balls, dip in well beaten eggs and then in finely rolled cracker; fry in hot lard or butter.— *Mrs. John M. Sumner.*

BAKED TOMATOES.

Wash, wipe, cut in two or leave whole. Place in a baking tin and season with pepper and salt, and place in a hot oven. Take up carefully when done and put bits of butter on each piece of tomato.— *Mrs. Clark Gapen.*

PARSNIP FRITTERS.

One-half cup of sweet milk, one table-spoonful of melted butter. Boil half a dozen medium-sized parsnips till very tender, mash them fine, add two eggs, three table-spoonfuls of flour and a little salt. Fry a delicate brown in hot drippings.— *Mrs. H. K. Edgerton, Oconomowoc.*

CROOK-NECKED SQUASH.

Cut in thin slices and let stand two or three hours in cold salt and water. Then let them drain in a colander and roll in flour; fry them in butter until brown.— *Mrs. David Atwood.*

RICE CROQUETTES.

Boil one cup of rice in one pint of milk or water till tender. While warm add a piece of butter size of an egg, two eggs and salt, make into rolls, and fry in hot lard like doughnuts.— *Miss Bertha Schaal.*

BOILED RICE.

One cup of rice, two cups of milk and one cup of water, one heaping tea-spoonful of salt, a piece of butter half the size of an egg; cover closely and steam one hour and a half.— *Mrs. B. E. Hutchinson.*

GREEN CORN OYSTERS.

To a pint of grated corn add two well-beaten eggs. one-half cup of cream and one-half cup of flour, with one-half tea-spoonful of baking powder stirred in, season with pepper and salt and fry in butter, dropping the batter in spoonfuls. Serve very hot as a relish with meats.— *Mrs. Darwin Clark.*

CORN CAKES OR MOCK OYSTERS.

One half dozen ears of sweet corn, grated, two eggs, pepper and salt. Fry in butter.— *Mrs. C. R. Riebsam.*

MACARONI WITH CHEESE.

Do not wash the macaroni, break into pieces and throw it into well-salted boiling water. Stir frequently to prevent adhering to stew-pan. As soon as tender, pour it into a colander and shake off all the water. Meantime melt butter size of an egg for half pound of macaroni, in a cup, and grate a handful of cheese. When the macaroni is well drained, place a little of it in a dish, pour over it some of the melted butter and sprinkle a little of the grated cheese; continue alternate layers, leaving butter and cheese on top. Brown in the oven. Serve immediately or the cheese will cool and harden. It requires about twenty minutes to boil macaroni.— *Mrs. C. Hawley.*

CHEESE FONDU.

Soak one cup of very fine dry bread crumbs in two scant cups milk, beat into this three eggs whipped very light, add one small table-spoonful melted butter, pepper, salt and half-pound old cheese grated. Butter a neat baking-dish, pour the fondu into it, strew dry bread crumbs over top and bake in a quick oven. Serve immediately, as it soon falls.— *Mrs. Clark Gapen.*

WELSH RARE-BIT.

Toast thin square or diamond shaped slices of bread; remove the crust. While hot, butter them slightly and dip in hot water just to moisten them. Sprinkle over a little salt, and pour over them rich new cheese, melted, enough to cover them. Serve very hot. Some serve a poached egg on each slice.— *Mrs. Harry Hobbins.*

CORN OYSTERS.

One-half can ot corn, two eggs, one-half cup of cracker crumbs, one-half tea-spoon salt. Form in little cakes about the size of an oyster and fry in lard.— *Mrs. S. E. Hood.*

RICE FRITTERS.

One cup of rice, boiled tender, butter size of egg. When cold stir in two eggs, flour enough to make a stiff batter.— *Mrs. R. J. McConnell.*

MACARONI CHEESE (ENGLISH).

Take as much macaroni as will half fill the dish in which it is to be served. Break it into pieces two and a half inches long. Put it into salted boiling water, and boil until perfectly soft, being careful it does not burn. Drain and put into a pudding dish; cover with grated cheese, and a table-spoon of melted butter; season with salt and pepper and pour over about a small cup of milk. Then cover with crisp bread crumbs dotted with pieces of butter and bake until browned on top.— *Miss M. George.*

MASHED CHESTNUTS.

Take one quart of chestnuts, make a small cut in the side of each shell, then throw them into boiling water; boil for five minutes, then shell, being careful to remove all the thin white skin under the shell. Cook in consomme (clear soup) with a little celery and three small lumps of sugar. When cooked strain through a fine sieve; then put into a saucepan and thin with soup (boullion or consomme), and add just before serving a lump of good butter. *Serve very hot*, with roast mutton. (From the French.) — *Mrs. Lucius Fairchild.*

COLD SLAW.

Shred a firm cabbage very fine; put into a bowl the yolks of three eggs, one-half cup of vinegar diluted with water, one table-spoon of butter, one-half tea-spoon each of mustard and pepper, and one tea-spoon each of sugar and salt. Beat them together. Place the bowl in a pan of boiling water and stir it until it becomes a little thickened. Pour this while hot over the cabbage and set it away to cool.— *Mrs. R. M. Bashford.*

SALADS.

CABBAGE SALAD.

Take two small heads of cabbage or one large one and chop fine. Then put in a jar or large pan, first a layer of cabbage, then one of salt, until all is in; let it stand two hours. Then take it out and rinse it in cold water once or twice, put back in the jar, and it is ready for the dressing, prepared as follows: For this quantity of cabbage beat four eggs, stir in a table-spoonful of mixed mustard, half a cup of butter, one cup of vinegar, and sugar to taste. Put in a bowl and set it over a tea-kettle of boiling water, and stir until it begins to thicken. When cold pour over the cabbage. This salad will keep for a week or two prepared in this way.— *Mrs. F. Durlin.*

CABBAGE SALAD.

Two eggs, three table-spoonfuls of sugar, butter size of an egg, two table-spoonfuls of ground mustard, a little salt; mix these well together, stir in one pint of cold vinegar, put on stove and continue to stir until it boils; pour hot over cabbage.— *Mrs. L. F. Kellogg.*

CHICKEN SALAD.

One large chicken, one dozen heads of celery, chop chicken and celery fine, and mix. Just before using pour over the following dressing: six eggs beaten light, one-half cup of melted butter, one cup of cream,

one cup of vinegar, one table-spoonful of made mustard, one table-spoonful of sugar; salt and pepper to
taste; mix well. Put the dish containing the mixture
into another of boiling water; stir constantly, and boil
until quite thick.— *Mrs. D. S. Comy.*

CHICKEN SALAD.

Two chickens, two heads of celery, four great spoons
of oil fried out of the fat of the chickens. Juice of
two lemons. Yolks of four eggs, raw. One whole egg.
One large half cup of vinegar, with mustard, pepper,
salt, sugar, butter and the eggs placed over a slow fire,
and stirred constantly until thickened; then add oil and
lemon juice, and just before serving mix it thoroughly
with the chopped chicken and celery.— *Mrs. W. G. Pitman.*

CHICKEN SALAD

Ten pounds of chicken before it is cooked, four
bunches of celery, twelve raw yolks of eggs beaten
stiff. Add slowly three-fourths of a bottle of sweet oil,
beating all the time, salt, pepper, made mustard, mixing these with some vinegar. When all beaten up, add
one-half cup of cold water; to whiten the dressing, add
very slowly the beaten whites of the eggs. Cut the
boiled chicken with a knife, the celery as well. This
makes salad enough for twelve persons. Do not pour
the dressing on to the chicken until ready for use.—
Mrs. C. A. Belden.

MAYONNAISE SAUCE.

Yolk of one egg — raw — beat with a fork, one-half
tea-spoonful of salt, one-half tea-spoonful of made mus-

tard, work one minute before adding the oil, add slowly a few drops of oil at a time, stirring constantly. When like jelly, add a few drops of lemon juice and vinegar. When the egg has absorbed a gill of oil add a pinch of red pepper and two tea-spoonfuls of vinegar.— *Mrs. C. A. Belden.*

SALAD DRESSING.

Two scant tea-spoons salt, one-half cup of vinegar, six eggs, two table-spoons of mixed mustard, one table-spoon butter, and six of salad oil, one and one-half cups cream. Beat whites and yolks separately, into them stir the oil gradually. Mix all the ingredients, except cream, in a new tin dish; cook until thick, stirring constantly. When cold add the cream, and pour over the prepared chicken and celery one hour before eating. This is sufficient dressing for two chickens.— *Mrs. James E. Moseley.*

SALAD DRESSING.

Three eggs, six table-spoons sweet cream or milk, three of melted butter, one tea-spoon pepper, one of salt, and two of mustard. Beat well together, and add a coffee cup of vinegar. Let it boil up and use when cold. In cool weather this will keep some days.— *Mrs. James R. Mears.*

FRENCH DRESSING FOR SALAD.

One table-spoon of vinegar, three table-spoons of olive oil, one salt-spoon each of pepper and salt, one even tea-spoon of onion, scraped fine. Mix the pepper and salt, then add the oil and onion, and then the vinegar; when well mixed, pour over the salad.— *Miss Emma Hawley.*

German Potato Salad

Boil two quarts potatoes with jackets until tender, peel and when very cool, slice very fine, add one onion diced very fine, one table-spoon salt one-half tea-spoon sugar, one-fourth tea-spoon pepper, make dressing as follows: take three slices bacon, try out, (then remove bacon,) into fat add one-half tea-spoon flour, let blend, but not brown; add three-fourth cup vinegar and one-fourth cup water; let boil a few minutes until smooth then pour all over potatoes immediately; mix well, taking care not to break potatoes too much.— *Mrs. H. Fauerbach.*

Grape Fruit Salad.

Cut two grape fruit in small peices, one small can pineapple cut up, arrange on lettuce and serve with a French dressing.— *Mrs. Albert Schmedeman.*

Shrimp Salad.

Use equal parts of shrimp and celery. Serve on lettuce with "Favorite Salad Dressing."— *Mrs. Frank Van Pierce.*

Favorite Mayonnaise Salad Dressing.

Four yolks, three table-spoons of olive oil or butter, three table-spoons of sugar, one tea-spoon dry mustard, one tea-spoon salt, a little cayenne, one-half cup of vinegar. Mix together. Boil until it thickens; when cold add a cup of whipped cream.— *Mrs. Frank Van Pierce.*

PICKLES.

COLD SLAW.

Cut the cabbage fine, take one heaping tea-spoon each of mustard and salt, one table-spoon butter, two of cream, two tea-spoons sugar, two-thirds of a cup of vinegar, yolk of one egg, beaten well; stir this all together on the stove till it thickens, then when cold pour over the cabbage.— *Mrs. Wm. F. Vilas.*

HOT SLAW.

Shave with a cabbage cutter a nice head of cabbage. Take half a cup of vinegar and put into a sauce-pan, add butter size of an egg, season highly with pepper and salt, and stir one raw egg into it.   Let it heat through, but not cook, then add the cabbage.   Do not let it boil. Serve hot.— *Mrs. E. R. Curtiss.*

CHILI SAUCE.

Six large tomatoes, two green peppers, one onion, one table-spoon salt, one-half cup sugar, two cups vinegar. Chop fine and simmer till well cooked.— *Mrs. L. B. Vilas.*

CHOW CHOW.

Four quarts of green tomatoes, one quart of green peppers, two good sized onions, chop all fine and mix together, stir in a cup of salt, and let them stand over night.   In the morning drain for a long time, put in one-half pint of white mustard seed, a cup of sugar, and cover with scalding vinegar.— *Mrs. James E. Burgess.*

Chow Chow.

One gallon green tomatoes after chopped fine, one cup salt, mix well, let stand over night, then drain through sieve, then add to the tomatoes twelve green peppers, one cup horse radish, one table-spoon cloves, one black pepper, three white mustard seed, one ounce mace, two table-spoon turmeric, four celery seed, dozen heads celery, eight large onions, cover with cold vinegar, and is ready for use.— *Mrs. J. W. Curtis.*

Cucumber Pickles.

Cucumbers sufficient to fill a four-gallon jar; pour boiling water over them, cover closely and let stand until cold. Turn the water off, and cover them with a weak cold brine for twenty-four hours. Take from this and put on, boiling hot, equal quantities of vinegar and water with two ounces of alum dissolved in it. Let this stand one week in a cool place, covered with cloth and weight. Then rinse the cucumbers in cold water, and drain. Take pure cider vinegar, with three pounds of sugar, one ounce each of pepper, cloves, mustard seed, and allspice, two ounces of cinnamon, a few blades of mace, rind of one lemon chopped, one cup of sliced horse-radish, one cup of nasturtian seeds, or two cups of the chopped leaf stems of the plant. Scald all this together in the vinegar, and pour boiling hot over the cucumbers. Keep closely covered with cloth and weight on them. If the vinegar is pure, this receipt will preserve the pickles two years or more.— *Mrs. A. Proudfit.*

FRENCH PICKLES.

One peck green tomatoes, and six large onions sliced, sprinkle a tea-cup of salt over them, and let them stand twenty-four hours. Drain well and boil fifteen minutes in two quarts of water and one quart of vinegar; drain again, and take four quarts of vinegar, two pounds of brown sugar, one-fourth pound of white mustard seed, ground, two table-spoonfuls of allspice, two table-spoonfuls of cloves, two table-spoonfuls of cinnamon, same of ginger and mustard, one-half table-spoonful of cayenne pepper; put all together and boil until tender, when it is ready for use.— *Mrs. J. W. Curtis.*

MIXED PICKLES.

Three hundred small cucumbers, eight green peppers, sliced thin, two heads cauliflower, two quarts string beans, very young and small, two quarts small onions, one root horse-radish, to vinegar enough to cover them. Add one-quarter pound each black and white mustard, one-quarter box black pepper, two tea-spoonfuls cayenne pepper, two ounces turmeric, a piece of alum the size of an English walnut, two table-spoonfuls black sugar, one-half pint ground mustard. Let the above mixture come to a boil, and then pour on the pickles hot or cold. Soak the cucumbers and cauliflower in strong brine that will bear up an egg, twenty-four hours.— *R. L. Garlick.*

GREEN TOMATO PICKLES.

Slice one peck tomatoes, strew them thickly with salt, let them stand all night, next morning drain off the green water, rinse the salt off by putting in a sieve and dashing water over them. Slice four large onions, have ready one ounce cloves, one of allspice and one of black pepper, all ground, half an ounce of celery seed, one-half ounce bruised coriander seed, one-quarter pound ground mustard. Put alternate layers of tomatoes, then onions and spices, till the kettle is two-thirds full. Cover with vinegar and boil till tender, then drain the vinegar off and throw it away; add fresh vinegar and put away in jars for use.— *Mrs. Wm. F. Vilas.*

GREEN TOMATO PICKLES.

Slice half bushel of tomatoes, add one tea-cup salt, and let stand twenty-four hours and drain. One gallon vinegar, two pounds sugar, two ounces cinnamon, two of allspice, one of cloves, two of black pepper; put the sugar, vinegar and spices on the stove and let it come to a boil, add tomatoes and let them also come to a boil. Put in jars for use.— *Mrs. E. S. McBride.*

TOMATO PICKLES.

One peck of green tomatoes, sliced, six green peppers, four onions, sprinkle with salt and let them remain over night; in the morning pour off the brine, boil with vinegar enough to cover them, add sugar to your taste, cloves, cinnamon, allspice and half an ounce of turmeric powder; boil all together until clear.— *Mrs. C. A. Belden.*

CUCUMBER CATSUP.

One dozen large ripe cucumbers, four onions. Pare the cucumbers, remove the seeds, and chop both onions and cucumbers very fine. Squeeze very fine; add pepper and salt to taste, and make very moist with cold vinegar. Put this in bottles or jars and seal.— *Mrs. D. S. Comly.*

TOMATO CATSUP.

One peck of fresh ripe tomatoes, four large white onions, four green peppers, one tea-cup of celery seed, one tea-cup of whole cloves, and one of allspice, one coffee-cup of brown sugar, and one of vinegar, a half tea-cup of salt, six cloves of garlic. Cook and strain.— *Mrs. Daniel Campbell.*

SPICED CANTELOPES.

Take ripe fruit and prepare as for eating, taking off the rind; let them soak in weak vinegar over night. To seven pounds of fruit add five pounds sugar and one quart vinegar. Mace and cloves to taste. Boil them three hours. Do not use vinegar that the fruit was soaked in, but fresh.— *Mrs. Robert B. Ogilvie.*

SWEET PICKLES.

Four pounds sugar, one quart vinegar, to eight pounds of fruit. Take about two tea-spoons cinnamon and cloves; pound and put in. Add fruit, and boil till tender; then put in jars, boil down the syrup and pour in.— *Mrs. S. H. Carpenter.*

4

SWEET PICKLE PEACHES.

Eight pounds of peaches, four pounds of sugar, one quart of vinegar, one level table-spoon of stick cinnamon broken very small, one level table-spoon of stick mace broken very small. Use no other spices. Have firm, sound peaches, wipe carefully and do not peel. When the sugar, vinegar and spices come to a boil in a porcelain kettle, drop in the peaches a few at a time, turn in the syrup with a silver fork until cooked through, but not soft; remove peaches from syrup as fast as cooked. Place peaches in a large stone bowl, and when the syrup has boiled until it will jell when tried, pour it over the peaches; press them down into the bowl under an inverted plate, and cover so as to entirely exclude the air. Look at them after a few days, and if syrup has become thin boil it down again.— *Mrs. David Atwood.*

TOMATO PRESERVES.

Peel tomatoes and weigh; allow three-fourths of a pound of sugar to one pound of tomatoes, five cents worth of ginger root and four lemons sliced to a half bushel of tomatoes; stew down well.— *Mrs. Robert J. McConnell.*

CHEESE.

CHEESE BALLS.

One large cup grated cheese (one month old is best); season with salt and red pepper; take the whites of two eggs well beaten; mix with cheese and roll into balls size of walnut; drop into hot lard and fry same as doughnuts. Makes eighteen balls.— *Mrs. A. B. Morris.*

CREAM CHEESE BALLS.

Add a little sweet cream to a cake of cream cheese; make into balls and roll in finely chopped salted almonds.— *Mrs. Albert Schmedeman.*

CHEESE SOUFFLES.

Cut a quarter of a pound of cheese into very small pieces; put in half cup of cream; season with a little salt and pepper; set on fire and stir in the yolk of an egg; put bits of toast in very small cups; pour the mixture over and set in oven one minute.— *Mrs. Frank Van Pierce.*

CHEESE STRAWS.

Sift six ounces of flour on the pastry board, make a hole in the center; into this hole put two table-spoons of cream, three ounces of grated rich cheese, four ounces of butter, half a tea-spoon of salt, quarter of a tea-spoon of white pepper, quarter of a tea-spoon of mustard, a very little cayenne. Mix all these ingredients with the tips of the fingers to a firm paste; knead it well; roll out to an eighth of an inch thick, and with a sharp knife cut it in straws about eight inches long and quarter inch wide; lay the strips carefully on a buttered tin, and bake them light straw color in a moderate oven. *Mrs. Charles D. Atwood.*

CHEESE TARTS.

One-half cup butter, one cup sugar, one cup currants, two eggs (not beaten), a dessert-spoonful of cornstarch; flavor with vanilla to taste. Put this in a dish altogether and mix; do not mix separately; drop in the tart, and bake crust and filling together.— *Mrs. A. B. Morris.*

WELSH RAREBIT.

One pound cheese, one table-spoon butter, one-half glass ale or beer, yolk of one egg, one tea-spoon Worcestershire sauce, one tea-spoon dry mustard, a dash of cayenne and paprica, one-fourth tea-spoon salt, six drops tabasco. Cut the cheese; put in dish with butter; when melted, add the other ingredients after mixing all together. Stir all the time. Serve on hot dipped buttered toast.— *Mrs. Frank Van Pierce.*

EGGS.

FRENCH OMELET.

One cup of boiling milk with one table-spoon of butter melted in it. Pour this on one cup of light bread crumbs, add salt, pepper and the yolks of six eggs well beaten, mix thoroughly, and lastly add the six whites cut to a stiff froth. Mix lightly and fry with hot butter. This will make two omelets. When almost done, turn together in shape of half moon.— *Mrs. J. W. Vance.*

LITTLE OMELETS.

Four eggs, two large iron spoons of flour, one cup of milk, one tea-spoon of salt. Beat yolks and whites separately and then put them together. Mix flour and milk and stir into the egg, add the salt. Bake in a hot greased frying pan, a ladleful at a time, on one side only. As soon as each one is done, roll it up (in the frying pan) and lay it on a flat dish. A little sugar may be sprinkled over them if desired. These are very nice, and do not grow heavy as they cool, like ordinary omelets. This makes enough for four persons.— *Miss Lois Robbins.*

OMELET.

Soak a tea-cup of bread crumbs in a cup of sweet milk over night; three eggs, beat yolks and whites separately; mix the yolks with the bread and milk, stir in the whites, add a tea-spoon of salt, and fry brown. This is sufficient for six persons.— *Mrs. Chas. E. Bross.*

OMELET.

Take three eggs, beats the whites and yolks separately; to the yolks after they are beaten, add a half tea-spoon salt, and a tea-cup rich cream in which a heaping tea-spoon of flour has been smoothly rubbed; lastly, stir in the whites which have been beaten as for cake, have ready a spider in which has been melted a table-spoon of lard, and which is as hot as can be, and not burned; pour in the mixture and let it stand till a rich brown on the bottom.— *Mrs. A. B. Braley.*

OMELET.

The yolks of eight eggs beaten light; one cup of milk: in part of this mix one table-spoon of flour, and add the remaining milk, with one tea-spoon of salt. Beat the whites to a stiff froth, in a large dish, and into this mix lightly the other ingredients, and turn immediately into a large spider in which has been melted a piece of butter, size of an egg; cover, and cook about fifteen minutes, taking care not to scorch; fold one-half over and serve on a hot platter.— *Mrs. James E. Moseley.*

OMELET.

For six people, use four eggs; separate whites and yolks; take an inch thick slice of bread, cut off the crust, and saturate with cream or milk; stir in yolks; add pepper, salt and parsley; beat whites to a stiff froth and stir in lightly with yolks and bread. Have a table-spoonful of butter in omelet pan; put over fire and let sputter, but not brown; pour in omelet; constantly shake, and let cook six minutes; turn over and cook two or three minutes; then slip off on to a hot platter.— *Miss Mary Louise Atwood.*

OMELET.

One cup of milk, one table-spoon of flour stirred into milk, four eggs, yolks and whites beaten separately; one-half table-spoonful of melted butter stirred into the mixture, a little salt; stir in the whites of eggs before putting into the spider; cook on top of stove about ten minutes.— *Mrs. J. W. Curtis.*

SCRAMBLED EGGS.

Separate the yolks and whites of six eggs; beat the yolks about two minutes, then add six table-spoons of milk, a tea-spoon of salt, and beat a little more; melt half a table-spoon of butter in a spider, pour in the yolks, and, when they thicken slightly, pour the whites in without beating; stir them constantly.— *Mrs. Edward P. Vilas.*

BREADED EGGS.

Boil hard and cut in round, thick slices. Pepper and salt; dip each in beaten raw egg, then in fine bread crumbs, or powdered cracker, and fry in nice dripping or butter hissing hot. Drain off every drop of grease and serve on hot dish.— *Mrs. G. W. Oakley.*

FRENCH EGGS.

Boil hard as many eggs as you wish; cut in halves, remove the yolks and make them fine with a knife. Make a dressing of a tea-spoonful of mustard, a wine-glass of vinegar, a table-spoon of cream, a wine-glass of oil, pepper and salt to taste, and the mashed yolks; mix well and fill each half of the white very full, and round nicely. These are very nice to garnish cold meats, or may be served alone.— *Mrs. Harry B. Hobbins.*

Egg Curry.

Take a pint and a half of good sweet milk, two table-spoonfuls of flour, and a dessert spoonful of curry powder, blended with a little butter or rich cream. Boil six eggs hard, peel and cut in two; have the rice prepared as for the chicken curry, line your dish with it, place eggs in center and pour the curry over them. Care should be taken not to pour the curry over the rice, as the whiteness of the wall of rice adds to its effectiveness; garnish with parsley or limes.— *Mrs. W. H. Fox.*

Baked Eggs.

Line muffin tin with bread crumbs made into a soft paste with hot milk; break an egg into each; season; cover with grated cheese and buttered bread crumbs. Bake six minutes, or until egg is set.— *Mrs. Frank Van Pierce.*

Curried Egg.

Boil six eggs hard, cut in half; place on slices of buttered toast, then pour on the following sauce: one and one-half cups milk, one table-spoon butter, one dessert-spoon corn starch; salt and pepper to taste; one tea-spoon curry powder. Boil five minutes.— *Mrs. A. B. Morris.*

MEXICAN EGGS.

One table-spoon of finely chopped (sweet preferred) green pepper (use only one-half if very peppery); one table-spoon of finely minced onion, one table-spoon of butter, in which stew the pepper and onion, adding one-third tea-spoon of salt; then one quart of tomatoes stewed before slightly, or if canned strain off the juice, using only the thick part; one table-spoon of good cider vinegar; stew together about five minutes in the chafing dish, then add ten eggs, and continue to cook until well scrambled. Serve on toast.— *Mrs. Lucius Fairchild.*

FRIED BOILED EGGS.

Boil eggs very hard; cut in slices; dip in raw egg and bread crumbs, and fry in hot lard.— *Mrs. A. B. Morris.*

SHIRRED EGGS.

Butter an egg shirrer, cover bottom and sides with fine cracker crumbs; break an egg into a cup and carefully slip into shirrer; cover with seasoned buttered crumbs and bake in moderate oven until the white is firm and the crumbs brown.— *Mrs. A. B. Morris.*

FRENCH OMELET.

Beat four eggs slightly; add four table-spoons milk, one-half tea-spoon salt, dash of pepper; put two table-spoons butter in hot omelet pan; when melted turn in the mixture.— *Mrs. A. B. Morris.*

STUFFED EGGS.

Cut hard boiled eggs lengthwise; remove yolks carefully, and powder; add to powdered yolk two sprigs

chopped parsley salt-spoon dry mustard and salt, two
tea-spoons lemon juice, two table-spoons melted butter
or olive oil, dash of cayenne. Mix thoroughly and fill
the whites. Lay on lettuce leaves.— *Mrs. Frank Van
Pierce.*

DRINKS.

COFFEE.

One and one-half quarts of boiling water, one-fourth of a pound of best ground coffee, one egg. Break the egg into the dry coffee, stir together until the coffee has entirely absorbed the egg, then put into the boiling water and let boil five minutes. Strain through a flannel into a china or porcelain coffee-pot and it is ready to serve.— *H. M. Kinsley, Chicago.*

TEA.

One tea-spoonful of best tea to one cup of water; pour boiling water into a china or earthen tea-pot; let it stand till heated through, then pour off the water, put in the tea, pour boiling hot water over it, and serve in three minutes.— *H. M. Kinsley, Chicago.*

CHOCOLATE.

Take two ounces (or squares) of Baker's chocolate, break it into a little boiling water and stir over the fire until it becomes a smooth paste; if unsweetened chocolate is used, add eight even table-spoonfuls of granulated sugar, then add little by little a pint of boiling water and a pint of scalded milk; stir it thoroughly and allow to simmer (not boil) for ten minutes, when it is ready to serve.

VIENNA BAKERY COFFEE.

Make coffee in the ordinary way; then to one pint of cream heated over boiling water allow the white of one egg beaten to a froth; add three table-spoonfuls of cold milk to the egg and mix well; then remove the cream, when hot, from the fire, and add the egg, stirring briskly for a few minutes. Serve the coffee in the usual manner, adding this mixture instead of cold cream.

BROWN BREAD.

Boston Brown Bread.

One cup of molasses, three cups of sour milk, one tea-spoonful salt, three tea-spoonful saleratus, five cups graham flour, two cups raisins. Steam three and one-half hours in pound baking powder can.— *Mrs. Agnus McConnell.*

Graham Bread.

Two cups graham flour, one cup white flour, one-half cup sugar, granulated or light brown, one-half tea-spoon salt and one-half tea-spoon soda sifted into flour. Mix thoroughly and add milk to make as stiff a batter as can be stirred with a spoon, about one and one-quarter cups, and one-third of a cake of yeast which has been dissolved and raised. Stir until thoroughly mixed, and turn at once into greased pan and let rise until it has about doubled its bulk. Bake in moderate oven about fifty minutes. This makes one loaf.— *Mrs. E. M. Fox.*

Steamed Bread

Two cups sweet milk, one cup sour milk, two cups meal, one cup flour, one-half cup molasses, one tea-spoon soda, little salt; scald sweet milk and pour on meal; when cool, mix; steam three hours; dry in oven — *Mrs. Adah Gibbs.*

BREAD.

POTATO YEAST.

Grate six good sized potatoes, pour over them two quarts of boiling water, two handfuls of hops, one-half cup of sugar, one table-spoonful of salt; let it boil until it thickens; when cool add yeast cakes that have been previously soaked, or yeast.— *Mrs. N. B. Van Slyke.*

YEAST.

Two quarts water, one good handful of hops, three or four potatoes, boil away one-half. One cup of flour, one cup of sugar, one table-spoon of salt, same of ginger; pour the boiling liquor over and stir well; cool, and put in the yeast to rise and bottle. It will keep two months.— *Mrs. L. B. Vilas.*

HOME-MADE HOP YEAST.

Pare and slice two good sized potatoes into a small stew pan. Add one pint of boiling water, and let cook until thoroughly done. Then mash fine in the water in which they were boiled, and pour it scalding hot on one small cup of flour; stir until smooth. Steep a small pinch of hops in one pint of water, and strain hot on the flour. When cool, add one tea-spoon sugar, two of salt, one-half of ginger, and one-half cup of yeast.— *Mrs. F. W. Oakley.*

WHITE BREAD.

Sift a pan of flour, stir into the center one quart of new milk, lukewarm; àdd one-half cup of home-made hop yeast; cover with flour, and let stand until light, when add one table-spoon of sugar, one table-spoon of butter, and one of lard. Mix thoroughly, keeping soft as possible, and put back in pan to rise again. When light, knead thoroughly once more, make into loaves, let rise again, and bake.— *Mrs. F. W. Oakley.*

SPONGE FOR BREAD.

Four good sized potatoes, peeled, boiled, and mashed fine; one table-spoon of lard, one table-spoon of sugar, one quart of warm milk or water; put these together, add three cups of flour, and beat up smoothly; use six table-spoons of yeast, and put to rise over night. In the morning knead fifteen or twenty minutes. For two dozen rolls knead in two table-spoons of lard.— *Mrs. Lyman.*

STEAMED BROWN BREAD.

One quart of sour milk, one quart of Indian meal, one pint of rye flour, one table-spoonful of soda, one cup of molasses, one tea-spoonful of salt. Steam four hours, and bake one hour.— *Mrs. Breese J. Stevens.*

STEAMED BROWN BREAD.

One cup of molasses, one cup milk, two cups Graham flour, one cup white flour, one tea-spoon soda. Steam two hours.— *Miss Kittie Bird.*

BOSTON BROWN BREAD.

One and one-half cups of Graham flour, two cups of corn meal, one-half cup of molasses, one pint of sweet

milk, one-half tea-spoon of soda. Steam three hours.—
Mrs. James Burgess.

BROWN BREAD.

Two cups rye meal, two cups Indian meal, one large
half cup molasses, one-half cup raisins, two cups sour
milk, two tea-spoons of soda. If sweet milk is used,
two tea-spoons cream of tartar, and one of soda. Boil
five or six hours.— *Mrs. L. B. Vilas.*

BROWN BREAD.

Prepare a sponge as for white bread, using potatoes
or white flour; put into a tray two parts Graham flour
and one part white flour, and to every quart of this add
a handful of Indian meal with a tea-spoonful of salt.
Wet this up with the sponge, and when it is mixed
add for each loaf half a tea-cupful of molasses; the
dough should be very soft. If there is not enough
of the sponge to reduce it to the desired consistency,
add a little blood-warm water; knead it diligently. It
will not rise so rapidly as white flour, having more
" body " to carry; let it take its time. Make into round,
comfortable loaves, and set down again for the
second rising; when you have again kneaded it, bake
steadily, taking care it does not burn, and do not cut
while hot. The result will well repay you for your
trouble. It will take a longer time to bake than white
bread. Graham flour should not be sifted.— *Mrs. W.
H. Hughes.*

BISCUIT.

Boil four good sized potatoes; mash fine while hot;
put in a tea-spoon of salt and two table-spoons of flour;

5

mash well together; pour on a quart of boiling water. Let it stand till milk-warm; put in half a cup of yeast; let it rise till morning; mix into stiff batter, putting in a little soda. Rise again; then beat up one egg; add half a pound of butter; mix and knead thoroughly half an hour; roll out and cut with biscuit cutter. Let them rise and bake.— *Mrs. J. C. Hopkins.*

LIGHT BISCUIT.

One quart of milk, three-fourths of a cup of lard or butter — half and half is a good rule; three-fourths of a cup of yeast, two table-spoonfuls white sugar, one tea-spoonful salt, flour to make a soft dough; mix over night, warming the milk slightly, and melting the lard or butter; in the morning roll out into a sheet three-quarters of an inch in thickness; cut into round cakes; set these closely together in a pan, let them rise for twenty minutes, and bake twenty minutes.—*Mrs. W. H. Hughes.*

PARKER HOUSE ROLLS.

Boil one pint of sweet milk; when partly cool melt in it one-half cup of sugar (some omit sugar) and one table-spoon of butter; when lukewarm add one-half cup of yeast; pour this mixture into the center of two quarts of flour. If for tea, set to rise over night; in the morning mix well and knead; set to rise again; in the afternoon knead again; roll; cut thinner than for biscuit; rub melted butter upon half the surface and fold it upon the other; set to rise again in pans, and, when light, bake twenty minutes.— *Miss Frank L. Clark.*

MUFFINS.

Two eggs, two table-spoons sugar, one tea-cup of milk and water, three tea-spoons of baking powder, one and one-half cups of flour.— *Mrs. J. H. D. Baker.*

PHILADELPHIA MUFFINS.

One quart of sweet milk, two quarts of flour, eight tea-spoonfuls of cream tartar, four tea-spoonfuls of soda; put the cream tartar in the flour, dissolve the soda in the milk, three-fourths of a cup of butter rolled in the flour. After the dough is well mixed, roll it out one-half an inch thick, cut with biscuit cutter and place two together (one on top of the other), and bake about twenty minutes. These are elegant if properly made.— *Mrs. D. S. Comly.*

RICE MUFFINS.

One cup of cold boiled rice, one pint of flour, two eggs, one quart of milk, or enough to make a thin batter, one table-spoon of lard or butter, one tea-spoon of salt. Beat hard and bake quickly.— *Mrs. Wm. F. Vilas.*

RUSK.

One cup of yeast, one cup of milk, one-half cup of sugar, one and one-half cups of flour; set at night. In the morning add yolks of two eggs, one cup of sugar, one-half cup of butter; let stand until very light. Mix very soft, bake them in small biscuits a light brown. Beat the whites and add two table-spoons of sugar for a frosting; set them in the oven to brown.— *Mrs. C. M. Macomber.*

BREAKFAST PUFFS.

One egg, a scant tea-cup of sweet milk, one cup of sifted flour, one tea-spoon of melted butter; break the egg, beat a little, add the other ingredients, beat lightly; have the gem pans hot. The secret of success is a moderate oven.— *Mrs. John C. Spooner.*

ROLLS.

One pint of scalded milk, cooled, one-half cup of yeast or one-third cake of compressed yeast, one table-spoon of sugar, a little salt, butter the size of an egg. Rub butter in one quart of flour; add the other ingredients, mixing thoroughly. Let stand in moderate heat till light, then flour till it can be easily kneaded on a board; mix and knead one-half hour. Rise again and roll out to the thickness of half an inch, cut in biscuits, and rub a little butter on one-half the upper side of each, fold the other half over and pinch down. Put in biscuit pans about two inches apart. Let them get very light and bake twenty minutes in a hot oven. These rolls set in the morning will be ready for tea. One measure makes fifty rolls.— *Miss Kate A. Chittenden.*

BATH BUNS.

One-half cup butter, and two of sugar, stirred to a cream, two eggs, one-half cup milk, three cups flour, one and one-half tea-spoon baking powder, three-fourths cup citron, cut fine and well dredged with flour. Bake in well greased muffin rings in a moderate oven. A little sugar sprinkled over the top of each bun is an improvement.— *Mrs. J. W. Hobbins.*

STEAMED CORN BREAD.

Two cups of sweet milk, one cup of sour milk, three cups of corn meal, one cup of flour, one-half cup of molasses, butter size of an egg, one tea-spoonful of soda, a little salt. Steam three hours and bake half an hour.— *Mrs. J. W. Curtis.*

CORN BREAD.

Two eggs, one-half cup of butter, two table-spoons of sugar, one cup of flour, one cup of corn meal, two tea-spoons of baking powder, one cup of sweet milk. Take the eggs, sugar and butter, and beat all together very light, then add the corn-meal, flour and milk.— *Mrs. Chas. E. Bross.*

JOHNNY CAKE.

One heaping tea-cupful of corn meal scalded to consistency of thin mush, a little salt, butter the size of a walnut, a small table-spoonful of sugar, four eggs, whites beaten separately, and stirred in the last thing.— *Mrs. N. B. Van Slyke.*

CORN BREAD.

Four table-spoons sugar, two table-spoons melted butter, four eggs, two cups of milk, two cups corn meal, one and one-half cups flour, four tea-spoons baking powder. Pinch of salt.— *Mrs. L. S. Ingman.*

CORN BREAD.

One-half pint of flour, one quart of corn meal, two eggs, lard size of an egg, two table-spoonfuls of molasses, two table-spoonfuls of baking powder, one bowl of milk, one tea-spoonful of salt.— *Mrs. R. J. McConnell.*

CORN MEAL MUFFINS.

One and one-half cups corn meal, same of white flour, one cup sugar, one-half cup shortening, two eggs, three tea-spoons baking powder. Add sweet milk to make not very stiff batter.— *Mrs. W. G. Pitman.*

CORN BREAD.

One pint sifted corn meal; one pint flour; one pint sour milk; two eggs beaten lightly; one-half cup sugar; piece of butter size of small egg. Add to beaten eggs the milk and meal alternately, then the butter and sugar; finally add tea-spoon of soda in sufficient milk to dissolve it. If sweet milk is used, add one tea-spoonful cream tartar. Bake twenty minutes in a hot oven.— *Mrs. E. Burdick.*

BREAKFAST GEMS.

One cup sweet milk; one and one-half cups flour; one egg; one tea-spoon salt; one tea-spoon baking powder; beaten together five minutes. Bake in hot gem pans in a hot oven fifteen minutes.— *Mrs. E. Burdick.*

GEMS.

One pint milk, two eggs, one table-spoon melted butter. Flour sufficient to make a good batter. One tea-spoonful of baking powder to each cup of flour. Bake quickly.— *Mrs. L. S. Ingman.*

BUCKWHEAT CAKES.

Take three slices of bread, and pour over them a pint of boiling water; then let it cool, and take a quart of cold water and make a batter with buckwheat flour; add the bread and a half cake of compressed yeast and a little salt; bake the next morning. After the first morning add a little soda and the same quantity of bread as before. Do the same every morning.— *Mrs. E. S. McBride.*

HYGIENIC GRIDDLE CAKES. (Substitute for Buckwheat.)

Three cups of purified middlings, one cup of Graham flour, one egg, one tea-spoonful saleratus, a pinch of salt; mix with sour milk. Use a hot griddle and serve immediately.— *Mrs. E. Burdick.*

POPOVERS.

Two cups of sweet milk, two eggs, two cups of sifted flour, one-half tea-spoon of salt; beat together very light and bake in gem pans in a quick oven.— *Miss Kittie Bird.*

HOME-MADE CRACKERS.

Three-fourths of a cup of butter or lard, one pint of sour milk, three tea-spoonfuls of baking powder. Stir all except the milk in with the flour, and when thoroughly mixed, put the milk in. Be careful not to knead them too much, as there is danger of their being tough. Roll thin and bake in a quick oven.— *Mrs. W. H. Hughes.*

FIVE HOUR BREAD.

One pint luke warm scalded milk, one and one-half spoon salt, one table-spoon butter, one tea-spoon sugar, one-half yeast cake; dissolve in one-fourth cup luke warm water; eight cups of flour. Bake about three-fourths hour.— *Mrs. Florence Bashford Spensley.*

CORN BREAD.

One pint cornmeal, one cup flour, one and one-half cups milk, one egg, two tea-spoons baking powder, one heaping table-spoon butter, one-half tea-spoon salt. Bake about one-half hour in a moderate oven.— *Miss Mary Louise Atwood.*

CORN BREAD.

One-half cup cornmeal, one and one-half cup flour, one cup sour milk, one-quarter cup sugar, two eggs beaten lightly, butter size of small egg, one tea-spoon of soda dissolved in a little milk. Bake twenty minutes in hot oven.— *Miss Kate A. Chittenden.*

FARINA BREAD.

Scald one-half cup milk; add one-half cup boiling water, and when luke warm three-quarters cake of compressed yeast softened in three table-spoons of luke warm water, half a table-spoon each of lard and butter, two table-spoons of molasses, 1 cup nut meats (English walnuts or pecans), one-half cup of white flour and entire wheat flour to knead. Finish and bake as ordinary bread.— *Mrs. Florence Bashford Spensley.*

FARINA CAKE.

Three-fourths cup farina, one-fourth cup brown grated bread, three-fourth cup chopped nuts, one cup sugar, one-half tea-spoon baking powder (heaping) six eggs; mix baking powder, farina, nuts and bread; mix yolks and sugar together aud then thoroughly into other mixture; last add well beaten whites of eggs; flavor with

vanilla and bake twenty minutes in moderate oven.—
Mrs. Florence Bashford Spensley.

POP OVERS.

Two cups flour, two cups sweet milk, three eggs, one-
half tea-spoon salt; grease pans and put in oven to get
hot; beat the eggs without separating them, very light;
add to them the milk and salt, then pour this gradually
on the flour, stirring all the time. Take pans from oven
and quickly fill them half full; put them in a quick oven
and bake twenty-five minutes.— *Miss Kate A. Chittenden.*

SOUR MILK PANCAKES.

Soak three slices of bread in sour milk over night;
next morning put this through colander, and to one
quart add a well beaten egg, one tea-spoon salt, one tea-
spoon soda, one table-spoon sugar; add flour enough to
make batter sufficiently stiff.— *Mrs. A. B. Morris.*

SOFT WAFFLES.

One quart sweet milk, one-half cup butter and lard
mixed, one tea-spoon sugar, one pint sifted flour, four
eggs.— *Mrs. A. B. Morris.*

BATH BUNNS.

One pint of milk scalded and cooled, one cup sugar,
one-half cup butter, three well beaten eggs, one tea-
spoon salt, two full cups flour, one cake compressed
yeast; set at night; in the morning add one-half nutmeg,
one cup currants, one tea-spoon grated lemon peel, two
pieces candied orange peel cut in small cubes, and flour
enough to make a moderately stiff dough; let it rise until

light; knead and roll out one-half an inch thick; cut out with a biscuit cutter; glaze the top with beaten egg, over which sift granulated sugar plentifully. Let them rise until light, and bake for twenty minutes in a moderately hot oven.— *Mrs. G. C. Comstock.*

RAISED COFFEE CAKE.

Two cups sponge, let raise over night; in the morning add one cup luke warm milk, three-quarter cup sugar, three-quarter cup shortening, two eggs, mix or beat well add flour to make stiffer: then spread cake in shallow pans about three-quarter inch thich, let raise almost double in height, spread over top melted butter, sprinkle sugar rather thickly over it and a trifle cinnamon, then chopped almonds over all. Bake about one-half hour.— *Mrs. H. Fauerbach.*

CLUB SANDWICHES.

Take slices of diamond shaped toast spread with butter, then cover with a crisp lettuce leaf, on this put a thin slice of the breast of the chicken, and then a thin slice of boiled ham or bacon, then another slice of bread. *Mrs. C. F. Spensley.*

PIES.

Philadelphia Butter Pie.

Cover a pie plate with crust as for a custard pie; take a piece of butter the size of an egg, two-thirds of a cup sugar, one cup sweet cream, one table-spoon of flour. Stir butter, flour and sugar together, then stir in the cream; pour in the plate. Bake till browned.—*Mrs. Clark Gapen.*

Cocoanut Pie.

Four eggs, the yolks used for pie, whites beaten to a froth after pie is baked; put on top and set in the oven till light brown. Three table-spoons of cocoanut, one of brandy or sherry, piece of butter size of a walnut, three table-spoons sugar, one pint milk — cream not taken off.— *Mrs. C. Hawley.*

Cocoanut Pie.

One scant pint of milk, heat until hot; beat three eggs very light (taking out the whites of two for top), sugar to taste, butter half the size of an egg, a pinch of salt, and a cup and a half of grated cocoanut. Put the cocoanut in the hot milk, then egg, etc. Beat the whites to a stiff foam, put on top, and brown slightly in the oven.— *Mrs. J. H. Palmer.*

Cocoanut Pie.

One cocoanut, grated, four eggs, two and one-half cups of sugar, two-thirds of a cup of butter, milk enough for two pies; stir butter and sugar to a cream, beat the eggs, and add the rest of the ingredients.— *Mrs. D. S. Comly.*

CREAM PIE.

Two pints of cream, two cups of sugar, and one egg, with four tea-spoons of flour; flavor with lemon and bake slowly. This quantity makes two pies; no top crust required. FROSTING: Whites of two eggs, and three-fourths of a cup of sugar; when pies are done, spread on the frosting and brown for a few minutes in the fire — *Mrs. E. Burdick.*

LEMON PIE.

One lemon (if small, one and a half lemons), one cup water, one cup sugar, two table-spoons of flour, five eggs (reserving whites of three for frosting); grate rind of lemon and express juice. Add all together, mixing thoroughly, and bake without top crust. FROSTING: Whites of three eggs, beaten to a stiff froth, and three table-spoons of white sugar. When pies are done, spread frosting over them, and brown slightly in oven. This makes one good-sized pie.— *Mrs. E. Burdick.*

LEMON PIE.

A nice paste, one cup sugar, one cup water, one table-spoon corn starch, two eggs, juice of two lemons, one cup of minced raisins; cover with a meringue.— *Mrs. I. C. Sloan.*

LEMON PIE.

One large lemon, juice and grated rind, one cup of sugar, five eggs, beaten separately. Stir carefully together; bake the crusts and then put in the filling; put back into the oven and bake slightly.— *Mrs. J. B. Bowen.*

LEMON CREAM PIE.

One cup sugar, one table-spoon of butter, yolks of four eggs, juice and grated rind of a lemon, one heaping table-spoon of corn starch, dissolved in a little cold water, stirred into a cup and a half of boiling water. Stir butter, sugar and eggs to a cream, then stir in gradually the hot corn starch. When cool add the lemon and bake in open shell. Make a meringue of the whites of the eggs and a cup of sugar, and put on the tops of the pies. This is enough for two pies.— *Miss Lois Robbins.*

MINCE MEAT FOR PIES.

Four pounds meat, ten pounds apples, two pounds currants, one ounce cloves, six pounds sugar, one pound suet, four pounds raisins, one-fourth pound allspice, one pint brandy, one quart cider, one pound citron.— *Mrs. Wm. F. Vilas.*

MARLBOROUGH PIE.

One tea-cup of dry grated or stewed apple, one tea-cup of milk, a lump of butter, sweeten to taste, yolks of two eggs; save the whites for frosting. Bake without upper crust. Beat the whites of the eggs, spread over the top, and set in the oven to brown. Flavor with brandy or lemon.— *Mrs. J. L. Whitcomb, Battle Creek, Mich.*

ORANGE PIE.

Juice and grated rind of one orange, one cup of milk or water, one cup of sugar, yolks of two eggs, one table-spoon corn starch; beat together, and bake like custard pie. Beat whites of two eggs to stiff froth; add four tea-spoons of sifted sugar to each egg, spread over pie after baking. Put back in oven, and let it get a light brown.— *Mrs. L. S. Ingman.*

PUMPKIN PIE.

Three pounds of pumpkin, add in bulk one-third apples, four eggs, half a pound of butter, two pounds sugar, two tea-spoons vanilla, one nutmeg, one wine-glass brandy. Beat the butter and sugar until light, then add the eggs, which must be beaten light first, then the flavoring; lastly add the pumpkin and apple, which must be previously rubbed through a colander. Bake in crusts.— *Mrs. Wm. F. Vilas.*

FINE PUFF PASTE.

One pound of flour, one and one-half pounds of butter, one-half pound of lard; cut the butter and lard through the flour, in small thin shells, and mix with sufficient ice water to roll easy. Touch with the hands as little as possible; put a little butter and lard on top and roll again; put in pie plates and bake as quickly as possible.— *Miss Lizzie Taylor.*

ORANGE PIE.

One cup of butter, two cups of sugar, stirred to a cream, four eggs beaten separately; add the juice of four oranges, the pulp and grated rind of three, one cup of milk, one table-spoon of flour.— *Mrs. D. S. Comly.*

WASHINGTON PIE.

One pound stale sponge cake, one pint milk, one-half pound currants, quarter of a pound butter, six eggs, cinnamon and brandy. Sweeten to taste. Bake.—*Mrs. Wm. F. Vilas.*

SQUASH PIE.

Three tables-poons of squash, one egg, half a cup of sugar, two table-spoons of syrup, one pint of milk, a little nutmeg.—*Mrs. C. M. Macomber.*

PIE CRUST.

For one pie. A cup of flour, two table-spoons of lard, a half tea-spoon salt, and three table-spoons of water. To make rub flour, salt, and lard together add water and roll. This crust is improved by making a day before it is to be baked and kept on ice until needed.— *Mrs. P. Frawley.*

BANANA PIE.

One cup of sifted banana pulp, one-half cup of sugar, one cracker powered fine, one-half cup of milk, one-half tea-spoon of salt, one-third tea-spoon of cinnamon, one egg, one-third cup of cream. Grated rind and juice of one-half lemon or two table-spoons of molasses. Mix the ingredients together and bake until firm in a pie-pan lined with pastry, as for a squash pie. The cracker may be omitted unless a rather firm pie be preferred.— *F. V. Pierce & Co.*

CHOCOLATE PIE.

Mix two table-spoons corn starch, one-half cup sugar, one-eighth tea-spoon salt, three heaped table-spoons chocolate. In a double boiler scald one cup milk and one-third cup cream; into this stir the chocolate mixture; cook until thick and smooth, then add the well beaten yolks of two eggs; cook one minute, stirring constantly. Let cool and turn into a baked puff paste crust; cover with a meringue made of two egg whites beaten stiff, and two table-spoons powdered sugar, one-half tea-spoon vanilla. *Mrs. Frances Clark Wood.*

CREAM PIE.

One pint of cream, one cup sugar, one table-spoon corn starch, two table-spoons flour, vanilla and salt, whites of three or four eggs.— *Mrs. R. M. Bashford.*

GREEN TOMATO PIE.

Three cups chopped apples, pint green tomatoes chopped, two cups sugar, two table-spoons flour, one-half cup vinegar or pickled peach syrup, one-half tea-spoon salt, one-half cup currants, one-half cup raisins, one-quarter pound citron, one-half tea-spoon each of cloves, cinnamon and allspice. This makes two pies and is very like mince.— *Mrs. Frances Clark Wood.*

LEMON PIE.

One cup sugar, one *full* tea-spoon corn starch, one *full* tea-spoon flour, butter size of hickory nut, one lemon grated rind and juice, a pinch of salt, two yolks of eggs. Stir all together; add one cup boiling water. Cook in double boiler until thick; bake lower crust; add filling and beaten whites of two eggs, with a *little* sugar and return to oven to brown lightly.— *Miss Kate A. Chittenden.*

MINCE MEAT.

Two pounds currants, two pounds raisins, two pieces citron peel, two pieces lemon peel, two pieces orange peel, one cup vinegar, one cup molasses, five cups white sugar, three table-spoons ground cloves, three table-spoons cinnamon, two allspice, two cups finely chopped suet, two tumblers jelly, one pound figs chopped fine, two pounds blanched almonds cut in two pieces, three and a half quarts sweet cider, twice as much apple as other ingredients, chopped very fine. Everything is thoroughly chopped except one pound raisins extra, that are seeded. After it begins to boil let boil thirty-five minutes, stirring all the time. When cold add two cups good brandy, thoroughly stirred in.— *Mrs. A. B. Morris.*

MINCE MEAT.

Six pounds beef and six pounds apples, chopped, four pounds sugar, two pounds citron, three pounds raisins, three pounds currants, one pound suet, chopped, two quarts boiled cider, one-half cup salt, two nutmegs, two table-spoons ground cloves, two table-spoons ground allspice, two table-spoons ground cinnamon. When used enough sweet cider should be used to make the mixture moist.— *Mrs. John Corscot.*

MOCK CHERRY PIE.

One coffee cup heaping full of cranberries cut in halves, one-half cup seedless raisins cut in small pieces; mix with raisins one cup sugar, one-quarter tea-spoon salt, one heaping table-spoon flour; add cranberries and two-thirds cup cold water, one tea-spoon vanilla. Bake in two crusts.— *Mrs. Frances Clark Wood.*

6

PUDDINGS.

APPLE PUDDING OR PIE.

Six eggs; add enough sugar to yolks to make quite thick, when beaten together; one quarter of a pound of butter, one and one-half cups of strained apples, one-half a nutmeg. Cook apples till soft; strain; add yolks, sugar, butter, and nutmeg, and lastly the beaten whites; bake in deep pie plate, with an undercrust. This will make two pies, and is to be eaten cold. Very nice.— *Mrs. Darwin Clark.*

BREAD PUDDING.

Soak one-half pint of bread crumbs in the same of milk for one hour. Squeeze with the hands, and mix with three table-spoons of sugar, four ounces of raisins, four ounces melted butter, yolks of four eggs, one ounce of citron. Beat the whites to a stiff froth, and stir in the last thing. Bake in a buttered mold forty minutes.— *Mrs. D. S. Comly.*

BATTER PUDDING.

Two eggs, one table-spoon of sugar, beaten together; one cup of milk, two cups of flour, one table-spoon melted butter; half a tea-spoon of soda; one tea-spoon of cream tartar; steam one hour and a quarter; serve with hot sauce or cream. Do not touch or jar while steaming.— *Miss Lizzie Taylor.*

BETSEY'S PUDDING.

One-half cup butter, one-half cup sugar, one-half cup molasses, three eggs, one cup milk, three tea-spoons baking powder, three cups flour, two pounds raisins, all kinds spices. Steam an hour, and keep till served. SAUCE: Butter size of an egg, two eggs, leaving the whites till after; one-half cup sugar. Stir all to a cream, then pour in two or three cups of hot water and stir briskly till all stirred up. Then beat the whites and stir in. Use brandy and lemon to flavor.— *Mrs. Wm. F. Vilas.*

BAKED BERRY ROLLS.

Roll biscuit dough thin, in the form of a large square or small squares. Spread over with berries. Roll the crust, and put the rolls into a dripping pan close together till full; then put into the pan, water, sugar and pieces of butter. Bake them. Serve any pudding sauce.— *Mrs. C. Hawley.*

CORN STARCH PUDDING.

One pint milk, two table-spoons corn starch, a scant half cupful sugar, whites of three or four eggs, salt, flavoring. Beat the eggs to froth. Dissolve the corn starch in a little of the milk. Stir the sugar into remainder of milk; place on the fire. When boiling add the dissolved corn starch. Stir constantly for a few moments. When it becomes a smooth paste stir in the whites, and let it remain a little longer to cook the eggs. Flavor with vanilla, put in a form, make a custard and pour over it.— *Miss Emma Hawley.*

CREAM PUFFS.

One pint water, half pound of butter, three-fourths pound flour. Boil butter and water together and stir in flour while boiling. Take it off to cool, and add ten eggs by breaking them in one at a time; be sure not to beat them. Add a tea-spoon of saleratus dissolved in a tea-spoon of water, just before baking. Drop on buttered tins, forming them the size of a cream cake, and bake in a quick oven twenty or twenty-five minutes. When cool, lift the edge and fill with the following mixture: One cup flour, two cups sugar, four eggs, one quart milk; boil milk; beat butter, sugar, flour and eggs together, and stir into the milk; let it thicken, and flavor with lemon.— *Mrs. L. B. Vilas.*

CORN STARCH PATTIES.

Three-fourths of a cup of butter, one cup of sugar stirred to a cream, four eggs (beaten separately), one cup of corn starch, one-half cup of flour, one heaping tea-spoon of baking powder; flavor; add the whites of the eggs last of all. A little water.— *Miss Lizzie Taylor.*

CHOCOLATE PUDDING.

One quart of milk, four table-spoons corn starch, one-half cup Baker's chocolate. Flavor with vanilla. Sweeten to taste; a little salt. Boiled; to be eaten with sugar and cream.— *Mrs. Fanny Smith.*

CREAM MANIOCA PUDDING.

Soak three table-spoons of manioca in water for about two hours, then put it into a quart of boiling milk; boil a half hour. Beat the yolks of four eggs with a cup of sugar; add three table-spoons of prepared cocoanut; stir in and boil ten minutes longer; pour into a pudding dish. Beat the whites of the eggs to a stiff froth; stir in three table-spoons sugar; put over the top; sprinkle cocoanut over the top and brown in the oven.— *Mrs. Clark Gapen.*

A SIMPLE, DELICATE PUDDING.

Heat one quart of milk nearly to boiling; beat together the yolks of four eggs, three table-spoons of sugar, three of corn starch, a little salt, and stir into the milk; when it thickens, remove from the stove and flavor with vanilla; pour into a dish suitable for the table. Beat the whites to a stiff froth; add four table-spoons sugar, a little vanilla; put on the top of the pudding and set it in the oven to brown.— *Mrs. L. B. Vilas.*

ESTELLE PUDDING.

Three eggs well beaten, two and one-half table-spoons sugar, two of butter, three-fourths cup of sweet milk, one table-spoon baking powder. Flour to make of the consistency of pound cake. Then take a cup of fresh berries of any kind, mix with a little sugar and stir in carefully. Steam forty-five minutes. Sauce: Three fourths cup sugar, one-fourth cup butter, one table-spoon flour and enough berries to season. Stir and pour on boiling water, and boil till the berries are done.— *Miss Bertha Schaal.*

FRENCH PUFF PUDDING.

One pint milk, four table-spoons flour, four eggs beaten separately, pinch of salt, the whites to be added the last thing before baking. Bake half an hour, and serve with wine sauce.—*Mrs. C. Hawley.*

FIG PUDDING.

One-half pound of figs, one-half cup of suet, one-half pound bread crumbs, one table-spoon of sugar, three eggs, one cup of milk. Chop the suet and figs fine, add cinnamon, nutmeg and wine to taste. Make an ordinary sauce without wine.— *Mrs. J. H. Palmer.*

FRUIT PUDDING.

One and one-half cups of milk, one-half cup of molasses, two eggs, three table-spoons melted butter, three cups of flour, one cup chopped raisins, one tea-spoon soda, a little salt. Steam two hours, and eat with a sweet sauce.— *Mrs. W. H. Hughes.*

GELATINE PUDDING.

Half box of gelatine dissolved in half a pint of water, stir in two tea-cups of sugar, juice of three lemons, whites of four eggs beaten to a stiff froth. Put in a mold to grow stiff. With the yolks, one quart of milk, a table-spoon of corn starch, make a boiled custard; flavor with vanilla, and pour over the pudding when cold.— *Mrs. H. K. Edgerton, Oconomowoc.*

GIPSY PUDDING.

Cut a stale sponge cake into thin slices, spread with currant jelly or preserves, put two pieces together like sandwiches, and lay in a dish. Make a soft custard, pour over while it is hot, and let cool before serving.— *Mrs. Clark Gapen.*

GRAHAM PUDDING.

One cup of sour milk, one-half cup of chopped suet, one-half cup of brown sugar, one-half cup of raisins, one-half tea-spoon of salt, one tea-spoon of soda, one egg, two cups of Graham flour. Steam two hours.— *Mrs. James Burgess.*

JENNY LIND PUDDING.

One pint of milk, one pint of blueberries, four eggs and a little salt. Bread crumbs enough to make a stiff batter; butter the size of an egg. Steam three-quarters of an hour.— *Mrs. James Robbins.*

JELLY PUDDING.

One quart of milk, one pint of bread crumbs, one-half cup of sugar, yolks of four eggs; bake about half an hour. When cool spread jelly over the pudding, and beat the whites of four eggs with a little sugar and spread over the top, and set back in the oven to brown. To be eaten with cream.— *Mrs. Edward P. Vilas.*

LIVERPOOL PUDDING.

One pint of milk thickened with two table-spoons of flour, two ounces of butter, one-fourth of a pound of sugar, three eggs well beaten, the juice and grated rind of one lemon. Line a dish with pastry, pour in the mixture, and bake slowly three-quarters of an hour.— *Miss Robbins.*

LEMON PUDDING.

One cup of sugar, four eggs, two table-spoonfuls of corn starch, two lemons, juice of both and rind of one, one pint of milk, one table-spoonful of butter. Heat the milk to boiling, stir in corn starch wet with a few spoonfuls of water, boil five minutes, stirring constantly; while hot mix in the butter and set away to cool. Beat the yolks light, add the sugar, and mix very thoroughly before putting in the lemon juice and grated rind; beat this to a stiff cream, and add gradually to the corn starch and milk when the latter is cold; stir all smooth, put in a buttered dish and bake. Eat cold.— *Mrs. W. H. Hughes.*

ORANGE PUDDING.

Peel, slice and seed five oranges; put in a dish; pour over them a coffee-cup of sugar; boil a pint and a half of milk, two table-spoons corn starch mixed in cold milk, yolks of three eggs, and a little sugar; pour the custard boiling hot over the oranges; make a meringue (one table-spoon of sugar to an egg); put over the top and brown; eat cold. The same can be made of peaches or strawberries.— *Mrs. H. K. Edgerton, Oconomowoc.*

ORANGE PUDDING.

Line the bottom of a pudding dish with stale sponge cake; slice upon the cake six oranges; make a custard of one quart of milk and five eggs (leaving out the whites of four), one small cup of sugar; pour the custard over the oranges; beat the whites to a stiff froth, and cover pudding, putting in the oven till slightly browned.— *Mrs. J. H. Palmer.*

POOR MAN'S PUDDING.

Four table-spoons rice to one quart milk; cooked on the stove in a little water, then sweetened and spiced; butter half the size of an egg, and bake.— *Mrs. J. N. Jones.*

PLUM PUDDING.

One pound of currants, one pound of raisins stoned and chopped a little, one pound of sugar, one pound of suet chopped very fine, one-half pound of flour, one-half pound of bread crumbs, one-fourth pound of candied lemon, one lemon, twelve eggs, one tea-spoon mixed spices, a little salt, and a little brandy; boil from four to five hours, and serve when done with brandy sauce.— *Mrs. Bromley.*

PLUM PUDDING.

Take half a pound of grated bread crumbs (must be fine) and half a pound of flour, mix them well together; one pound of suet, chopped fine, one pound of raisins, one pound of currants, the yolks of eight eggs and whites of four, well beaten, one-half pound brown sugar, one-half a nutmeg, one tea-spoon ginger, two ounces sweet almonds, cut fine, quarter of a pound of candied citron, same of candied lemon, quarter ounce of mixed spice, the grated rind of one lemon, a little salt, one wine-glass full of wine, one wine-glass of brandy. Mix all together, adding a little milk, remembering that when mixed it must be thick. Steam five hours. Serve with wine sauce.— *Mrs. J. H. Palmer.*

PLUM PUDDING.

Two pounds of currants, two pounds of raisins, two pounds of sugar, two pounds of suet, two pounds of crumbs, sixteen eggs, two nutmegs, one pound of candied citron cut into thin strips, a very little milk, three-fourths of a cup of flour, wine-glass of best brandy. Add the eggs, milk and brandy when you are going to put the pudding to boil. Have a cloth that will not let the water soak, and butter very thoroughly. Place a plate on the bottom of the kettle. The water must be boiling and kept so. Boil six hours.— *Mrs. J. D. Gurnee.*

PLUM PUDDING.

One cup of suet, one cup of molasses, two eggs, one cup of raisins, two cups of milk, one tea-spoon of soda, salt and spices to taste, flour to make thick enough to drop from the spoon. Steam three hours. SAUCE: Five eggs beaten separately, one-half pound of sugar, one-half cup of wine, butter size of an egg, one-half cup of water. Heat wine, water and butter, adding nutmeg, yolks and sugar beaten together, and whites, just before stirring the whole into the wine, etc. Serve immediately.— *Mrs. L. Fairchild.*

PLUM PUDDING.

One cup of molasses, one cup of chopped suet, one cup of milk, three cups of flour, one cup of stoned raisins, add currants and citron, one tea-spoonful of soda, same of cinnamon, cloves and nutmeg. WINE SAUCE: One cup of butter stirred to a cream, two cups of sugar, one cup of wine, added slowly; set the bowl in a kettle of hot water three-quarters of an hour before using. It must not be stirred nor poured out of the bowl.— *Mrs. L. F. Kellogg.*

THE QUEEN OF PUDDINGS.

One and one-half cups of white sugar, two cups of fine, dry bread crumbs, five eggs, one table-spoonful of butter, one quart of fresh, rich milk, one-half of a cup of jelly or jam, vanilla, rose, or lemon seasoning. Rub the butter into a cup of sugar, beat the yolks very light, and stir these together to a cream. The bread crumbs soaked in milk come next, then the seasoning. Bake this in a buttered pudding dish — a large one, and but two-thirds full — until the custard is set; draw to the mouth of the oven, and spread over with jam or other nice fruit conserve; cover this with a meringue made of the whipped whites and half a cup of sugar; shut the oven until the meringue begins to color. Eat cold with cream. You may in strawberry season substitute the fresh fruit for the preserves. It is then truly delightful.— *Mrs. W. H. Hughes.*

RAISIN PUFFS.

Two eggs, half cup butter, three tea-spoons baking powder, three cups flour, two table-spoons sugar, one cup milk, one cup raisins seeded and chopped fine; steam in small cups thirty or thirty-five minutes; if left in too long they become heavy. Eaten with wine sauce.— *Mrs. L. B. Vilas.*

SAGO PUDDING.

Six apples, six table-spoons of sago, one cup of sugar, one quart of water. Bake two hours.— *Mrs. S. H. Carpenter.*

SOUR CREAM PUDDING.

One pint of sour cream, thoroughly whipped, one-half tea-spoonful of soda in the cream, six eggs, four table-spoonfuls of flour; bake an hour. Serve cold with wine sauce.— *Mrs. N. B. Van Slyke.*

SUET PUDDING.

One tea-cup of suet, chopped fine, one tea-cup of molasses, one tea-cup of sweet milk, three cups of flour,
one tea-cup of fruit, one tea-spoon of soda. Steam two
hours. WINE SAUCE: One cup of sugar, one-half cup
of butter, one-half cup of wine, one egg; beat butter,
sugar and egg together; set it on the stove and heat,
pour in the wine, add a little nutmeg. Pour from one
dish to another.— *Mrs. Edward P. Vilas.*

SUET PUDDING.

One cup of suet, one cup of raisins, one cup of molasses, one cup of sour milk, one tea-spoon of soda, flour
enough to make a stiff batter; boil or steam two hours;
serve with brandy sauce.— *Mrs. C. M. Macomber.*

SWEDISH PUDDING.

One-half pound flour, same of butter and of sugar,
eight eggs, a little salt. Rub sugar and butter to a
cream; add yolks well beaten, the salt, flour, and lastly
the whites, beaten to a froth. Put the batter three-
fourths of an inch deep in tea-cups; steam half an hour;
the batter will fill the cups. Turn out on a hot platter;
serve with strawberry sauce. Half the amount for a
small family. STRAWBERRY SAUCE: Half cup butter,
one cup sugar, the beaten white of an egg, one cup
strawberries, mashed. Rub butter and sugar to a cream,
add the beaten white of the egg, and the strawberries,
thoroughly mashed.— *Mrs. C. Hawley.*

TAPIOCA PUDDING.

Soak one tea-cupful of tapioca in one pint of cold
water, one hour; add the yolks of three well beaten

eggs, one cup sugar, small piece of melted butter, three pints of milk and a little nutmeg. Bake, and when done frost with the whites of the three eggs, and four table-spoonfuls of sugar; flavor with lemon.— *Mrs. W. G. Pitman.*

TAPIOCA PUDDING.

One cup tapioca, three pints water, one-half cup sugar, one small tumbler jelly. Soak tapioca over night; cook in double boiler one hour. Add sugar and jelly, mix well, and pour in mold. Serve with sugar and cream.— *Mrs. John Bascom.*

TROY PUDDING.

Two and one-half cups of flour, one-half cup of corn meal, one cup of beef suet chopped, one cup of sweet milk, one cup of molasses, one cup of currants rubbed in flour, one even tea-spoon of soda dissolved in the milk, a little salt. Steam two hours.— *Mrs. Edmund E. Thompson.*

WHEELER PUDDING.

Two cups of flour, one cup of sweet milk, one-half cup of molasses, one-half cup of butter, one cup of stoned raisins, one egg, one tea-spoon of soda. Steam two hours. To be eaten with liquid sauce.— *Miss Kate A. Chittenden.*

PUFF PASTE.

One pound butter, one pound flour. Mix the flour into a paste with *cold* water; roll it out and place four ounces of the butter over it in small pieces; fold it in a square, roll it out again, and so on until all the butter is used. Set it in the refrigerator for one hour. Bake puff balls always in a *hot* oven.— *Mrs. R. M. Bashford.*

CHRISTMAS PLUM PUDDING.

One and one-half pounds of raisins, one-half pound of currants, one-half pound of mixed fruit peels, three-fourths pound bread crumbs, three-fourths pound beef suet, eight eggs, one wine glass of brandy. Mix the dry ingredients well together, then add eggs and brandy. Press into a buttered mold and steam six hours. Make some days before needed, and steam for two hours on the day used. Serve with wine sauce.— *Mrs. Charles D. Atwood.*

ENGLISH PLUM PUDDING.

Six eggs, two cups sugar, three cups suet, three cups currants, three cups raisins, chopped, one cup sweet milk, half cup brandy or whiskey or extra half cup sweet milk, one tea-spoon cinnamon, one tea-spoon essence cloves, one nutmeg, two cups mixed peel; stir as stiff as fruit cake. Boil four hours if in two puddings, if in one pudding boil six hours.— *Mrs. A. B. Morris.*

FRENCH PASTRY.

One tea-spoon butter, two white sugar, three tea-spoons flour, four eggs beaten separately, one-half tea-spoon of soda, dissolved in half tea-cup of sour cream; bake in jelly cake pans; put a layer of cake on a pie plate and spread strawberry preserves upon it, then a layer of meringue; set in the oven till a light brown, continuing in the same way with three or four layers, finishing with preserves and meringue on top. Serve with sauce of butter, sugar and whites of eggs. For the meringue beat the whites of six (6) eggs to a stiff froth, and sugar until almost as thick as frosting.— *Mrs. R. M. Bashford.*

GRAHAM PUDDING.

One cup graham flour, one-half cup sour milk, one-half cup molasses, one-half cup fruit, one egg, one-half tea-spoon soda, a little salt, spices to taste. Steam one and one-half hour; liquid sauce.— *Miss Kate A. Chittenden.*

PINEAPPLE SAGO PUDDING.

Soak one-half cup sago in one cup water over night; cook sago in three cups water till clear; add one-half tea-spoon salt, and one cup sugar; let cook and add the well beaten whites of three eggs; stir well, then add one-half can grated pineapple. Serve with cream.— *Mrs. Frances Clark Wood.*

RUM PUDDING.

Bake a medium sized sponge cake in a round pan. Several hours later, or the next day, remove the center of the cake, leaving sides and bottom about an inch thick. Beat together the yolks of two eggs; two table-spoons of sugar and a dash of salt; add one-half cup of scalded milk, and cook in a double boiler, stirring constantly until as thick as boiled custard. Take from the fire, add one level table-spoon of granulated gelatine which has been soaked in one-quarter of a cup of cold water, and stir until dissolved; strain, and when cold add one tea-spoon of vanilla and three table-spoons of rum. When the mixture is quite thick mix in lightly one and one-half cups of cream whipped to a stiff froth; pour into the prepared sponge cake, garnish with angelica and chopped candied fruits, and set in a cool place for two or three hours to stiffen.— *Miss Mary Louise Atwood.*

Sago Pudding.

One-half cup sago, three cups water; cook until clear, then cool; add a pinch of salt, one cup sugar, beaten whites of two eggs, one-half can pineapple.— *Mrs. C. F. Lamb.*

Sponge Pudding.

Six eggs, two ounces of flour, two ounces of sugar, one pint of milk, piece of butter size of an egg. Cook the sugar, flour and milk together until it thickens, then pour in the melted butter; stir into this the yolks of the eggs beaten very light; lastly, gently mix in the beaten whites. Have an earthen pudding dish buttered and placed in a pan of hot water and bake half an hour. Do not let it stand after pouring into dish nor after pudding is baked. Serve with wine sauce.— *Mrs. Frank G. Brown.*

7

CAKES.

ANGEL CAKE.

Whites of twelve eggs, one and one-half tumblers of sifted granulated sugar, one tumbler of sifted flour, one tea-spoon of vanilla, one level tea-spoon cream tartar. Sift the flour seven times and add the cream tartar. Beat the eggs to a stiff froth in a mixing bowl, then while beating add the sugar very lightly, then the flour very gently, and lastly the vanilla. Do not stop beating until ready to pour into the pan. Bake forty minutes in a moderate oven. When done turn the pan upside down till the cake is cold. Use a pan that has never been greased. Be sure the tumbler holds two and one-fourth gills.— *Mrs. David Atwood.*

ALMOND CAKE.

Six eggs, two cups of sugar, one small cup of butter, two large cups of flour. Mix butter and sugar to a cream and beat eggs separately, one-half tea-spoon baking powder. Spread in tins one inch deep; lay the split almonds on the top, brown side up. As soon as taken out of the oven sift pulverized sugar over it.— *Mrs. L. S. Ingman.*

ALMOND CAKE.

Two cups of sugar, one cup of butter, one cup of milk, three and one-half cups of flour, five eggs, three

tea-spoons of baking powder; bake in jelly pans; spread
with a custard of one cup of cream, four eggs, one-half
pound of almonds blanched and pounded to a paste; ice
on top.— *Mrs. E. Perry.*

APPLE CAKE.

The cake made in two layers and put together with a
preparation like the following: Grate three large apples, the grated rind and juice of one lemon, one cup of
sugar. Stir together and cook ten minutes.— *Mrs. J.
W. Vance.*

BOSTON OR BROWN CAKE.

One pound of butter, one pound of sugar, one pound
of flour, six eggs, one quart of milk, a teaspoonful each
of soda, cinnamon, cloves and nutmeg, and a wine-
glass of brandy.— *Mrs. N. B. Van Slyke.*

BREAD CAKE.

On baking day take from your dough after its second rising two cups of risen dough; have ready also
two cups of white sugar, one cup of butter creamed
with the sugar, three eggs, yolks and whites separate,
one tea-spoonful of soda dissolved in hot water, two
table-spoonfuls of sweet milk (cream is better), one-half a
pound of currants well washed and dredged, one teaspoonful of nutmeg, one tea-spoonful of cloves. Beat
the yolks of the eggs very light, add the creamed butter
and sugar, the spices, milk, soda and dough; stir until
all are well mixed, put in the whites (well beaten), and
lastly the fruit. Beat hard five minutes, let it rise
twenty minutes in two well buttered pans, and bake half
an hour, or until done.— *Mrs. W. H. Hughes.*

CARDAMON CAKES.

One pound of good brown sugar, one pound of flour, three ounces of butter, three eggs, two table-spoonfuls of cinnamon, one of ginger. Put all the ingredients in a dish before mixing them, beat the eggs separately, knead up and roll very thin; cut them in squares the size of a soda cracker, put blanched almonds, halved, on each corner; bake quickly.— *R. L. Garlick.*

CHOCOLATE CAKE.

Two cups of sugar, two-thirds of a cup of butter, three eggs, one cup of sweet milk, three cups of flour, one and one-half tea-spoons of baking powder, add a little salt and flavoring. Put one-half of the above into two jelly tins, and bake. To the other half add a cup of grated Baker's chocolate, one-half tea-spoon of cloves, one tea-spoon of cinnamon, one-half tea-spoon of allspice, and bake in two jelly tins. Put the dark and light layers together alternately with jelly or frosting.— *Mrs. Edward P. Vilas.*

CARAMEL CAKE.

One and one-half cups of sugar, three-fourths of a cup of butter, one-half cup of milk, two and one-fourth cups of flour, three eggs, one and one-half heaping tea-spoons baking powder. CARAMEL: Butter the size of an egg, one pint of sugar, one-half cup of milk or water, one-half cake of chocolate. Boil twenty minutes without stirring, and pour over the cake.—*Mrs. L. F. Kellogg.*

CHOCOLATE CAKE.

One cup sugar, one-half cup butter, one-half cup sour milk, one and one-half cups flour, one-half tea-spoon soda, whites of three eggs; salt to taste; season with lemon extract. DARK PART: One cup sugar, one-half cup butter, one-half cup sour milk, one and one-half of flour, one-half tea-spoon soda, yolks of three eggs, one-half cake chocolate. PASTE FOR FILLING: One pint milk, yolks of two eggs, and enough corn starch to thicken; season with vanilla, and a little salt.— *Mrs. A. B. Braley.*

CHILD'S FEATHER CAKE.

Three cups of light dough, two cups rolled sugar, three well beaten eggs, mixed with the sugar and butter; one-half cup of warm milk, or a little less; one tea-spoonful of soda in two great-spoonfuls of water, and put in the milk; one cup of melted butter worked into the sugar; the grated rind and juice of one lemon; work all together, adding the lemon juice just before putting it in buttered pans. If you have no lemons, use one nutmeg and a table-spoon of sharp vinegar, added just before putting it in pans; one and one-half spoonfuls, if the vinegar is weak. Some think this improved by standing to rise fifteen minutes.— *Mrs. James Burgess.*

CLOVE CAKE.

One cup butter, two and one-half cups sugar, one cup milk, one quart flour, four eggs, one tea-spoon soda, two of cream tartar, cinnamon and cloves to taste, one pound raisins, stoned and chopped.— *Mrs. John N. Jones.*

COFFEE CAKE.

One cup of butter, one and one-half cups of brown sugar, one cup of molasses, one cup of strong coffee, four cups of flour, two eggs, one-half tea-spoon of ground cloves, one nutmeg, two tea-spoons of baking powder, one pound of fruit, raisins and currants.— *Miss Robbins*.

CONNECTICUT ELECTION CAKE.

Three cups milk, one of yeast, two of sugar, five of flour. Stir together, and put in a warm place to rise over night. Next morning add two cups sugar, and two cups butter, two nutmegs, and one pound raisins. Put in round tins, and raise until light. Bake in a slow oven. Much improved by icing.— *Mrs. James E. Moseley*.

COCOANUT CAKE.

Three eggs, two cups of sugar, one cup of sweet milk, two table-spoons of melted butter, two and one-half cups of flour, one tea-spoon of soda, two of cream tartar Flavor with lemon, bake like jelly cake. PREPARATION: One grated cocoanut, two eggs, juice and grated rind of one lemon, one-half cup of sugar. Mix the preparation, heat it through and spread on each layer. *Mrs. L. S. Ingman*.

CREAM CAKE.

One cup sugar, butter size of an egg, two cups flour, one cup milk, two tea-spoons of baking powder, and last the whites of three eggs. Bake in layers. CREAM: One cup sweet cream, beaten, sweetened, flavored and put between the cake.— *Mrs. W. M. Foresman*.

CREAM CAKE.

Two cups of powdered sugar, two-thirds of a cup of butter, four eggs, one-half of a cup of milk, one-half tea-spoonful of soda, one tea-spoonful of cream tartar, three cups of flour. Bake in thin layers as for jelly cake, and spread between them, when cold, the following mixture: One-half pint of milk, two small tea-spoonfuls of corn starch, one egg, one tea-spoonful of vanilla, one-half of a cup of sugar. Heat the milk to boiling and stir in the corn starch wet with a little milk; take out a little, and mix gradually with the beaten egg and sugar; return to the rest of the custard, and boil, stirring constantly until quite thick; let it cool before you season and spread on the cake. Season the icing also with vanilla.— *Mrs. W. H. Hughes.*

Cup Cake.

One cup of butter, two cups of sugar, one cup of milk, four cups of flour, four eggs, two tea-spoons baking powder.— *Miss Robbins.*

Dover Cake.

One pound of flour, one pound of white sugar, one-half pound of butter rubbed with the sugar to a very light cream, six eggs, one cup of sweet milk, one tea-spoon of soda dissolved in vinegar, one tea-spoon powdered cinnamon, one table-spoon of rose-water. Flavor the frosting with lemon juice.— *Mrs. W. H. Hughes.*

Delicate Cake.

One and one-half cups of sugar, one-half cup of butter, whites of four eggs, three-fourths of a cup of sweet milk, two cups of flour, one tea-spoon of baking powder. Flavor with bitter almonds.

DELICATE CAKE.

One pound of sugar, one pound of flour, three-quarters of a pound of butter, whites of sixteen eggs. Flavor to taste.— *Mrs. James R. Mears.*

FRENCH CAKE.

Three and one-half cups of flour and two cups of sugar, one cup of milk, one and one-half cups of butter, four eggs, one tea-spoon of soda, two tea-spoons cream tartar.— *Mrs. J. W. Vance.*

FRUIT CAKE.

One and one-half pounds of flour, one and one-half pounds of granulated sugar, one and one-half pounds of butter, two pounds of citron, sliced, soaked in one-half pint liquor over night; four and one-half pounds currants, rolled in flour, two pounds raisins, stoned and chopped, fifteen eggs, beaten separately, one cup of syrup, two pounds of figs cut fine, one and one-half tea-spoons of soda, one table-spoon each of allspice, cloves, cinnamon, nutmeg.— *Mrs. Abijah Abbott.*

PLAIN FRUIT CAKE.

Four cups flour, one cup molasses, one cup sugar, two cups seeded raisins, chopped, one tea-spoonful cloves, citron to taste, one tea-spoonful soda dissolved in water and added last.— *Mrs. John Bascom.*

FRUIT CAKE.

One pound of flour, one pound of brown sugar, three-fourths of a pound of butter, two pounds of raisins, two pounds currants, one pound of citron, twelve eggs, two table-spoons cinnamon, four nutmegs, one cup of sweet milk, one cup of molasses, one tea-spoon of soda, one wine-glass of brandy; bake two hours in a slow oven.— *Mrs. J. E. Davies.*

FRUIT CAKE.

One pound each of sugar, butter and flour, twelve eggs, two pounds dried currants, two of stoned raisins, one large spoonful mace, one of cinnamon, four nut-megs, two glasses of Sherry wine, one each of brandy and rose-water, one pound citron. Beat sugar and butter to a cream, then add yolks of eggs well beaten, alternately with the flour, by degrees, then add fruits, spice, and add whites of eggs last.— *Mrs. J. B. Bowen.*

WHITE FRUIT CAKE.

One cup butter, two of sugar, and one small cup sweet milk, whites of five eggs, one grated cocoanut, one pound blanched almonds, cut fine, one pound citron, cut fine, three and one-half cups sifted flour, two heap-ing tea-spoons baking powder; flour the fruit, adding it last.—*Mrs. Harry Hobbins.*

FRUIT CAKE.

One and one-half pounds of dark brown sugar, one pound of butter, three pounds of raisins, two pounds of currants, one pound of citron, two pounds of figs, chopped fine, one pound of candied lemon, one and one-half pounds of flour, one dozen eggs, one cup of cold coffee, one cup of molasses, one cup of brandy, one tea-spoonful of soda, three table-spoonfuls of cinnamon, two table-spoonfuls of cloves, three nutmegs.— *Mrs. J. W. Curtis.*

FRUIT CAKE — FRENCH LOAF.

One pound sugar, three-fourths butter, five eggs, two tea-spoons soda, one pound flour, two of fruit, one gill brandy, cloves, cinnamon and nutmeg.— *Mrs. McBride.*

FRENCH CREAM CAKE.

One cup of sugar, one and one-half cups of flour, three eggs, two tea-spoons baking powder, two table-spoons of cold water. Bake in jelly tins. CUSTARD: Dissolve in a little cold milk two heaping table-spoons of corn starch, add two eggs, beaten well, one small cup of sugar. Add to nearly a pint of boiling milk when nearly done, one-half cup of butter, and flavor with vanilla.— *Mrs. J. E. Davies.*

FRUIT CAKE.

One pound of flour, one pound of brown sugar, three pounds of currants, three pounds of raisins, one pound of citron, fourteen ounces of butter, ten eggs, one wine-glass of wine, one wine-glass of brandy, one tea-cup of buttermilk, one tea-spoon of soda, one tea-spoon of cloves, one table-spoon of mace, same of cinnamon, same of molasses. First put together butter and sugar, then yolks of eggs, then buttermilk, then flour, whites of eggs, spices, and last fruit.— *Mrs. Geo. Fox.*

HICKORY-NUT CAKE.

One and a half cups sugar, two-thirds cup butter, one-half cup of sweet milk, two cups flour, whites of four eggs, three tea-spoonfuls baking powder, small bowl hickory nuts.— *Mrs. J. W. Curtis.*

HICKORY-NUT CAKE.

One-half cup of butter, one and one-half cups of sugar, whites of four eggs, three-fourths of a cup of milk, one-half tea-spoon of soda, one tea-spoon cream tartar, three cups of flour; flavor with vanilla. Large coffee-cup of hickory nuts.— *Mrs. James Burgess.*

HICKORY-NUT CAKE.

Two cups sugar, one-half cup butter, one cup sweet milk, two and one-half cups flour, one tea-spoon of cream tartar, two and one-half tea-spoons soda, whites of eight eggs. After mixing butter and sugar to a cream, put in the other ingredients, alternately, reserving the soda till the last. Bake in layers; spread each layer with soft frosting, and add nuts. Put nuts in your cake, if you like.— *Mrs. Wm. F. Vilas.*

HICKORY-NUT CAKE.

Three-fourths of a cup of butter, two cups of sugar, one cup of milk, three cups of flour, three eggs, three even tea-spoons of baking powder, one cup of nuts. BOILED FROSTING: One cup of granulated sugar, one-half cup of water; boil till it grains; add beaten whites of two eggs. Stir in sugar quickly till it cools.— *Mrs. L. F. Kellogg.*

HICKORY-NUT CAKE.

One cup of nut meats (broken), one and one-half cups of sugar, one-half cup of butter, two cups of flour, three-fourths of a cup of sweet milk, two tea-spoons of baking powder, whites of four eggs, well beaten. Add meats last.— *Mrs. R. J. McConnell.*

ICE CREAM CAKE.

Two cups of sugar, one cup of butter, one cup of corn starch, one cup of milk, two cups of flour, the whites of eight eggs, three tea-spoonfuls of baking powder. ICING: The whites of four eggs, four cups of sugar; pour half a pint of boiling water over the sugar, and boil until when dropped in cold water it is very stiff, but not brittle; pour this over the beaten whites, stirring constantly, and while hot add a very scant tea-spoonful of citric acid; beat occasionally until cold and very stiff. Flavor with vanilla or almond.

This recipe, with four table-spoonfuls of grated French chocolate dissolved in a little water and added to the frosting, makes a fine chocolate cake.— *Mrs. David Atwood.*

LAYER NUT CAKE.

One cup of butter, two cups of sugar, three cups of flour, one cup of sweet milk, one tea-spoon of baking powder, whites of five eggs. Bake in jelly cake tins. LAYER: One cup of nut meats, one cup of chopped raisins; mix with syrup made of half a cup of sugar in water and juice of one lemon.— *Mrs. H. K. Edgerton, Oconomowoc.*

LEMON JELLY CAKE.

One cup of sugar, one-half cup of butter, three eggs, beaten separately, one-half cup of sweet milk, two cups of flour, two tea-spoons of baking powder. Bake in jelly tins. JELLY FOR CAKE: Grated rind and juice of one lemon, one cup of sugar, yolks of two eggs. Cook in a bowl in boiling water ten minutes.— *Mrs. J. E. Davies.*

LEMON CAKE.

One cup of butter, three cups of sugar, rub them to a cream, stir in the yolks of five eggs, well beaten, one tea-spoon of soda dissolved in a cup of sweet milk, juice and grated rind of one lemon, whites of five eggs well beaten, sift in four tea-cupfuls of flour, and bake half an hour.— *Mrs. E. S. McBride.*

ORANGE CAKE.

Two cups of flour, one and one-half cups of sugar, yolks of five eggs and whites of four, beaten separately, juice and rind of one orange, one tea-spoon of cream of tartar, one-half tea-spoon of soda. ICING: White of one egg, juice and rind of one orange, sugar to taste.— *Mrs. John Bascom.*

ORANGE CAKE.

Two cups of sugar, two cups of flour, one-half cup of cold water, five eggs, two tea-spoons baking powder. Beat the yolks with the sugar, add the water, then the flour mixed with the baking powder, then the beaten whites of the eggs; lastly the juice and grated rind of one orange. Bake in three layers. ICING: The beaten whites of two eggs, sugar, and juice and grated rind of one orange.— *Mrs. L. S. Ingman.*

ORANGE CAKE.

One cup sugar, two eggs, one-half cup butter, one-half cup sweet milk or water, two cups of flour, one tea-spoon cream of tartar, one-half one of soda. Bake as for jelly cake. MIXTURE TO PUT BETWEEN: One orange, grated, and the juice; white of one egg, beaten to a froth, four table-spoons powdered sugar. Mix and spread between the layers.— *Mrs. James R. Mears.*

PACIFIC CAKE.

Whites of eight eggs, two cups pulverized sugar and one small cup butter mixed thoroughly to a cream, one cup sweet milk, three cups sifted flour, three small tea-spoons of baking powder.

If desired as a "layer-cake," either of the following recipes will be found good:

CHOCOLATE: Whites of three eggs, one and one-half cups of pulverized sugar, three table-spoons grated sweet chocolate, one tea-spoon vanilla.

ICE CREAM: One pint sugar, water enough to boil until it "ropes," whites of three eggs; stir sugar into eggs by degrees; one tea-spoon of vanilla, one tea-spoon of pulverized citric acid.— *Mrs. E. Burdick.*

PLAIN CAKE.

One cup of sugar, one table-spoon of butter; cream together; one egg, one cup of milk, two cups of flour, two tea-spoons baking powder. FROSTING: One square of chocolate (Baker's No. 1), grated, and melted over tea-kettle, after which add one egg, one half cup of pulverized sugar, one-half table-spoon of cream, and one-half tea-spoon of vanilla.— *Mrs. L. S. Ingman.*

POLONAISE CAKE.

Boil over a slow fire one and one-half pints of cream; stir while boiling. Have ready the yolks of six eggs beaten with two table-spoons of arrowroot; stir into the boiling cream and boil ten minutes. Divide into two parts. FIRST PART: Stir in six ounces of chocolate, two ounces of sugar, one-fourth of a pound of macaroons, rolled fine. SECOND PART: One ounce of citron, four ounces of sugar, six ounces of almonds, blanched and chopped, or rolled very fine; flavor with rose. Use a sponge cake recipe and bake in layers (or if liked better, a gold and silver cake). Put together with a dark and light filling alternately. MERINGUE FOR THE TOP: Whites of nine eggs, one table-spoon of sugar to an egg. Color one-half of the meringue pink, and put on the cake first a layer of white, then one of pink; have the white on top; then drop large drops of the pink and white alternately over the top.— *Mrs. D. S. Comly.*

POUND CAKE.

Mix a pound of sugar with three-fourths of a pound of butter, put in the yolks of eight eggs (when the sugar and butter are worked white), beaten to a froth, and then the whites. Add a pound of sifted flour, and mace or nutmeg to the taste. If you wish to have your cake particularly nice, stir in just before putting in the pan a quarter of a pound of citron or almonds blanched and powdered fine in rose-water.— *Mrs. W. H. Hughes.*

MEASURE POUND CAKE.

One and one-half cups of sugar, one cup of butter, two cups of flour, one-fourth of a cup of sweet milk, four eggs, one tea-spoon of baking powder; flavor.— *Mrs. Charles S. Mears.*

POUND CAKE.

One pound of sugar, one pound of flour, one pound of butter and ten eggs.— *Mrs. C. M. Macomber.*

RAISIN CAKE.

Three-fourths of a cup of butter, one and one-half cups of sugar, two eggs, two and one-half cups of flour, one-half cup of molasses, one-half cup of cold water, one-half tea-spoon of soda, one-half tea-spoon each of cloves, cinnamon and nutmeg, three-fourths of a pound of chopped raisins, citron.— *Mrs. Charles Riebsam.*

ROCHESTER JELLY CAKE.

Two cups of sugar, two-thirds of a cup of butter, three eggs, one cup of sweet milk, three cups of flour and one and one-half tea-spoonfuls of baking powder; add a little salt and flavoring. Put one-half of this into two jelly cake tins, and bake. To the other half add one large cup of raisins, stoned and chopped fine, one table-spoonful of molasses, one-fourth of a pound of citron, chopped, one-half tea-spoonful of cloves, one tea-spoonful of cinnamon, one-half tea-spoonful of all-spice, a little nutmeg; add a table-spoonful of flour; bake in two tins as above. Put the dark and light together alternately, with jelly between, and frost the top.— *Mrs. David Atwood.*

SNOW CAKE.

Whites of ten eggs beaten together to a stiff froth; one and one-half tumblers of pulverized sugar and one of flour; one tea-spoon of cream tartar mixed well in the flour. Flavor with lemon and a little salt.— *Mrs. W. K. Barney.*

8

SILVER CAKE.

One-half cup of butter, one cup of sugar, one-half cup of milk, two cups of flour, whites of four eggs, one tea-spoon of baking powder, one-half tea-spoon of vanilla. Citron, if you like.— *Miss Robbins.*

SPICED CAKE.

One cup of new milk, one tea-spoonful of soda, one large cup of sugar, two eggs, three cups of flour, half a cup of butter; mix in order named; add a tea-spoonful each of cinnamon and allspice, and half a tea-spoon of cloves, one cup of raisins, and a little citron, if desired.— *Mrs. E. Burdick.*

SPONGE CAKE.

Two coffee-cups of sugar, four eggs; beat fifteen minutes with hands; two cups of flour, and last, three-fourths of a cup of boiling water.— *Mrs. W. M. Foresman.*

SPONGE CAKE.

Six eggs, three cups of sugar, mix yolks with sugar, three cups of flour, one cup of cold water, a pinch of salt, two heaping tea-spoons of baking powder; flavor with lemon or vanilla. Makes two loaves of cake.— *Mrs. C. M. Macomber.*

SPONGE CAKE.

Nine eggs, three-quarters of a pound of sugar, half a pound of flour, two lemons; beat eggs and sugar together over a kettle of hot water until very light; add grated rind of lemon, then the flour, beating lightly; finally add juice of lemons. If lemons are large, one will suffice.— *Mrs. E. Burdick.*

SPONGE CAKE.

Nine eggs; take the yolks, and beat with three cups of sugar to a cream; add three-quarters of a cup of lukewarm water; then put in three full cups of flour; whites of the eggs beaten to froth, and stirred in the last thing; flavor with vanilla or lemon. Makes two cakes.— *Mrs. E. R. Curtiss.*

SPONGE CAKE.

Six eggs; their weight in sugar; half their weight in flour; flavor with rose-water, nutmeg or lemon.— *Mrs. N. B. Van Slyke.*

MISS CLARK'S SPONGE CAKE.

Three-fourths pound sugar, one-half pound flour, seven eggs. To the sugar, add half a tumbler of cold water, let that boil, beat the eggs light, then pour the boiled sugar over them, beating hard all the time; continue to beat till cold, add the flour gently, then add one tea-spoon vinegar. Bake in a cool oven.— *Mrs. Wm. F. Vilas.*

SPONGE CAKE.

Two cups of sugar, two cups of flour, six eggs, one tea-spoon cream tartar, one-half tea-spoon soda dissolved in one-half cup warm water, rind and juice of one lemon; break the eggs on the sugar and beat very light; then add the flour and water, put cream tartar in flour, soda in water, lastly the lemon.— *Mrs. R. B. Ogilvie.*

SPONGE CAKE.

Seven eggs, two cups of soft granulated sugar, two full cups of sifted flour, two-thirds of a cup of cold

water, flavor to taste, a pinch of salt. Beat yolks and
sugar to a cream, add water, then add the flour, lastly
the whites cut to a stiff froth, stirred in lightly. A
moderate oven.— *Mrs. J. C. Spooner.*

TEA CAKE.

One and one-half cups of sugar, one-half cup of butter, four table-spoonfuls of milk, two eggs, whites and
yolks beaten separately, two and one-half cups of flour,
one tea-spoon of cream of tartar, one-half tea-spoon of
soda, raisins, currants and spices to taste.— *Mrs. John
Bascom.*

WHITE CAKE.

Three cups of sugar, one cup of butter, one cup of
sweet milk, four (light) cups of flour, whites of twelve
eggs, two tea-spoons of baking powder, flavor with
almond extract; before putting into pan to bake, add
half a pound of sweet almonds blanched and split.—
Mrs. A. J. Ward.

WHITE CAKE.

Two cups sugar, one-half cup butter, whites of four
eggs, one cup sweet milk, three cups flour, and three
small tea-spoons baking powder. Beat butter and sugar
to a cream, and then stir in milk and flour slowly; add
whites last. Bake in two square tins and frost.— *Miss
Bertha Schaal.*

WALNUT CAKE.

One pound of sugar (two coffee-cups), one pound of
flour (one quart), one-half pound of butter (one coffee-
cup), six eggs, one cup of sweet milk, one tea-spoon of
soda in milk, two tea-spoons of cream tartar in flour,

one pint of English walnut meats, one pint of stoned raisins. One-half cup of brandy improves it (it can be left out if desired). Mix butter and sugar, yolks of eggs, milk and soda together, thoroughly; add flour, cream tartar, nuts, raisins, etc., with the whites of the eggs. This makes a four-quart loaf, or two two-quart loaves. It will keep a long time in a close tin cake-box.— *Mrs. J. E. Davies.*

WALNUT CAKE.

Two cups sugar, one-half cup butter, three-fourths cup milk, whites five eggs, three cups flour, three tea-spoons baking powder. Chop a pound of walnuts, leaving out twenty-eight halves for the outside, with a cup of raisins, and stir into cake. Bake in two square tins, put frosting between and on the top, then cover with the remainder of the nuts.— *Miss Kittie Bird.*

FROSTING WITHOUT EGGS.

Dissolve a large pinch of gelatine in six table-spoons of boiling water, strain and thicken with sugar. This is enough to frost two cakes.— *Mrs. Edward P. Vilas.*

BOILED CHOCOLATE FROSTING.

One pint granulated sugar, whites of two eggs, one cake of grated Baker's chocolate, just enough hot water to wet the sugar; let it boil until it is stiff, but not brittle; add the chocolate and remove from the stove. Stir in the beaten whites.— *Mrs. Edward P. Vilas.*

SAND JUMBLES.

One cup of butter, one cup of sugar, three cups of flour, two eggs, and two tea-spoons of baking powder;

reserve one white to put over the cakes before baking; then sift sugar and cinnamon, and cut in squares or diamonds.— *Mrs. J. H. Palmer.*

COOKIES.

One cup of butter, two cups of sugar, two eggs, one-half a nutmeg, one cup of sour cream, two tea-spoons of cream tartar, one tea-spoon of soda.— *Mrs. S. H. Carpenter.*

COOKIES.

One and one-half cups of sugar, one cup of butter, one tea-spoonful of soda, one-half cup of sweet milk. Mold very stiff and roll thin.— *Mrs. James E. Burgess.*

JUMBLES.

One pound of flour, three-fourths of a pound of sugar, one-half of a pound of butter; three eggs.— *Mrs. James E. Burgess.*

RING JUMBLES.

One pound butter, one pound sugar, four eggs, one and one-fourth pounds flour, small wine-glass of rose-water. Mix sugar and butter to a cream, then add the yolks, then the rose-water, next, half the flour, lastly, the whites stirred in very lightly, alternately with the remaining flour. Use broad, flat tins for baking and buttered paper to put the cake on; using a table-spoon to put the dough on the paper in the form of regular rings, leaving a hole in the center; when done sift fine sugar over; for substitute for rose-water use lemon or vanilla.— *Mrs. Wm. F. Vilas.*

GINGER SNAPS.

One pint boiling molasses, one cup shortening stirred in the hot molasses, three tea-spoons of soda. Ginger or cinnamon to taste. Flour enough to make as soft dough as can be rolled out.— *Mrs. Charles S. Mears.*

GINGER SNAPS.

One cup of molasses, two-thirds of a cup of lard, one heaping tea-spoon of soda, one table-spoon of ginger, a pinch of salt; flour enough to roll out thin, and bake in a quick oven.— *Mrs. C. R. Riebsam.*

GINGER SNAPS.

One large cup butter and lard, mixed. One coffee-cup sugar, one cup molasses, one-half cup water. one table-spoon ginger, one of cinnamon, one tea-spoon cloves, one of soda dissolved in hot water. Flour for pretty stiff dough. Roll out rather thinner than sugar cakes, and bake quickly. These will keep for weeks if kept in a dry place.— *Mrs. F. W. Oakley.*

ENGLISH GINGER SNAPS.

Two pounds of molasses, two pounds of flour, one pound of dark brown sugar, three-fourths of a pound of butter, a few drops of essence of lemon; melt the butter, add a little ginger, mix well together, then add the molasses and sugar, lastly the flour; mix all well together, let it stand all night, and drop in tins in the morning to bake. Do not roll them out; they will spread in the oven themselves.— *Mrs. Geo. F. Taylor.*

GINGER BREAD.

One cup of sugar, one cup of molasses, one cup of sour milk, one cup of butter, four cups of flour, four eggs, one tea-spoon of soda, one table-spoon of ginger; improved by adding half a cup of sour cream. Bake in two cakes.— *Mrs. George A. Mason.*

SPONGE GINGER BREAD.

One cup of sugar, one cup of sour milk, one small tea-spoonful of soda, one cup of molasses, four eggs — the yolks and whites beaten separately,— one cup of butter, one table-spoonful of ginger, one cup of raisins, four cups of flour. In place of sour milk and soda, you may use sweet milk and baking powder.— *Mrs. W. H. Hughes.*

GINGER CAKE.

One-half cup of sugar, one egg, one cup of buttermilk, one cup of molasses, over half a cup of butter and lard, mixed, or butter alone, one heaping tea-spoon of soda, one tea-spoon of ginger, one tea-spoon of cinnamon.— *Mrs. L. S. Ingman.*

LEMON CHEESE-CAKES.

One-fourth of a pound of butter, one pound white sugar creamed together; six eggs, whites and yolks beaten very light; two lemons, juice and grated rind. Beat all together well, and put into a stone jar placed within a kettle of boiling water, and heated until of the consistency of honey, stirring very often. When wanted for use, make open shells of puff paste, and fill with a spoonful of the mixture.— *Mrs. J. W. Hobbins.*

LEMON CHEESE-CAKES (English).

One pound of loaf sugar, broken, six eggs, omitting two whites, juice of three lemons, grated rind of two; put in a jar, and place the same in boiling water; stir gently till mixture becomes stiff like honey; tie down with brandy, and keep for use. Do not grate lemons on grater; take lumps of sugar and rub the rind with them. Be sure and have rich puff paste, about a spoonful for each patty pan.— *Miss Lizzie Taylor.*

CONNECTICUT DOUGHNUTS.

One quart milk, one pound sugar, three-fourths pound half lard and half butter, three eggs, one-half cup yeast; melt the lard and butter; stir them into the milk with the sugar, eggs, and half tea-cup yeast, and some nutmeg; add flour till as thick as pancakes; then set in a warm place to rise; when light, mold as stiff as biscuit and set to rise the second time; when very light, pour the dough out on the molding-board and pat the rolling pin over it, leaving it two inches thick; with a sharp knife cut it in squares, and fry in hot lard.— *Mrs. J. C. Gregory.*

DOUGHNUTS.

Two eggs, one cup of sugar, one cup of thick sour milk, one tea-spoon of saleratus, four table-spoons of melted lard and butter; salt, and mix soft.— *Mrs. L. B. Vilas.*

DOUGHNUTS.

Three eggs, one cup sugar, two cups sweet milk, one-half cup lard, two tea-spoons baking powder. Cut half an inch thick.— *Mrs. Daniel Campbell.*

DOUGHNUTS.

Two eggs beaten light, one cup of sugar, one table-spoon of butter, one cup of sweet milk, one and one-half tea-spoons of baking powder, one tea-spoon of salt, spices; mix soft.— *Mrs. Charles S. Mears.*

FRIED CAKES.

One cup of sugar, two and a half table-spoons of melted butter, one cup of milk, two eggs, two tea-spoons of baking powder, a little salt; mix quite soft.— *Mrs. J. C. Freeman.*

OLY KOEKS.

Three eggs, one coffee-cup of milk, one and one-half cups of sugar, two tea-spoons of baking powder; flavor with lemon; flour to thicken sufficiently to drop from a spoon into plenty of hot lard, to form balls; drop raisins, a few at a time, into mixture, and turn them into the center of each cake. Roll in pulverized sugar when a little cooled.— *Mrs. A. J. Ward.*

CRULLERS.

One cup butter, two cups sugar, two of milk, three eggs, one tea-spoon saleratus; flour till stiff enough to roll out.— *Mrs. R. W. Hurd.*

WAFFLES.

One quart of milk, five eggs (whites beaten separately and added the last thing), two table-spoons of butter, heaping full, two tea-spoons baking powder, one quart of flour and a pinch of salt.— *Mrs. J. H. Palmer.*

WAFFLES.

Take a quart of flour, six eggs, a spoonful of melted butter, a tea-spoon of salt, half a nutmeg, and four ounces of sugar; milk enough to make a stiff batter. Beat well until it looks light.— *Mrs. R. W. Hurd.*

WAFFLES.

One quart of flour, one-half pint of milk, four eggs beaten separately, two heaping tea-spoonfuls of baking powder, butter the size of an egg.— *Mrs. L. F. Kellogg.*

FRITTERS.

One-half pint of sweet milk, two eggs well beaten, one pint of flour, one tea-spoon of baking powder. Serve warm with maple syrup.— *Mrs. C. R. Riebsam.*

STRAWBERRY SHORT-CAKE.

Two quarts flour, one tea-spoon salt, four tea-spoons baking powder, four table-spoons shortening, two eggs, two and one-half cups milk. Mix soft. Divide dough and roll in two layers size of pan; spread butter on one of them, putting the other on top, and bake together. When done, separate and place berries mixed with sugar between.— *Mrs. Charles S. Mears.*

GRANDMA'S SHORT-CAKE.

One pound of flour dried and sifted, one-fourth pound of butter, and half as much lard, one salt-spoonful of salt, a pinch of soda thoroughly dissolved in just enough vinegar to cover it and well worked in; enough ice-water to enable you to roll out into paste half an inch thick; cut into squares, prick with a fork, and bake light brown; split, butter, add berries, and eat while hot.— *Mrs. W. H. Hughes.*

CRANBERRY SHORT-CAKE.

Little more than a quart of flour, three tea-spoonfuls baking powder, butter the size of egg, the same of lard. Mix quite soft with milk; bake in layer tins (two layers); split and spread with butter, then fill with cranberries, cooked to a jelly and well sweetened. Place on the top whipped cream, sweetened.— *Mrs. J. C. Freeman.*

BLUEBERRY CAKE.

One cup of sugar, one cup of sweet milk, two-thirds of a cup of butter, one and one-half pints of flour, two eggs, two heaping tea-spoonfuls of baking powder, one cup of blueberries, well floured.— *Mrs. B. E. Hutchinson.*

HUCKLEBERRY CAKE.

Two-thirds of a cup of butter, one and one-half cups of sugar, three eggs, one cup of sour milk, one tea-spoon of soda, four cups of flour, one quart of huckleberries.— *Mrs. John N. Jones.*

BIRTHDAY CAKE.

One and one-half cups sugar, two-thirds cup butter, one cup sweet milk, two level tea-spoons baking powder, two and one-half cups flour, three eggs, one tea-spoon vanilla. Bake in two tins, adding to one half one heaping tea-spoon cinnamon, one-half tea-spoon each of cloves and allspice, one table-spoon brandy, a little nutmeg, one and one-half cups raisins, quarter pound citron; put together with frosting.— *Mrs. Geo. C. Comstock.*

Angel Food.

Whites of thirteen eggs, one and one-half cups granulated sugar, three-fourths of a tea-spoon of cream of tartar one cup of flour, one tea-spoon of vanilla, a pinch of salt; sift the flour and cream of tartar together three times; beat whites of eggs to a stiff froth and add sugar, stirring all of the time until well mixed; add vanilla and salt, and lastly fold the flour and cream of tartar into this mixture without beating. Bake fifty minutes in a moderate oven.— *Mrs. Phillis Frawley.*

Apple Jelly Cake.

Cut fine and stew enough apples to make about a pint of sauce; add juice and rind of one lemon, half a cup of sugar and one egg well beaten; beat all together well, then set to cool until cake is ready. Take three eggs, stir whites and yolks separately; half a cup sugar, butter size of egg, half a cup sweet milk, three cups flour and three tea-spoons baking powder. Bake in three jelly pans. Use the prepared apples between each layer and on top.— *Mrs. Robert McConnell.*

Bread Cake.

Three cups of raised dough, two cups of sugar, one cup of butter, two or three eggs, one glass of brandy, one-half tea-spoon soda, and a little flour.— *Mrs. R. M. Bashford.*

Chocolate Nougat Cake.

One cup sugar creamed with half cup butter; add the yolks of two eggs well beaten, one cup of buttermilk or thick sour milk. in which has been dissolved one level tea-spoon of soda, one and one-half cups of flour, one-half cup chopped walnut meats, one-half cup chopped and seeded raisins, two squares of melted chocolate, one-half tea-spoon vanilla, the beaten whites of the eggs; bake in two layers, put together with boiled icing. Frosting: Boil two cups sugar with scant half cup water until it hairs on a fork, then pour slowly on the whites of two egg which have been beaten up very stiff, and add one-half tea-spoon vanilla.; stir constantly with Dover egg beater.— *Mrs. Calvert Spensley, Mineral Point.*

COFFEE CAKE.

One cup sugar, one cup molasses, one tea-spoon soda stirred in molasses, three eggs, one cup cold coffee, four cups flour, one tea-spoon cinnamon, one-half nutmeg, grated, one pound raisins, one pound currants, if desired. — *Mrs. John Corscot.*

ENGLISH SEED CAKE.

One cup butter, two cups sugar, one cup sweet milk, three and one-half cups flour, two tea-spoons baking powder, one-third of a nutmeg, one table-spoon caraway seeds; cover the top closely with blanched almonds and sift a little granulated sugar over the top. This makes two loaves, or about three dozen little cakes, which are nice to serve with afternoon tea.— *Mrs. Geo. C. Comstock.*

FRUIT LAYER CAKE.

Yolks of three eggs beat well, one half cup sugar beat well in eggs, butter size of an egg, one-half cup New Orleans molasses, one level tea-spoon soda, dissolved in a little boiling water, one small tea-spoonful cinnamon, one-half small tea-spoonful cloves, or to taste, two scant cups of flour, two-thirds cup of coffee, cold, and added last. Filling: whites of two eggs, then boil together one-half cup boiling water, and one large cup of sugar; whip the boiled sugar into the whites of the eggs; chop one cup of raisins fine, then sprinkle over the frosting after it has been put on the cake. Make in three layers; try a small cake; if right it will have a fine grain and be very light. The batter should be rather thin.— *Miss K. Foran.*

HASH CAKE.

One-half cup of butter, two cups of sugar, two cups of sweet milk, four eggs, three cups of flour, one tea-spoonful of baking powder. Filling. One pound of blanched almonds, one pound of figs, one pound of raisins, all chopped, mix with sweet milk to the consistency of jelly. This filling will make two cakes.— *Mrs. R. M. Bashford.*

SCRIPTURE CAKE.

1 cup of butter,	Judges, 5,	verse 25
3½ cups of flour,	I Kings, 4,	" 22
3 cups of sugar,	Jeremiah, 6,	" 20
2 cups of raisins,	I Samuel, 30,	" 12
2 cups of figs,	I Samuel, 30,	" 12
1 cup of water,	Genesis, 24,	" 17
1 cup almonds,	Genesis, 43,	" 11
6 eggs,	Isaiah, 10,	" 14
1 tea-spoonful of honey	Judges, 14,	" 18
A pinch of salt	Leviticus, 2,	" 13
Spices to taste,	I Kings, 10,	" 10
2 tea-spoonfuls baking power,	I Corinthians, 5,	" 6
Follow Solomons advise for	Proverbs, 23,	" 14

making good boys and you will make a good cake.

Or proceed as in the ordinary rules for cake baking, putting in the fruit and nuts last of all. The raisins should be seeded, the figs chopped and the almonds blanched and sliced; all of these well floured to prevent sinking to the bottom.— *Mrs. Lucius Fairchild.*

SPICE CAKE.

One cup sugar, one-half cup melted butter, one egg, white and yolk beaten seperately, one cup thick sour milk (butter milk is best), not quite two cups flour, one cup chopped raisins, one level tea-spoon of soda, one level ground cinnamon, one-quarter ground cloves, one-quarter ground nutmeg. Put soda with flour, put all the spices with raisins, and flour them a little; also a little pinch of baking soda. Beat hard in order given and be careful not to get this cake too stiff with flour.—*Mrs. A. B. Morris.*

WAUPUN SPONGE CAKE.

Five eggs, two-third cup sifted sugar, one half cup flour, sift before measuring and four or five times afterwards; juice of half a lemon. Beat yolks very light; when thick add sugar gradually and juice of lemon. Beat whites very light turn yolk mixture into them and beat fully. Add the flour a little at a time; just poke it in.— *Miss Voila Hooker Bell.*

LUNCH CAKES.

Two eggs, two cups of sugar, two cups of flour, one cup of butter, one-half cup of milk, one cup of chopped raisins, two tea-spoonfuls of baking powder, nutmeg, cinnamon and cloves. Bake in patty-pans.— *Miss Kate C. Morton.*

CHOCOLATE GINGER BREAD.

Cake without eggs: one cup molasses, one cup sour milk, one-half tea-spoon ginger, one tea-spoon cinnamon, two table-spoons sugar. Dissolve one tea-spoon soda, in one tea-spoon cold water add the mixture with two table-spoons each of melted lard and butter, stir in two cups sifted flour then add three table-spoons melted chocolate, with one table-spoon melted butter. Bake in layers use chocolate or white icing.— *Mrs. A. B. Morris.*

CHOCOLATE ICING.

Two squares chocolate, one cup white sugar, one-half cup milk one-half tea-spoon vanilla. Stir all together till cold and thick; spread on with silver knife.— *Mrs. A. B. Morris.*

GINGER BREAD.

Two cups flour, one cup molasses, one-half cup boiling water, two table-spoons butter, one-half table-spoon ginger, one-half tea-spoon salt, one tea-spoon soda, one egg beaten.— *Mrs. C. F. Lamb.*

CRULLERS.

Two cups brown sugar, one and one-third cups butter, six eggs, one-half nutmeg, one tea-spoon cinnamon, flour to roll rather stiff.— *Mrs. C. F. Lamb.*

BOSCOBEL DOUGHNUTS.

One coffee cup sugar, two coffee cups sour or butter-milk, one level tea-spoon soda, two full tea-spoons baking powder, two table-spoons lard melted, one table-spoon butter melted, two eggs, salt, nutmeg, flour to mix.— *Miss Kate A. Chittenden.*

9

HONEY SNAPS.

One pound honey (one cup), one-half pound granulated sugar (one cup), one-half pound butter (one cup), one-half tea- spoon of salt, one-half tea-spoon soda, grated peel of one or two oranges, enough flour to make a stiff dough, roll thin and bake in slow oven. Boil honey, sugar, butter, peel, salt, together; add soda and flour and let get cold before rolling out.— *Mrs. Angus Mc Connell.*

OATMEAL COOKIES.

One-half cup butter, one and one-half cups sugar, four eggs beaten separately, one and one-half cups quaker oats, one-half cup chopped raisins, one tea-spoon soda, one tea-spoon baking powder, two cups of flour Drop on well greased tins; bake a light brown.— *Mrs. Calvert Spensley, Mineral Point.*

GINGER WAFERS.

Heat to boiling point one cup of butter, one cup of molasses, two cups brown sugar, one table-spoon ginger, and one scant table-spoon of soda. Remove from the fire and beat until cool, then add two beaten eggs and enough flour to make a stiff dough. Roll very thin, and bake in a quick oven.— *Mrs. C. F. Lamb.*

ENGLISH COOKIES.

Two cups brown sugar, one cup lard and butter, one cup cold coffee, two eggs, one level tea-spoon soda, one level tea-spoon baking powder, three cups sifted flour, one tea-spoon cinnamon. one tea-spoon nutmeg, two cups raisins (seeded), one cup English walnuts. Drop off spoon in greased pan. Bake in quick oven.— *Mrs. Albert Schmedeman.*

COOKIES.

One cup butter, two cups sugar, two-thirds cup sweet milk, two eggs, one tea-spoon soda, two tea-spoons cream tarter, nutmeg, salt, flour enough to roll thin and smoothly; sprinkle with sugar and bake in a quick oven.— *Mrs. Mary Chittenden Hurd.*

SOFT COOKIES.

Two coffee cups of sugar, one cup butter packed full; rub sugar and butter to a light cream, then add three well beaten eggs; dissolve one tea-spoonful of soda in one cup sour cream, then add to creamed butter and stir in four cupfuls of sifted flour; add grated nutmeg and vanilla to taste. Roll not too thin, and bake in quick oven. A nice finishing touch can be given by sprinkling with granulated sugar, rolling lightly with rolling pin; cut out and press whole raisin in center of each.— *Mrs. Angus McConnell.*

HERMITS.

One and one-half cups sugar, three-quarters cup of butter, three eggs, one tea-spoon cloves, cinnamon, allspice, one tea-spoon soda and a little salt, one good cup raisins chopped; add salt to flour and make thick enough with flour to roll soft.— *Mrs. A. B. Morris.*

SNOW BALLS.

One cup of sugar, butter half the size of an egg, two eggs, one cup of sour milk, one tea-spoon of soda, nutmeg to taste.— *Mrs. S. E. Hood.*

ROCKS.

One cup butter, one and one-half cups sugar, three eggs, two and one-half cups flour, one tea-spoon soda dissolved in table-spoon warm water, three-quarters of a pound of dates, chopped fine, meats of one and a half pounds English walnuts, cut up, one tea-spoon allspice, one tea-spoon cinnamon. Drop on buttered tins and bake.— *Mrs. John Corscot.*

CUSTARD. CREAMS, ETC.

CHARLOTTE RUSSE.

One pint of cream, whipped light, one-half ounce of gelatine, dissolved in one gill of hot milk, whites of two eggs, beaten to a stiff froth, one small cup of powdered sugar. Flavor with almond or vanilla. Mix cream, eggs and sugar, flavor and beat in the gelatine, and milk last. It should be quite cold before this is added.— *Miss Sue M. Ingman.*

CHARLOTTE RUSSE.

One cup cream, one cup milk, two eggs, quarter box gelatine, two-thirds cup sugar. Boil milk and gelatine together; yolks and sugar as for boiled custard. Let stand until a little cool, then beat up the whites and put in. Let stand till it begins to harden, then beat up cream and stir in. Flavor with vanilla.— *Mrs. J. W. Curtis.*

CHARLOTTE RUSSE.

One ounce gelatine, one pint sweet milk, one pint cream, four eggs, sugar to taste; beat the sugar and yolks of eggs together till light; dissolve the gelatine in the milk, then boil and strain over the eggs and sugar. Whip the cream — which must be very cold — to a stiff froth, and add it to the above; flavor with vanilla; line the serving dish with sponge cake, and pour in mixture; then set on ice till wanted.— *Mrs. E. Burdick.*

CHARLOTTE RUSSE.

One pound lady fingers, one quart rich sweet cream, three-fourths cup powdered sugar, two tea-spoonfuls vanilla or other extract.   Split and trim the cakes, and fit neatly in the bottom and sides of two quart molds. Whip the cream to a stiff froth in a syllabub churn, when you have sweetened and flavored it; fill the molds, lay cakes closely together on the top, and set upon the ice until needed.— *Mrs. W. H. Hughes.*

CHARLOTTE RUSSE.

Dissolve in a half pint of milk one-half an ounce of gelatine; let it cool but not congeal. Stir into one pint of whipped cream, well sweetened and delicately flavored. Beat very light the whites of seven eggs, and mix thoroughly with above, and pour over slices of sponge cake in a mold.   Leave a little of the whipped cream to pour over the top.— *Miss Kittie Bird.*

PINE-APPLE CHARLOTTE RUSSE.

One half box of gelatine dissolved in a cup of milk, one pint of cream, whites of four eggs, one-half can of grated pine-apple; beat the whites of the eggs very light, also the cream; add one and a half cups of sugar to the whipped cream, then the pine-apple; strain in the gelatine, and then the whites of the eggs stirred in lightly; line your dish with sponge cake, pour in the mixture and set away to cool. Stir the mixture till it begins to thicken before pouring in the mold.— *Mrs. James E. Burgess.*

SNOW CUSTARD.

One-half package Cox's gelatine, three eggs, one pint of milk, two cups of sugar, juice of one lemon. Soak the gelatine one hour in a tea-cupful of cold water. To this, at the end of this time, add one pint of boiling water, stir until the gelatine is thoroughly dissolved, add two-thirds of the sugar and the lemon juice. Beat the whites of the eggs to a stiff froth, and when the gelatine is quite cold whip it into the whites, a spoonful at a time, for at least an hour; whip steadily and evenly, and when all is stiff pour into a mold, previously wet with cold water, and set in a cool place. In four or five hours turn into a glass dish. Make a custard of the milk, eggs and remainder of the sugar; flavor with vanilla or bitter almond, and when the meringue is turned out of the mold, pour this about the base.— *Mrs. W. H. Hughes.*

BAVARIAN CREAM.

One quart of sweet cream, yolks of four eggs, one-half an ounce of gelatine or isinglass, one small cup of sugar, two tea-spoonfuls of vanilla or bitter almond extract. Soak the gelatine for an hour in just enough cold water to cover it. Drain and stir into a pint of the cream made boiling hot. Beat the yolks smooth with the sugar, and add the boiling mixture, beating in a little at a ti ne; heat until it begins to thicken, but do not actually boil; remove from the fire, and while still hot stir in the other pint of cream, whipped or churned in a syllabub churn to a stiff froth. Beat this whip, a spoonful at a time, into the custard until it is the consistency of a sponge cake batter. Dip a mold into cold water, pour in the mixture and set on ice to form.— *Mrs. W. H. Hughes.*

COCOANUT CREAM.

One pint of cream, two ounces of gelatine, one cocoanut, ten ounces of powdered sugar, two lemons. Whip the cream, add to it the sugar, the cocoanut, grated fine, and the milk of the nut; dissolve the gelatine in a gill of water, and let it boil two minutes; then stir it gently into the cream; add the lemon juice and put into molds.— *Mrs. D. S. Comly.*

VELVET CREAM.

Nearly a box of gelatine soaked in a cup of Sherry wine over night; melt it over the fire with a cup of sugar; when it is warm, add a quart of cream, and strain into molds. If wine is too hot it will curdle the cream.— *Mrs. J. H. Palmer.*

SPANISH CREAM.

One quart of milk, five eggs, one-half box of gelatine, two cups of sugar, one tea-spoon of vanilla. Beat yolks and sugar together until creamy; dissolve gelatine in a little cold milk, add it, the sugar and yolks, to the quart of milk, and make a soft custard; beat whites of eggs very stiff, add them and vanilla to the custard, stirring fast for five minutes, and put into a mold as quick as possible. Serve with cream.— *Miss Frank L. Clark.*

CREAM BLANC MANGE.

Dissolve one-half package of gelatine in one-half pint of milk. Boil one-half pint of milk in a custard boiler. Strain the milk off from the gelatine into the boiling milk and boil all together. Add to this the dissolved gelatine with two tea-spoonfuls of vanilla and one-half cup of sugar. When partly cool add a large cup of cream, and beat well. Turn into a mold and set away to cool. Serve with sugar and cream.— *Mrs. Breese J. Stevens.*

BLANC MANGE.

One quart milk, put into a double boiler, dissolve two heaping table-spoons corn starch in a little cold milk, then put it into the hot milk, stirring all the time; then stir in the whites of three beaten eggs, after you take from the fire, and beat quickly a few minutes; wet a mold and pour in. Serve with sugar and cream.— *Mrs. John N. Jones.*

CHOCOLATE MANGE.

Dissolve one box of Cox's gelatine in one pint of water; boil together one quart of milk, one pound of sugar, one large coffee-cup of grated chocolate and gelatine, for five minutes. Add one pint of cream, flavor with vanilla, pour into molds, and cool quickly on snow or ice.

APPLE SNOW.

One pint of strained apple, one-half pint of powdered sugar, whites of three eggs; beat the eggs to a stiff froth, then add apple and sugar alternately, a spoonful at a time of each; beat all together until it stands stiff on the spoon.   Serve with custard made of the yolks of the eggs.— *Miss Lois Robbins.*

LEMON SPONGE.

Two ounces gelatine; pour over one pint of cold water; let it stand fifteen minutes; add half pint boiling water, three-quarters of a pound white sugar, and juice of four lemons.   When the gelatine is cold, before it begins to get firm, add the well beaten whites of three eggs.   Beat the whole twenty minutes, till it is quite white and very light; then put in a mold, wet in cold water.— *Mrs. A. B. Braley.*

FRUIT SALAD.

Half a dozen oranges, cut fine; a quart of strawberries, or red raspberries; a tea-cup each of grated pineapple and cocoanut.   Sweeten to taste.   Place in layers in a glass dish.— *Mrs. Herbert W. Chynoweth.*

WINE JELLY.

Two pounds white sugar; three lemons; grate rind of one, and use juice of three; four ounces gelatine, soaked in a pint of cold water for an hour and a quarter; one pint Madeira wine.   Dissolve the whole in a quart of boiling water; strain through a jelly bag, and pour into molds, and set in a cool place.— *Mrs. E. Burdick.*

WINE JELLY.

One box Cox's gelatine, one pint Sherry wine, one and three-fourths pounds sugar, two lemons.   Pour over the gelatine one pint of cold water, and let it stand one hour; then pour over that one pint and coffee-cup of boiling water; add one and three-fourths pounds sugar, one pint Sherry wine, rind and juice of two lemons. Stir the ingredients thoroughly, and strain through a fine strainer, and place on ice.— *Mrs. J. C. Gregory.*

PINE-APPLE JELLY.

One package of gelatine dissolved in one pint of boiling water; when dissolved add the juice of one or two lemons, one quart of boiling water, two cups of sugar, one-half can of grated pine-apple.— *Mrs. James E. Burgess.*

LEMON JELLY.

Soak one-half box of gelatine in a cup of water, juice and grated rind of two lemons, three cups of sugar, three cups of boiling water; mix all together, let come to a boil, strain and put in molds.— *Mrs. Darwin Clark.*

LEMON JELLY.

Squeeze the juice of two lemons on one pound of sugar; add two table-spoonfuls of wine or brandy; pour a scant quart of boiling water on one-half of a paper of Cox's gelatine, after it has soaked twenty minutes in enough cold water to cover it; then add to it the lemon, sugar, and brandy; when thoroughly dissolved pour into a mold (which has been dipped into cold water), and put in a cool place to form.— *Mrs. W. H. Hughes.*

ICE CREAM.

One quart of milk, one pint of cream, one and one-half cups of sugar, two eggs; flavor to taste; pour into a freezer and put in a cool place, with plenty of ice around it.— *Mrs. W. H. Hughes.*

St. Nicholas Ice Cream.

To two quarts of milk put eight eggs, one and one-half pounds of white sugar, and boil the whole. Stir it well. When boiled, strain it through a sieve into the ice cream freezer. Put freezer into a mixture of rock salt and pounded ice; then whip four quarts of sweet cream until thick, mix it with the rest, shut freezer and turn until stiff. Take care not to let salt into cream.— *Mrs. J. C. Hopkins.*

Ice Cream.

One quart of cream, two eggs, one and one-half cups of sugar; eggs beaten separately, the sugar in the yokes, then beat very hard together; stir into the cream. Flavor to taste, and freeze.— *Mrs. Edward P. Vilas.*

Peach à la Mode.

Make a syrup of one pound of sugar and half a pint water. When boiled and skimmed, place in it six large peaches, halved and peeled, with the kernels blanched; let boil gently until clear. Skim your syrup. Squeeze the juice of three lemons with gelatine which has been soaked half an hour (or until dissolved); one ounce of gelatine to a quart of syrup. Wet a mold, pour in jelly, then a layer of peaches; alternate layer of jelly and peaches until mold is full. Put mold on ice to harden.— *R. L. Garlick.*

Lemon Ice.

Juice of six lemons; put to it three pints water, let it boil quite a while, two cups sugar, strain; put into a freezer, and beat up whites of four eggs, and stir in when it begins to harden.— *Mrs. S. H. Carpenter.*

WATER ICE.

One quart water, one pound sugar, the outer rind of one lemon, and juice of two. Same for orange or pine-apple (one pine-apple). Put in a can, pack ice and salt around it, and freeze. Scrape it down till all is frozen. *Mrs. Wm. F. Vilas.*

PINE-APPLE SNOW.

One can of pine-apple (grated is best), one quart of water, sugar to taste, whites of four eggs, well beaten. Mix well together and freeze.— *Mrs. D. S. Comly.*

DIMPLES.

Beat the whites of three eggs very dry, add gradually three-fourths of a pound of sugar, and beat well until well mixed; blanch three-fourths of a pound of almonds, cut them into pieces as small as peas, and stir into the egg and sugar; drop the mixture in spots as large as a half-penny on white paper upon a tin, and bake in a cool oven.— *Mrs. J. W. Curtis.*

CHOCOLATE PUFFS.

One-half pound refined sugar, one-half ounce chocolate, grated; mix well. Beat the white of one egg to a froth and stir in sugar and chocolate; beat well and drop on well sugared paper. Bake slowly.— *Mrs. J. H. D Baker.*

SODA CREAM.

Two and one-half pounds white sugar, one-eighth pound tartaric acid, both dissolved in one quart of hot water; when cold add the beaten whites of three eggs, stirring well; bottle for use. Put two large spoons of this syrup in a glass of cold water, and stir in it one-fourth of a spoon of bicarbonate of soda; any flavor can be put in the syrup desired.— *Mrs. John M. Sumner.*

FROZEN PEACHES.

One quart of sweet cream, six ounces ot sugar, one teaspoon of vanilla; mix well and freeze; when nearly frozen add one quart of peaches, crushed, with sugar to taste; then finish freezing. This will make about three pints, enough for seven or eight people.— *Mrs. W. M. Foresman.*

APPLE PRESERVE.

Ten pounds of apples, ripe and sweet, ten pounds of sugar, six lemons, sliced; boil the sugar with a very little water; skim until clear; then add the apples chopped fine, and the lemons. Let it boil until the apple is quite clear.— *Mrs. J. D. Gurnee.*

RED RASPBERRY JAM.

To the raspberries, add the juice of about one-third as many currants as you have berries. Use one pound of sugar for each pound of fruit. Press the berries until broken, in an earthen dish, with a wooden or silver spoon. Add the currant juice, and boil a few minutes, or until the seeds begin to soften, stirring to prevent burning. Then add the sugar, and boil ten minutes. Try a little by cooling on a plate; if watery, boil a little longer. Put up in cups with brandy papers pressed closely on the top of the fruit. Paste paper carefully over the cups.— *Mrs. A. Proudfit.*

CREAM CANDY.

To each pound of sugar allow a cup of boiling water, three-fourths of an ounce of butter, and one-fourth of a tea-spoon of vanilla. Dissolve the sugar before allowing it to boil; as soon as it commences to boil, add the butter, and when nearly done, the vanilla. To try, drop a little into cold water; if it hardens, it is done. Do not stir after it commences to boil, and have a hot fire, so that it will cook quickly and steadily to the end. Pour from the kettle (do not scrape it out) onto a greased marble table. When cool enough to handle, pull until hard.— *Miss Lois Robbins.*

BUTTER SCOTCH.

Three cups of molasses, two cups of sugar, one cup of butter, and one small tea-spoon of soda before taking off.— *Mrs. J. W. Curtis.*

MOLASSES CANDY.

One cup of molasses, three-fourths of a cup of sugar, one-fourth of a cup of butter, four tea-spoonfuls of vinegar, and a little vanilla.— *Miss Helen Julia Kellogg.*

MOLASSES CANDY.

One and one-half pounds of sugar, one-half pint of molasses, one-fourth tea-spoon of cream tartar, butter the size of a walnut. As soon as the water and sugar comes to a boil, add the cream tartar dissolved in water, and boil until it candies; then add the molasses and butter; boil until it hardens in water, and pull when cool.— *Miss Kittie Bird.*

MOUSSE.

Heavy cream beaten until stiff; sweeten and flavor. Pack in ice and salt and allow to stand for three or four hours.— *Mrs. A. B. Morris.*

COFFEE ICE CREAM.

One cup black coffee, one cup granulated sugar, one quart cream, one pint milk, pinch salt, half tea-spoon vanilla.— *Mrs. A. B. Morris.*

PEACH ICE CREAM.

One quart cream, one pint milk, two cups sugar, one dozen ripe peaches, whites two eggs; pare and mash peaches, add sugar; let stand until the rest is all ready, then add cream and milk; add just before freezing the whites of eggs, beaten.— *Mrs. A. B. Morris.*

CLARET SAUCE FOR ICE CREAM.

Boil together, without stirring, one-half pound sugar and one gill of water until it will spin a heavy thread, adding one salt-spoon of cream of tarter. Take from fire and add one gill of claret and juice of half a lemon. Stand aside till very cold.— *Mrs. Albert Schmedeman.*

CHIPPED PEAR.

Eight pounds pears not too ripe, eight pounds granulated sugar, one and one-half pounds candied ginger, four lemons; chip pears and ginger; boil together with sugar one hour. Boil lemons whole in clear water until tender, cut in small pieces, removing seeds; add to pears; boil one hour more. Serve with ice cream.— *Mrs. Florence Bashford Spensley.*

CAFE PARFAIT.

Mix two cups *double* cream, one cup clear black coffee, three-quarters cup sugar. *Chill thoroughly;* then beat with Dover egg beater until thick to bottom of bowl, or keep reversing fork until all is beaten. Fill ice cream freezer, fitting cover tightly; stand in ice and salt three or four hours. Serve in glasses with cherries on top.— *Mrs. Florence Bashford Spensley.*

LEMON SPONGE.

Stir together the grated rind and juice of two large lemons, one cup sugar; add the beaten yolks of four eggs. Put into a double boiler in which water is *boiling;* stir for three minutes; add one-quarter box gelatine that has been soaked in one-quarter cup cold water for two or three minutes; stir well; remove from fire; add well beaten whites of eggs; put into mold and allow it to get very cold. Serve covered with whipped cream. —*Mrs. C. F. Lamb.*

PINEAPPLE SALAD.

Cut off top of big pine leaving green handle on lid, scoop out carefully, put shell on ice, or fill with cracked ice, to cool; make fruit salad of pineapple, peaches, oranges, or as many small fruits as can be had, mix with thick sugar syrup, marischino or sherry; chill; fill pineapple shell and serve ice cold.— *Mrs. Florence Bashford Spensley.*

TEA WITH LEMON SYRUP.

Mix English breakfast and gunpowder of teas in the proportion of two to one respectively. Take from this

10

tea one tea-spoonful, pour over it a cup of boiling water and let stand in a hot place three minutes. To make the lemon syrup, boil a cup of sugar and one-third cup water five minutes; add one-third cup strained lemon juice after taking from fire. The punch is a mixture of equal parts of tea, syrup and water. The mellowness of flavor is due to using the cooked syrup and blended tea.— *Mrs. J. S. Paige.*

PINEAPPLE SHERBERT.

Three quarts water, two quarts sugar, make syrup; add two cans pineapple (shredded), and juice of ten lemons; whites four eggs added last. This makes two gallons.— *Mrs. A. B. Morris.*

TUTTI FRUTTI.

To one pint best French brandy, ten pounds fruit and ten pounds granulated sugar, adding same amount of fruit and sugar together, for instance four pounds pineapple and four pounds sugar, etc., following with other fruits in their season. Put in a gallon stone jar with cover on; keep in cool place, and stir with wooden spoon *every day* until all fruits are in and sugar well dissolved. Do not be alarmed if it ferments, it will be all the better.— *Mrs. A. B. Morris.*

CURRANT CONSERVE.

One quart red currant juice, one quart red raspberry juice; this takes four boxes each; two pounds raisins (seeded), six oranges, eight pounds sugar; dice the orange peel, remove seeds and white rind, as this tastes bitter;

use pulp and juice of orange. Cook this all together three-quarters of an hour. Makes 15 tumblers.—*Mrs. A. B. Morris.*

LEMON PUNCH.

One dozen lemons, one orange, cut up, one banana, sliced, one-quarter pint shredded pineapple, three cups sugar, one quart weak tea, five quarts water. Serve on ice.— *Mrs. A. B. Morris.*

ORANGE MARMALADE.

Twelve oranges, two lemons, four pounds rhubarb. Cut rhubarb in small peices without removing skin. Cut oranges and lemons, skin and all, very fine. Measure fruit and add the same amount of sugar. Cook half or three quarters of an hour. Put in glasses and cover. — *Mrs. Albert G. Schmedeman.*

ENGLISH ORANGE MARMALADE.

One dozen oranges, nine lemons sliced very thin, remove seeds; to every pint of fruit add one quart cold water, let stand twenty-four hours, then boil till thick and tender, let stand again twenty-four hours, then measure pound for pound of fruit and granulated sugar and boil one hour and a quarter, after it reaches boiling point; put in jars while hot; do not peel fruit but wash thoroughly.— *Mrs. A. B. Morris.*

GRAPE FRUIT MARMALADE.

Six large oranges, grape fruit to equal them in weight, take out seeds and pips, slice very fine and let stand twenty-four hours in six quarts of water, then boil in the same water, very slowly for two hours; when tender add eight pounds of sugar, boil one hour and a half or until it will jelly, put in glasses and seal when cool, same as jelly.— *Mrs. Calvert Spensley, Mineral Point.*

Bar-le-duc.

Make a good currant jelly, when half boiled, add large ripe currants one-fourth as many cups as there are cups of jelly, let boil for five or ten minutes.   They must not shrivel one bit.   Then take them from the liquor with a wire spoon, spread on a plate to cool and cook the jelly until it will harden, and is ready to put in glasses. When it has reached this stage, add the currents let them get hot, then take from the fire and fill a small glasses, seal same as other jellies.   This will do for both red and white currants.— *Mrs. Calvert Spensley, Mineral Point.*

Fudges.

Two cups of sugar, one-half cup of cream, one-half cup of boiling water, one or two squares of unsweetened chocolate, a piece of butter the size of a small egg, one-half tea-spoon of vanilla.   Boil until of some body when tried in water.   When a little cool beat with a fork until it begins to stiffen when pour onto buttered plates.— *Miss Mary Louise Atwood.*

Musk Melons.

Select small round melons, scrub well with brush, cut top off carefully.   Scoop balls out of melon with round scoop, squeeze a little lemon juice in each melon, add sugar if needed.   Serve without top very cold.— *Mrs. Florence Bashford Spensley.*

PECAN CANDY.

To a pound of light brown sugar add two-thirds of a cup of boiling water and two even table-spoons of butter; stir until it melts; add a pinch of cream of tartar and let the syrup boil without stirring until a drop will make a soft ball but not stick to the fingers; then extinguish the flame and pour in a cupful of pecan kernels and pour into buttered tins.— *Miss M. L. Atwood.*

POP CORN BALLS.

For three quarts pop corn, boil one-half pint molasses for twelve minutes, then put the popped corn into a large pan; pour the molasses over it; stir thoroughly together and make into balls with your hands, which should be slightly buttered. — *Mrs. Florence Bashford Spensley.*

MISCELLANEOUS.

TIME TABLE.

BOILING MEATS.

Mutton......... .... per pound,   15 minutes.
Corned beef.... ....   "   30 to 35 "
Ham... ... .   "   20 "
Turkey............... ....   "   15 "
Fowl...........................   "   20 to 30 "
Tripe ....   "   3 to 5 "

BAKING MEATS.

Beef ribs, rare.. .... per pound, 8 to 10 "
Beef boned and rolled ....   " 12 to 15 "
Mutton leg, rare   ....   "   10 "
Lamb, well done..............   "   15 "
Veal...........................   "   20 "
Pork.... . ...   "   20 "
Venison, rare ....   "   10 "
Chicken ... .   "   15 "
Goose ....   "   18 "
Fillet, hot oven............................   30 "
Braised meats .... 3 to 4 hours.
Turkey, 8 pounds..........................   2 "
Birds, small, hot oven .. .. 15 to 20 minutes.
Tame ducks................................ 2 hours.
Large fish .... 1 and 1-2 hours.

BROILING MEATS.

Steak 1 and 1-2 inch thick................ 10 to 15 minutes.
Mutton chops, French ....   8 "
   "   "   English.... .... 10 "
Spring chicken... .... 30 "
Quail...................................... 30 "
Squabs .... 30 "
Shad, Bluefish .... 30 "

VEGETABLES.

Potatoes............................	30 minutes.
Asparagus................................	45 "
Peas	30 to 40 "
String beans	45 to 60 "
Lima "	60 "
Spinach........................... ...	45 to 60 "
Turnips...............	1 h. and 15 "
Beets......	1 h. and 30 "
Cabbage	2 hours.
Brussels sprouts........................	45 "
Onions..................................	2 hours.
Parsnips	1 hour.
Green corn..........	15 to 20 "
Bread	1 hour.
Biscuits..................................	20 minutes.
Cake	20 to 45 "
Custards, very slow oven	1 hour.

FOOD FOR INFANTS WITH IMPAIRED DIGESTION.

One pint of water, one coffee cup of milk, two inches square of gelatine, one table-spoonful of arrow root; boil all ten minutes; when cold add one gill of new milk. This has been found excellent in extreme cases. —*Mrs. E. Burdick.*

FOR A BURN.

A cornmeal poultice covered over with young nyson tea, softened with hot water, and applied as hot as can be borne, relieves pain in a few minutes.—*Mrs. Wm. F. Vilas.*

FOR A BURN.

Wring out a cloth in a thick mixture of bi-carbonate of soda and water, and bind on the burn, changing often. This will relieve almost immediately.—*Miss Mary Louise Atwood.*

COLD IN THE HEAD.

Tri-nitrate of bismuth, six drachms; pulverized gum arabic, two drachms; hydrochlorate of morphia, two grains. To be used as a snuff.— *Mrs. H. K. Edgerton, Oconomowoc.*

FOR A COUGH.

Make a syrup of figs and sweeten with maple sugar or common brown sugar.— *Mrs. H. K. Edgerton, Oconomowoc.*

MORRIS SALVE.

One and one-half ounce olive oil, one ounce spermacite, one ounce virgin wax, two ounces honey, one ounce camphor; break in small pieces. Put all ingredients in white bowl, and put bowl in pan boiling water until all is dissolved; then stir till cold with a silver fork. Put in screw-top jar.— *Mrs. A. B. Morris.*

MOTH PREVENTIVE.

A pleasant perfume, and also good for moths, may be made as follows: Take one-quarter ounce each of cloves, caraway seed, nutmeg, mace, cinnamon and longuin bean, then add as much Florentine orris root as will equal all these ingredients; put together; grind the whole together to a powder, and put in small bags or powders among your clothes, etc.—*Mrs. A. B. Morris.*

BAKING POWDER.

One-half pound baking soda, one pound and two table-spoons of cream tartar, two table-spoons cornstarch. Sift together twenty times; keep in old baking powder cans. If at all lumpy from standing, just sift over, and it will be all right.— *Mrs. A. B. Morris.*

PASTE.

Put a tea-spoon brown sugar with a quart of paste and it will fasten labels on tin cans as well as on wood.— *Mrs. A. B. Morris.*

SPICE BAG.

Six ounces orris root, one-half ounce lavender, one-half ounce jockey club, one-half ounce heliotrope, one-half ounce jassamine, a pinch of cloves, allspice and cinnamon, all ground.— *Mrs. A. B. Morris.*

A GOOD TONIC.

One ounce Peruvian bark, one ounce thoroughwort, one ounce hops, one quart good whiskey, put in two quart jar and let stand ten days, stir every day. Take one tea-spoon every day before meals.— *Mrs. A. B. Morris.*

FURNITURE POLISH.

To one pint turpentine, two pints raw linseed, one table-spoon vinegar, one tea-spoon litharge. Shake well before using. Apply with flannel cloth and rub dry with clean cloth.— *Mrs. A. B. Morris.*

FOR COUGH.

Four ounces honey, one ounce balsam copaiva, one ounce spirits nitre, one ounce syrup squills, one ounce paregoric. A dessert-spoonful night and morning; shake bottle.— *Mrs. A. B. Morris.*

USEFUL HINTS.

Anything being cooked for the second time needs an extra hot oven.

Crumbs grated from fresh loaf give a more delicate color than dried crumbs, to fry.

Dried crumbs absorb more moisture and are better for watery dishes.

Crumbs spread on top of dishes should be mixed with melted butter evenly over the fire; this is better than having lumps of butter dotted on top.

A few drops of rose water to almonds to prevent their oiling when chopped or pounded.

To skim sauces draw the sauce pan to one side of stove throw in a tea-spoon of cold water and the grease will rise, so that it can be easily taken off.

Chop suet in cool place and sprinkle it with flour to prevent its oiling or sticking together. Remove all membrane before chopping.

Before you cook cabbage always soak for an hour, in a bowl before cooking.— *Mrs. A. B. Morris.*

To make coffee for parties one pound to a gallon.

For ice cream six or seven persons to a quart.

Butter, sugar, flour and meal are measured by the rounding spoonful.

Salt, pepper, mustard and spices by the level spoonful.— *Mrs. R. M. Bashford.*

How To Cook Husbands.

A good many husbands are utterly spoiled by mismanagement. Some women go about as if their husbands were bladders, and blow them up. Others keep them constantly in hot water; others let them freeze by their carelessness and indifference. Some keep them in a stew by irritating ways and words. Others roast them. Some keep them in a pickle all their lives.

It cannot be supposed that any husband will be tender and good, managed in this way; but they are really delicious when properly treated. Be sure to select your husband yourself, as tastes differ, and it is far better to have none unless you will patiently learn how to cook him. A preserving kettle of the finest porcelain is best, but if you have nothing but an earthenware pipkin, it will do, with care. See that the linen in which you wrap him is nicely washed and mended, with the required number of buttons and strings tightly sewed on. Tie him in the kettle by a strong silk cord called comfort, as the one called duty is apt to be weak. They are apt to fly out of the kettle and be burned and crusty on the edges, since, like crabs and lobsters, you have to cook them while alive. Make a clear, steady fire out of love, neatness and cheerfulness. Set him as near to this as seems to agree with him. If he sputters and fizzes, do not be anxious; some husbands do this until they are quite done. Add a little sugar in the form of what confectioners call kisses, but no vinegar or pepper on any account. A little spice improves them, but it must be used with judgment. Do not stick any sharp instrument into him to see if he is becoming tender. Stir him gently, watching the while lest he lie too flat and close to the kettle, and so become useless. You cannot fail to know when he is done. If thus treated you will find him very digestible, agreeing nicely with you and the children, and he will keep as long as you want, unless you become careless and set him in too cold a place.

In Trying any of the Recipes

In this book, it is very important that you should use only the best and purest ingredients:

> The purest Olive Oil
> The fresh selected shelled nuts
> The finest, richest cheese
> The best imported macaroni
> The highest grade of flour
> The purest and best molasses
> The best selections of raisins,
> figs and dates.

In fact everything depends on the quality of the goods you use.

Be safe
Order them at

Piper Bros.
Our watchword is Quality

COOKERY AMERICANA

Each of the following titles includes an Introduction and Revised Recipes by Chef Louis Szathmáry.

Along the Northern Border: Cookery in Idaho, Minnesota, and North Dakota. New York, 1973.

Cooking in Old Créole Days by Célestine Eustis. New York, 1904.

Cool, Chill, and Freeze: A New Approach to Cookery. New York, 1973.

Directions for Cookery, in Its Various Branches by Miss Eliza Leslie. 31st edition. Philadelphia, 1848.

Fifty Years of Prairie Cooking. New York, 1973.

Hand-Book of Practical Cookery by Pierre Blot. New York, 1869.

High Living: Recipes from Southern Climes. Compiled by L. L. McLaren. San Francisco, 1904.

Home Cookery & Ladies' Indispensable Companion: Cookery in Northeastern Cities. New York, 1973.

The Improved Housewife, or Book of Receipts by Mrs. A. L. Webster. 6th edition. Hartford, 1845.

The Kansas Home Cook-Book. Compiled by Mrs. C. H. Cushing and Mrs. B. Gray. 5th edition. Leavenworth, Kansas, 1886.

Midwestern Home Cookery. New York, 1973.

Mrs. Porter's New Southern Cookery Book by Mrs. M. E. Porter. Philadelphia, 1871.

One Hundred Recipes for the Chafing Dish by H. M. Kinsley. New York, 1894.

Six Little Cooks by Elizabeth Stansbury Kirkland. Chicago, 1879.

Southwestern Cookery: Indian and Spanish Influences. New York, 1973.